NONSENTENTIAL CONSTITUENTS

Pragmatics & Beyond
New Series

Editors:

Jacob L. Mey
(Odense University)

Herman Parret
(Belgian National Science Foundation, Universities of Louvain and Antwerp)

Jef Verschueren
(Belgian National Science Foundation, University of Antwerp)

Editorial Address:

Linguistics (GER)
University of Antwerp (UIA)
Universiteitsplein 1
B-2610 Wilrijk
Belgium

Editorial Board:

2

Ellen L. Barton

Nonsentential Constituents

NONSENTENTIAL CONSTITUENTS

A Theory of Grammatical Structure
and Pragmatic Interpretation

Ellen L. Barton
Wayne State University

JOHN BENJAMINS PUBLISHING COMPANY
AMSTERDAM/PHILADELPHIA

1990

Library of Congress Cataloging-in-Publication Data

Barton, Ellen L.
  Nonsentential constituents : a theory of grammatical structure and pragmatic interpretation / Ellen L. Barton.
      p.   cm. -- (Pragmatics & beyond; new series ; ISSN 0922-842X; 2)
  Includes bibliographical references.
  1. Grammar, Comparative and general -- Syntax. 2. Generative grammar. 3. Pragmatics. 4. Context (Linguistics). I. Title. II. Series.
  P291.B295   1990
  415 -- dc20   90-31712
  ISBN 90 272 5008 1 (Eur.)/1-55619-045-X (US) (alk. paper)

To my parents,
Thomas and Virginia P. Barton

Table of Contents

Acknowledgments

I want to thank my colleague, Steven Lapointe of Wayne State University, who painstakingly reviewed several drafts of this volume; his work improved my work immeasurably, and I am grateful for his intellectual and emotional support. I also wish to thank Gregory Ward, who commented on an earlier draft of this material, and James McCawley, Martha Ratliff, Ruth Ray, and Ruth Yontz, who offered helpful comments on portions of this work. I alone, of course, am solely responsible for the remaining shortcomings in the material presented here.

In addition, I would like to thank Suzanne Ferguson, former chair of the Department of English at Wayne State University, who arranged for a Research Development Fund grant which allowed me to attend the 1987 Linguistic Institute at Stanford University. I also wish to thank Judy Levi, former chair of the Department of Linguistics at Northwestern University, who helped me find a publisher for this volume.

Finally, I want to thank my sister Mary Jo Barton, who edited this manuscript and compiled the bibliography, not once, but twice. I also want to thank my friends Deborah Ward and Dorothy Huson, who encouraged me in countless discussions. I am most grateful to my husband Michael Kraut, who lived through the daily process of writing and revising this book.

Introduction

Participants in a discourse regularly use utterances that are smaller than grammatically complete sentences; the traditional term for such a nonsentential utterance is 'fragment', and the typical exemplar of a fragment is an independent major lexical category as an answer to a question:

(1a) A: What happened in 1974?
     B: A scandal in the White House.
(1b) A: What did President Nixon and his Executive staff try to do?
     B: Obstruct justice.

Linguists traditionally have assumed that full sentence sources truncated by ellipsis rules account for the grammatical structure as well as the semantic interpretation of fragments: within the grammar, a sentential structure dominated by the initial node of S is reduced to a fragment by the operation of ellipsis, and it is the full sentential source that provides the semantic interpretation for the remaining fragment. In contrast to previous ellipsis analyses, I argue here against both of these assumptions. I claim that independent major lexical categories like the examples in (1) are generated within a grammar as syntactic structures dominated by the initial node of NP, VP, and so on, rather than S; I call these independent structures dominated by a major lexical category initial node 'nonsentential constituent structures'.[1] I also claim that the major part of the interpretation of an independent constituent utterance takes place within a pragmatic context, rather than in the semantic component of a grammar. In this work, I present a theory of nonsentential constituents by developing two interacting models: an autonomous competence model of the grammar of nonsentential constituent structures and a modular pragmatic model of the interpretation of independent constituent utterances in context.[2]

The focus of this work is an investigation of the interaction between these competence and pragmatic models as components of a comprehensive theory; nonsentential constituents are particularly suited for such an investigation because a full explanation of their structure and interpretation requires a theory that integrates syntax and semantics within the context of discourse and pragmatics. By specifying the exact contribution of each component, the development of a theory of nonsentential constituents has to examine central and controversial issues in linguistics, such as the autonomy of syntax, the interaction between grammar and pragmatics, and the nature and development of a pragmatic model.

The theory of nonsentential constituents is presented in five chapters. After an overview of the theory is given here in the Introduction, Chapter One considers the properties of the interacting competence and pragmatic models, discussing the issues of autonomy and modularity as they are related to the development of each model. Chapter Two motivates a nonsentential constituent structure analysis of independent constituents dominated by major lexical category initial nodes, and Chapter Three develops a competence model of the grammar of these nonsentential constituent structures. Chapters Four and Five develop a pragmatic model of the interpretation of independent constituent utterances in context. This work describes the structure and interpretation of nonsentential constituents in English, although the general points of the theory should apply to a description of nonsentential constituents in other languages as well.

To develop a comprehensive theory encompassing the structure and interpretation of nonsentential constituents, I am adopting a general framework suggested by Chomsky:

> It makes sense, I think, to analyze the mental state of knowing a language into further components, in particular, to distinguish what is sometimes called "grammatical competence" from "pragmatic competence". . . .By "grammatical competence" I mean the cognitive state that encompasses all those aspects of form and meaning and their relation, including underlying structures that enter into that relation. . . .Pragmatic competence underlies the ability to use such knowledge along with the conceptual system to achieve certain ends or purposes. (1980: 59)[3]

These two competencies are related to the central questions of linguistics as posed by Chomsky:

(i)   What constitutes knowledge of language?
(ii)   How is knowledge of language acquired?
(iii)   How is knowledge of language put to use?
(1986a: 3)

A competence model provides an answer to the first and second questions by specifying the context-free principles and rules that generate paired representations of the sound and the meaning of a syntactic structure; I suggest that a pragmatic model provides a partial answer to the third question by specifying the principles and operations that describe a representation of the context-based interpretation of an utterance. Together, then, the models provide a theory of the structure and interpretation of language, although in this case the enterprise of developing models is limited to developing a theory describing the grammar of nonsentential constituent structures and the context-based interpretation of independent constituent utterances. Chapter One describes the interaction between the competence model and the pragmatic model in terms of their contributions to the theory of nonsentential constituents.

Motivating a nonsentential constituent structure analysis requires arguments against an ellipsis analysis, and these are presented in Chapter Two. The central claim of a nonsentential constituent structure analysis is that independent major lexical categories like the examples in (1) are dominated by major lexical category initial nodes; in (1a) the initial node is NP, and in (1b), the initial node is VP:

(2a) $[_{N''} [_{DET} a] [_{N'} [_{N} scandal] [_{P''} in the White House]]]$
(2b) $[_{V''} [_{V'} [_{V} obstruct] [_{N''} justice]]]$

This analysis contrasts with an ellipsis analysis, which assumes that independent major lexical categories like the examples in (1) are derived from a full sentence source:

(3a) What happened in 1974?
       A scandal in the White House (happened in 1974) →
       A scandal in the White House.
(3b) What did President Nixon and his Executive staff try to do?
       (President Nixon and his Executive staff tried to) obstruct justice
       →
       Obstruct justice.

In §2.1, after reviewing some of the relevant literature on deletion in a generative grammar, I describe the extension of an intrasentential deletion framework to an intersentential ellipsis analysis aimed at accounting for independent major lexical categories, concentrating mainly upon the work of Morgan (1973). In §2.2, extending the work of Yanofsky (1978) and Napoli (1982), I present arguments that demonstrate the inadequacy of previous ellipsis analyses. The arguments rest upon the difference between examples like (4a) and (4b):

(4a) A: What stops the White House staff from visiting House Speaker Tip O'Neill in his Congressional office?
B: Old grudge.
(4b) A: The White House staff doesn't visit Tip O'Neill in his Congressional office.
B: Old grudge.

An ellipsis analysis easily generates the answer in (4a), analyzing the NP as the remainder of a full sentence source:

(5) (An) old grudge (keeps the White House staff from visiting Tip O'Neill in his Congressional office). →
Old grudge.

An ellipsis analysis, however, cannot generate the same NP in (4b) because the NP is not a demonstrably straightforward remnant of some previous sentence or question in the linguistic context, and any deletion rules generating such a structure would violate the Condition of Recoverability on Deletion. In contrast to an ellipsis analysis, a nonsentential constituent structure analysis automatically accounts for the NP in (4a) as well as the one in (4b) because it describes either NP as deriving from a major lexical category initial node:

(6) $[_{N''} [_{N'} [_{ADJ'} \text{ old}] [_N \text{ grudge}]]]$

In §2.2, I discuss similar examples from each of the major lexical categories, concluding that a nonsentential constituent structure analysis is the best-motivated analysis to account for the entire range of independent major lexical category structures.

In Chapter Three, I develop a competence model of the grammar of nonsentential constituent structures using the Government-Binding theory of Chomsky (1981, 1982, 1986a,b) within the general framework of transformational generative grammar. Early research in generative grammar initiated a significant shift in the object of research on language. As Chomsky describes it, "The shift in focus was from the study of [External] E-language to the study of [Internal] I-language, from the study of language regarded as an externalized object to the study of the system of knowledge of language attained and internally represented in the mind/brain" (1986a: 24). A competence model of grammar is a description of this internally represented knowledge of language, a significant component of which is attributed to a language faculty common to all humans and described by Universal Grammar. Chomsky's subsequent development of Government-Binding as a theory of Universal Grammar changed the concept of the I-language: "UG [Universal Grammar] consists of interacting subsystems. . . . From one point of view, these are the various subcomponents of the rule system of grammar. From another point of view, which has become increasingly important in recent years, we can isolate subsystems of principles" (1981: 5). Current research attempts to articulate the theory of Universal Grammar and its interaction with grammars of individual languages by exploring the properties and interactions of the subsystems of principles within Government-Binding theory.

These shifts in perspective have important implications for developing a competence model of the grammar of nonsentential constituents. First, in terms of the shift from E-language to I-language, it is interesting to note that research in generative grammar has concentrated almost exclusively upon the sentence, perhaps because the notion of sentence traditionally and historically has occupied a privileged position in grammatical research. The shift of focus from the external language to the internal language, though, allows a corresponding shift in emphasis from sentences as objects of the external language to structures as constructs of the internal language. Within a consideration of the structures of a language, sentences and constituents have equal status, and defining the initial node of a generative grammar so that it includes both sentences and constituents, as I propose in this work, reflects their equivalent status as structures within grammatical theory. Second, in his research developing the theory of Government-Binding, Chomsky often emphasizes the far-reaching effects of the interaction of principles within the subsystems of Government-Binding, pointing out that "small changes in the characterization of the principles and concepts have wide-ranging and complex consequences for some particular language under investigation and for others as well" (1986a: 148). Incorporating the generalization that sentences and constituents have equal status as initial nodes in a generative grammar requires adding only one generalization to the principles of X-bar theory, namely, the statement that X^{max} is the initial node of a grammar. Working out the effects of incorporating this generalization illustrates the interaction of principles in the description of well-formed nonsentential constituent structures; it also has implications in terms of general issues in research on X-bar theory.

In Chapter Three, I propose that the X-bar construct of X^{max} is the initial node of a generative grammar. This proposal accounts for all of the structures generated by a grammar, including sentence structures as well as nonsentential constituent structures: a sentence structure is dominated by the initial node of S (INFL"); a nonsentential constituent structure is dominated by the initial node of a major lexical category within the set represented by X" (in English, NP, VP, ADJP, PP, and (possibly) ADVP). Tracing out the consequences of integrating X^{max} as an initial node, I describe the grammar of nonsentential constituent structures within each component of a generative grammar, considering their representation at D-structure in §3.1, their representation at S-structure in §3.2, and their representation at Logical Form in §3.3. In Chapter Three, I also consider the contributions that this research makes to the theory of Government-Binding, exploring the theoretical implications arising from the generalization that the initial node of the grammar is X^{max}. Specifically, I propose that contrasts between the major non-lexical category of Sentence (INFL") and the major lexical category of VP (V") indicate that they are integrated as contrasting members of the total set of major syntactic categories within X-bar theory, arguing against the notion that the category of Sentence is a maximal projection of the lexical category of V. I also explore the relationship of major and minor categories within X-bar theory, arguing in support of a constraint limiting the participating categories in X-bar theory to major categories, which accounts for a number of differences in the distribution and properties of major vs. minor categories, including the contrast in their ability to function as the initial node in the derivation of a nonsentential constituent structure.

Within the theory of nonsentential constituents, the competence model and the pragmatic model interact in order to provide a modular account of the meaning of independent constituents: the output of an autonomous competence model is context-free semantic meaning narrowly defined as a Logical Form representation, which becomes the input to a pragmatic model; the output of a pragmatic model is a representation of meaning broadly defined as interpretation within context. In this work, I develop a pragmatic model which accounts for the context-based interpretation of independent constituent utterances by making inference its central mechanism.[4] The specific operations of inference within the pragmatic model are based on the notion of non-deductive inference in the work of Grice (1957, 1968, 1975), who suggests that there is a gap between what is said and what is meant (in a total sense) and that discourse participants arrive at an interpretation of what is implicated by making inferences. These inferences are based on the Cooperative Principle and its maxims of Quality, Quantity, Relation, and Manner, and there are two types of implicated meaning: generalized implicatures, which are calculated for an expression in all contexts, and particularized implicatures, which are calculated for expressions in specific contexts.

To provide an account of the context-based interpretation of independent constituent utterances within a Gricean framework, I propose that a pragmatic model has two submodules generating representations of implicated meaning; the submodules are separate because each one incorporates a different type of inference which is based on a different kind of contextual information. This internal structure of the pragmatic model reflects the differences in interpretation between examples like those in (4a) and (4b), repeated here as (7):

(7a) A: What stops the White House staff from visiting House Speaker Tip O'Neill in his Congressional office?
      B: Old grudge.
(7b) A: The White House staff doesn't visit Tip O'Neill in his Congressional office.
      B: Old grudge.

The first submodule of the pragmatic model, the submodule of linguistic context, describes the discourse-based interpretation of the example in (7a). Here, the NP *old grudge* could be interpreted as functioning in the discourse role of Agent for the predicate *stop*:[5]

(8)   A: $[_S$, what $[_S$ x $[_{VP}$ $[_V$ stops$]$
           ⟋ AGENT   [AGENT, PATIENT]
         $[_{NP}$ the White House staff]
           PATIENT
         $[_{PP}$ from visiting Tip O'Neill in his Congressional office]]]]]
      B: $[_{NP}$ old grudge]

The first submodule of the pragmatic model accounts for this interpretation by generating a representation of linguistic context through a generalized operation of discourse inference; the interpretation is based solely on the linguistic context of the independent constituent utterance.

The second submodule of the pragmatic model, the submodule of conversational context, describes the information-based interpretation of the example in (7b). Here, the NP *old grudge* has to be interpreted using information from beyond the linguistic context; depending upon the particular information shared by the interlocutors, the NP could be interpreted in one of (at least) two ways (the symbol + ⟩ means 'implicates'):[6]

> (9a) A: The White House staff doesn't visit Tip O'Neill in his Congressional office.
>
> B: Old grudge.
>
> + ⟩ The White House staff doesn't visit Tip O'Neill in his Congressional office because the White House staff holds an old grudge against Tip O'Neill.
>
> (9b) A: The White House staff doesn't visit Tip O'Neill in his Congressional office.
>
> B: Old grudge.
>
> + ⟩ The White House staff doesn't visit Tip O'Neill in his Congressional office because Tip O'Neill holds an old grudge against the White House staff.

The second submodule of the pragmatic model accounts for these interpretations by generating a representation of conversational context through a particularized operation of cooperative inference aimed at explaining the relevance of the utterance as a cooperative contribution to the conversation. In this case, the interpretations are based on the shared knowledge of the interlocutors about the relationship between Tip O'Neill and the White House staff. In general, the submodule of conversational context accounts for interpretation based on information within domains of relevance, which include the physical context of a discourse, the topic of conversation, the shared knowledge of interlocutors and their general knowledge about the world.

Although the two submodules of the pragmatic model describe different types of interpretation, interpretation based upon the linguistic context and interpretation based on the conversational context, the internal organization of each submodule is similar. Each submodule has a principle that describes the structure of context (linguistic or conversational), and each principle has an associated operation of inference that describes the elaboration of that structure of context (generalized discourse inference or particularized cooperative inference). Each principle also has an associated condition of acceptability that governs the results of the operation of inference. Figure 1 illustrates the two submodules of the pragmatic model; the

Figure 1

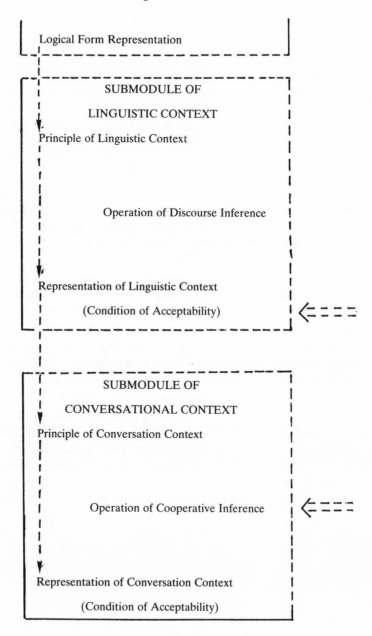

horizontal dotted lines indicate where the interactions within the pragmatic model take place, and the right-hand dotted lines and double arrows indicate where the pragmatic model interacts with external systems of information. Together, the two submodules of the pragmatic model provide an account of the context-based interpretation of independent constituent utterances. Two chapters describe the submodules of the pragmatic model in detail: Chapter Four describes the submodule of linguistic context, and Chapter Five describes the submodule of conversational context. The chapters investigate the relationship of inference and context within each submodule of the pragmatic model, arguing that the context of an utterance provides information which triggers an operation of inference, elaborating the structure of context.

In the development of the competence and pragmatic models within the theory of nonsentential constituents, I use both constructed and attested discourse sequences, the latter coming mainly from *The Presidential Transcripts* of the Watergate conversations between President Richard Nixon and members of his Executive staff.[7] In the development of the competence model, I mostly use constructed examples for ease of exposition. In the development of the pragmatic model, however, I rely on constructed examples only when I need a set of contrasting examples or when I need an example without a complex context for the illustration of a theoretical point. I recognize that the version of the *Transcripts* I am using presents regularized data; in other words, the transcripts do not include intonation, pauses, overlap, lengthened syllables, and other features as do the detailed transcripts of conversation analysis (cf. Ochs 1979, for a discussion of the superior nature of such close transcripts). My use of the published *Transcripts* is a compromise: on the one hand, it is a problematic source of conversational data because the method of transcription is deficient; on the other hand, it is a rich source of conversational data with many interesting examples of independent constituent utterances. In the development of the pragmatic model, I use the *Transcripts* because the consideration of natural discourse sequences and their interpretation provides the data that a pragmatic model is supposed to account for.

1. Interacting Models in a Theory of Nonsentential Constituents

1.0 Introduction

Most research on nonsentential structures has been done as a consideration of sentence fragments, and a review of the literature on the topic of fragments reveals three general positions, each one with adherents within different traditions of linguistic research.

The first position simply dismisses fragments as unworthy of consideration. Sweet, for example, in his descriptive grammar, says: "From a grammatical point of view these condensed sentences are hardly sentences at all, but rather something indeterminate between word and sentence" (1900: 57). In his traditional grammar, Follett seems to agree with Sweet, remarking that a fragment is "only a part masquerading as a whole" (1966: 293). And in a text on generative grammar, P. Matthews claims: "Fragments are of no concern to syntax, except as a source of confusion in our data" (1981: 14).

The second position emphasizes the role of deletion or ellipsis in the creation of fragments. Grammarians and linguists typically use answers to questions as the data for their investigations of fragments, claiming that answers to questions are truncated versions of full sentence sources:

(1a) A: What happened in 1974?
      B: A scandal in the White House.
          A scandal in the White House (happened in 1974).
(1b) A: What did President Nixon and his Executive staff try to do?
      B: Obstruct justice.
          (President Nixon and his Executive staff tried to) obstruct justice.

Traditional and descriptive grammarians suggest rules of ellipsis (e.g., Quirk et al. 1972), and generative grammarians essentially adopt this framework by suggesting that ellipsis rules constrained by a Condition of Recoverability on Deletion account for fragments (e.g., Morgan 1973; Sag 1976). Within the literature, this position is the standard explanation of the structure and interpretation of fragments.

The third position, which occurs sporadically throughout the literature, suggests that some nonsentential structures may not be the result of deletion or ellipsis. In traditional grammar, Fowler (1926) and Curme (1931) claim that certain utterances, exemplified by exclamations like "Beautiful!", do not seem to derive from ellipsis because the meaning is complete within the utterance. In his descriptive grammars, Jespersen (1924, 1933, 1949) suggests a three part classification of articulate sentences, semi-articulate sentences, and inarticulate sentences: the first class includes full sentences; the second class includes sentences with elliptical constructions; and the third class includes expressions that do not derive from ellipsis, including sayings like "Ladies first" and "One man, one vote" (1949, Vol. VII: 123-124). Recent work in generative grammar by Yanofsky (1978), Brame (1979), and Napoli (1982) also has challenged the assumption that deletion rules produce all nonsentential structures.

In this work I present a theory of nonsentential constituents that arises from this third perspective concerning the nonsentential origin and derivation of independent major lexical categories like the examples in (1a) and (1b). In this chapter, I discuss the defining characteristics of the interacting models within this theory: the autonomous and modular nature of the competence model of the grammar of nonsentential constituent structures, and the partially autonomous and partially modular nature of the pragmatic model of the interpretation of independent constituent utterances.

1.1 The competence model and autonomy

A theory of nonsentential constituents has to account for independent major lexical categories like the examples in (2):

    (2a) A: What happened in 1974?
           B: A scandal in the White House.
    (2b) A: What did President Nixon and his Executive staff try to do?
           B: Obstruct justice.

(2c)   A: When was Nixon elected President?
       B: In 1968 and 1972.
(2d)   A: How did he feel when he was forced to resign?
       B: Very angry.
(2e)   A: Has a U.S. President resigned before?
       B: Never.

Morgan suggests two analyses in order to account for examples like these:

> Two alternatives come immediately to mind: to generate them directly, or
> by ellipsis from full sentences. First of all, the traditional terms for these
> sequences — 'fragments' — reflects the commonsense judgment that they
> are remnants of full sentence, large portions of which have been annihi-
> lated by ellipsis. . . .[The alternative] course is to enlarge the inventory of
> initial symbols in the grammar to include at least S, NP, VP, AdjP, Adv,
> and probably several others. Then just as the grammar makes available to
> the speaker an infinite set of objects labeled S, it would also make avail-
> able an infinite set of well-formed sequences labeled NP, VP, Adv, and so
> on. (1973: 721, 723)

In his article, Morgan argues in favor of the first alternative, extending the
ellipsis analysis of traditional grammar to account for independent major
lexical categories within the framework of transformational generative
grammar.

I argue against an ellipsis analysis, developing Morgan's alternative
analysis that major lexical categories function as initial nodes in a generative grammar and providing a constituent-based rather than a sentence-
based account of nonsentential major lexical categories like the examples in
(2). The central claim of the theory of nonsentential constituents presented
here is that independent major lexical categories are nonsentential in their
grammatical structure and pragmatic interpretation. The grammatical component of the theory consists of a competence model of the grammar of
nonsentential constituent structures within the framework of transformational generative grammar.

One defining characteristic of a competence model within the
framework of transformational generative linguistics is the constraint of
autonomy of syntax, which specifies that rules in a generative grammar are
"essentially independent of factors relating to any other linguistic system or
to extralinguistic considerations" (Hale et al. 1977: 379). Thus, a competence model of the grammar of nonsentential constituent structures
describes the well-formedness or ill-formedness of nonsentential con-

stituents solely as syntactic structures: the rules of the grammar generate a structural description of D-structure, S-structure and Logical Form representations. Chomsky describes the major limitation upon these representations:

> [These] structure[s] must provide whatever information about an expression is available to the person who knows the language, *insofar as this information derives from the language faculty*; its representations must specify just what the language faculty contributes to determining how the expression is produced, used, and understood. (1986a: 46; my emphasis)

The restriction to information specific to the language faculty limits the domain of an autonomous grammar to operating over a single syntactic structure out of context: to assign a representation to a structure, an autonomous grammar does not use information from discourse or from the physical context of situation or from any other cognitive or social system.

In *Syntactic Structures*, Chomsky stated "grammar is autonomous" (1957: 17), and this claim has been debated ever since, mostly by researchers who argue that language is better explained in terms of social or conceptual systems. (Cf. Halliday 1973, 1978, 1985; Hymes 1964, 1972, 1974; Labov 1972; Gumperz 1982 *inter alia* for arguments from the perspective of language as a social system. Cf. Grossman et al. 1975; Bolinger 1977; Givón 1979a,b; Foley and Van Valin 1984 *inter alia* for arguments from the perspective of language as a functional system. Cf. van Dijk 1972, 1977; Johnson-Laird 1983; Lakoff 1987 *inter alia* for arguments from the perspective of language as a conceptual system.) In response, researchers, including Chomsky, have presented arguments from a variety of perspectives in support of the autonomy of syntax.

From the philosophical perspective of theory construction, Chomsky characterizes knowledge of language as a mental structure, one that is biological as well as psychological. Looking at the study of other biological systems, he points out that physiologists study anatomical systems, such as the cardiovascular and renal systems, as independent systems before they study their interaction and suggests that such an approach is valid for the study of language as an independent and autonomous mental structure: "In short, there seems little reason to insist that the brain is unique in the biological world in that it is unstructured and undifferentiated" (1980: 39). Chomsky also notes that there currently is no evidence to choose between internally or externally motivated theories, so the best way to choose between them is to see which one builds the stronger case for itself: "The choice between these alternatives cannot be settled by *a priori* argument, but only by trying to refine each of them to the point where we can ask how they fare as theories that explain some significant range of facts" (1980: 48). For Chomsky, autonomy is a justified assumption in the study of language.

From the perspective of theoretical linguistics, Newmeyer reviews the empirical and theoretical arguments in support of autonomy, defining autonomy as follows:

> [T]he grammar of a language is characterized by a formal *autonomous system*. That is, the phonology, syntax, and those aspects of meaning determined by syntactic configuration form a structural system whose primitive terms are not artifacts of a system that encompasses both human language and other human facilities or abilities. (1983: 2; author's emphasis)

His most persuasive arguments consider a variety of empirical evidence from grammatical constructions. One example is the system of grammatical gender in Indo-European languages, in which, for instance, *sonne* "sun" is feminine and *mond* "moon" is masculine in German, while in French *soleil* "sun" is masculine and *lune* "moon" is feminine. Within gender systems, words also cross natural categories, such as the German *Mädchen* "girl," which is neuter rather than feminine. Newmeyer argues that facts like these cannot be logically related to culture, belief systems, communicative functions, cognitive strategies, or conceptual categories, concluding that no externally motivated system can account for the wide range of grammatical data in a consistent or principled way. He points out that an autonomous grammar, in contrast, constructs simple structural rules to account for grammatical gender and other phenomena best described as internal to languages.

From the perspective of cognitive science, Fodor argues in support of the notion of a language faculty as an autonomous cognitive module, claiming that a modular view of an autonomous language faculty accounts for the unconscious, automatic, and extremely rapid operation of language comprehension:

> So the present proposal is that the language-input system specifies, for any utterance in its domain, its linguistic and maybe its logical form. It is implicit in this proposal that it does no more than that. (1983: 90)

According to Fodor, the defining characteristic associated with an autonomous module is its informational encapsulation, which means that the information within a modular system is strictly limited and closed to additional information. In the case of the language faculty, the information is limited, essentially, to an autonomous generative grammar assigning representations to structures; the grammar is closed to information from other cognitive systems of information and thinking.[1]

The competence model of the grammar of nonsentential constituent structures developed in this work respects the constraint of autonomy, which contrasts with the operation of an ellipsis theory. An ellipsis analysis strongly violates autonomy by requiring direct input from a discourse context in order to determine the grammatical well-formedness of independent major lexical categories. From the perspective of current research in transformational generative linguistics, however, a powerful argument motivating the nonsentential analysis of independent constituents is that it describes the well-formedness or ill-formedness of independent major lexical categories solely according to grammar-internal criteria, thereby preserving the autonomy of syntax.

1.2 The pragmatic model and modularity

The defining feature of a competence model is the constraint of autonomy, which limits its operations and representations to the domain of the description of the grammatical derivation of a single structure out of context. The domain of pragmatics, in contrast, is not constrained by the same kind of condition of strict autonomy, which allows its operations and representations to describe the interpretation of utterances within specific contexts. This presence or absence of context determines the domains of the competence model and the pragmatic model as they make their contributions to the larger theory of nonsentential constituents.

The term 'pragmatics' is a cover label for a variety of research, but one area of relative agreement among practitioners is that it explores the use of utterances in context. Morris (1938) originally defined pragmatics as "the relation of signs to their users" (1969 ed.: 107); Carnap (1939) broadened that definition to encompass "the action, state, and environment of a man who speaks or hears [a linguistic sign]" (1969 ed.: 146); and Stalnaker sums up pragmatics as "the study of linguistic acts and the contexts in which they are performed" (1972: 383). Preparing to review fifty years of work in the field, Levinson describes pragmatics as "linguistic investigations that make necessary reference to aspects of the context" (1983: 5). Consequently, the emphasis here upon certain aspects of the context-based interpretation of independent constituent utterances should not be a controversial one.

The term 'pragmatic model', however, is a controversial one, and there is not general agreement about my proposed focus on context-based interpretation as its domain. I use the term 'model' as Chomsky defines it: a model is a description of the knowledge underlying a native speaker's ability to produce and understand expressions of his or her language (1965: 9; 1986a: 3). I use the term 'pragmatic model' in opposition to the term 'competence model'. Again following Chomsky, I take a competence model to be a description of the knowledge underlying a native speaker's ability to generate paired representations of the sound and meaning of syntactic structures (1965: 8; 1981: 4). I suggest that a pragmatic model is a description of the knowledge underlying a native speaker's ability to formulate context-based interpretations of utterances. Both a competence model of grammar and a pragmatic model of interpretation are necessary components of a comprehensive theory that attempts to account for the ability to produce and understand expressions of a language, in this case, nonsentential constituents.

These remarks limiting the domain of the pragmatic model to context-based interpretation are not intended to indicate that this is the only theoretically interesting aspect of pragmatics or that a pragmatic model necessarily has to account for this aspect and no others. Context-based interpretation, however, is one crucially important aspect of pragmatics given the general goal of developing a theory of nonsentential constituents that accounts for their grammar and their meaning (or, in other words, given the goal of describing the structure and interpretation of nonsentential constituents within a theory that accounts for native speaker ability to produce and understand these expressions). The crucial aspect of meaning that an autonomous grammar does not specify is context-based interpretation; thus, the emphasis on this aspect of pragmatics grows out of the attempt to build a particular kind of theory within the broad framework of Chomskyan linguistics.[2]

The distinction between a competence model and a pragmatic model corresponds in part to a theoretical distinction between semantics and pragmatics as differently-based competencies. Semantics, as a component of an autonomous grammar within a Chomskyan framework, is narrowly defined as the Logical Form representation of meaning that is strictly determined by the grammar. Pragmatics, as suggested above, is broadly defined as meaning that consists of interpretation within context. In a survey of possible approaches to pragmatics, Levinson arrives at the roughly similar definition of pragmatics as "Meaning minus semantics," and argues persuasively that this distinction is appropriate for research:

> [S]uch a theory recommends itself to the pragmaticist for the following reasons. First, it is the only kind of theory now available that is precise and predictive enough to make [investigatable] the nature of a semantics/pragmatics boundary, or the interaction between the two components. Secondly, it is arguable that most other theories, e.g., those based on semantic components, can be subsumed within it, in so far as they are built on consistent and logical lines. Thirdly, it is perhaps still the kind of theory with the most support in linguistic and philosophical circles, despite many dissenters and many unresolved problems. Finally, many of the issues in pragmatics have arisen historically from this particular vantage point, and to understand them one must at least at first approach [them] from the same direction. . . .[T]here remains the hope that with two components, a semantics and a pragmatics working in tandem, each can be built on relatively homogeneous and systematic lines. (1983: 15)

In this work, I use an extremely narrow definition of semantics as Logical Form representation in a Government-Binding grammar because this definition fits in with the particular goal of my research, which is to develop a theory of nonsentential constituents within the theoretical framework of Chomskyan linguistics. This is not a generally accepted definition of semantics, however, because it ignores a great deal of work in other frameworks, including theories of truth conditions and other work in formal semantics. Levinson, for example, points out that a standard definition of semantics is a truth conditional theory of meaning, citing Gazdar's slogan, "Pragmatics = Meaning — Truth Conditions" (Gazdar 1979: 2; quoted in Levinson 1983: 12). Recent work by Heim (1982) and Kamp (1981) also develops a theory of meaning incorporating truth conditional representations as well as discourse representations into a formal theory of semantics, although they may not agree with the exact division between semantics and pragmatics as proposed by Gazdar. Many linguists might see the relationship between truth conditional semantics and pragmatics as one of the leading issues of research in the field of pragmatics, and could criticize my work for not addressing this issue. But even though the relationship of independent constituents to truth conditional semantics raises many issues, including the interesting question of whether a semantic proposition must be uniquely related to a sentential utterance, it is, unfortunately, beyond the scope of this volume to compare different semantic theories in terms of their relationship with pragmatics.

Within the general framework of Chomskyan linguistics, the pragmatic model under development here is an attempt to construct a model of pragmatic competence along the systematic and homogeneous lines that Levinson recommends, using a Gricean notion of non-deductive inference. Developing a pragmatic model of the general ability of native speakers to make inferences in order to interpret utterances in context would be a vast task; the model presented here is only a small part of such an undertaking. In a way that is similar to describing a portion of the grammar of English, as I do in developing the competence model of the grammar of nonsentential constituent structures, I am describing a small portion of the pragmatic knowledge of speakers of English — their ability to interpret independent constituent utterances in context.

As descriptions of knowledge underlying ability, competence models and pragmatic models contrast in the information that they utilize to generate structures and to interpret utterances. A competence model uses information that is internal to an autonomous grammar, specifically, the elements and principles within each module of Government-Binding. A pragmatic model, in contrast, uses information from a wide variety of contextual sources. Competence models and pragmatic models also contrast in their operations: in a competence model within the framework of generative grammar, the central mechanism is derivation; in the pragmatic model under development here, the central mechanism is Gricean inference. These contrasts in information and operation account for what I see as the most significant difference between the two types of models: a competence model is determinate while a pragmatic model is essentially indeterminate. A competence model is determinate because the rules of the grammar apply in a derivation to specify a binary value, either well-formed or not well-formed, for the representation of each syntactic structure. The representations of a pragmatic model, in contrast, are indeterminate because the non-deductive inferences that generate an interpretation of an utterance are essentially hypotheses, calculations, guesses, insights, conclusions, or intuitions about meaning. These interpretations can differ across speakers; they also can differ as a result of varying contextual factors. In short, the representations of a pragmatic model are not unique and stable entities. A pragmatic model has to encompass and explain indeterminacy, and it does so by incorporating its diverse sources of contextual information and by making the operation of Gricean inference its central mechanism.

Pragmatic interpretation depends upon a great deal of information from a variety of sources, including the linguistic context, the physical context of situation, the topic of conversation, the shared background knowledge of the interlocutors, and their general knowledge about the world. Furthermore, each area of information can in and of itself be enormous and complex. In describing the physical context of situation for an utterance, for instance, Brown and Yule, following Hymes (1964, 1972, 1974), mention some of the factors within a communicative event: addressor, addressee, audience, topic, setting (time, place, physical relations of addressor and addressee), channel (oral, written), code (language, dialect), and message-form (genre: debate, sermon, fairy-tale) (1983: 38).

Based on this variety of information, pragmatic interpretation takes place through the process of non-deductive inference, a process which is not, in general, very well understood. Researchers have pointed out that the possible inferential connections between bits of information are complex and never-ending, even leading to the absurd. Fodor, for example, discussing the interpretation of the word *panther* in Ogden Nash's saying "If you're called by a panther/don't anther," comments: "Given enough context, practically everything I know can be construed as panther related" (1983: 70-71). Searle, explicating the sentence *George Bush wants to run for the presidency*, mentions two types of background knowledge necessary for the interpretation of the sentence: specific knowledge about elections, including "such things as that the United States is a republic, they have an election every four years, in these elections there are candidates of the two major parties, the person who gets the majority of the electoral votes becomes president," plus a network of interconnected knowledge that underlies seemingly straightforward interpretation:

> If you try to follow out the threads of the network, if you think of what you would have to know in order to understand the sentence [above], you eventually reach a whole lot of stuff that looks really weird if you try to say that [it is] part of your knowledge or belief. For example, you will get to things like: people generally vote when conscious, or there are human beings, or elections are generally held at or near the surface of the earth. (1986: 16)

Levinson, too, notes that non-deductive inference is a "mysterious process" (1987b), and Fodor seems to concur: "[T]he closer we get to what we are pretheoretically inclined to think of as the 'higher,' 'more intelligent' . . . cognitive capacities . . . the less anybody understands [them]" (1983: 107).

Some researchers regard this situation as discouraging, arguing that the two characteristic features of pragmatic interpretation, its wide-ranging information base and its operation of non-deductive inference, constitute a block to the entire enterprise of developing pragmatic models. Hornstein (1986), for instance, claims that a psychologically significant feature of a competence model of grammar is that it breaks down the seemingly complex ability to judge the grammaticality of a sentence into simple sub-capacities explicitly connected to local properties of sentences; as an example, he cites the Binding principles in Government-Binding, which explain a variety of judgments about the well-formedness or ill-formedness of anaphoric relations within sentences (cf. §3.3). Turning to pragmatics, however, Hornstein has two objections to the state of the art. First, he criticizes the open-ended variety of information that it is possible and sometimes necessary to use in pragmatic interpretation: "In a word, anything at all that might act as background information is . . . relevant to the interpretation of an utterance" (1986: 240). He also criticizes the fact that the process of pragmatic inference, which uses this variety of information, is not well-defined or described:

> Though as a practical matter we have no trouble picking up, weighing, juggling and using vast amounts of information relevantly, quickly, and appropriately in many varied contexts we simply do not understand how this sort of holistic enterprise is carried out. We simply do not understand *in general* what sorts of capacities a person must have in order to make all-things-considered judgments and effortlessly exploit beliefs in drawing the conclusions that are regularly drawn in the way relevant to the situation at hand. (1986: 241; author's emphasis)

Because pragmatic theories have not broken down the complex ability of interpretation into narrowly constrained subcapacities, Hornstein concludes that they have "contributed relatively little" to current linguistic theory and that linguistics should, therefore, "scrap" pragmatics from its domain of research (1986: 234).

Somewhat ironically, Hornstein's arguments echo earlier objections to including a semantic component within linguistics, especially his criticism of the quantity and quality of information required for pragmatic explanation. His objection is that the incorporation of outside information contaminates linguistic theory:

> [O]nce one exploits general knowledge, beliefs, desires, hopes, dreams, etc., as vital parameters in one's linguistic theory then the theory becomes intractable. (1986: 240)

Hornstein here sounds remarkably like Bloomfield in his famous argument against the study of meaning:

> The situations which prompt people to utter speech include every object and happening in their universe. In order to give a scientifically accurate definition of meaning for every form of a language, we should have to have a scientifically accurate knowledge of everything in the speakers' world. . . . The statement of meanings is therefore the weak point in language-study, and will remain so until human knowledge advances very far beyond its present state. (1933: 139-140)

In response to Hornstein, I suggest that the principled addition of a pragmatic component to linguistic theory has to be similar to the principled addition of a semantic component to generative grammar (as, e.g., through arguments in early work by Katz and Fodor (1963) and in more recent work by Marantz (1984), Hornstein (1984), and May (1985) *inter alia*). The pragmatic component has to be incorporated with constraints that limit its domain, specify its interactions with other systems, and govern its operations and representations. In the approach to be developed here, the pragmatic model has specific points of interaction between its operations and representations and the systems of information and knowledge that interact with them. This specified interaction provides the constraint that restricts pragmatics to the limited domain of the context-based interpretation of utterances rather than the unlimited domain of all information. The pragmatic model thus does not have to incorporate or encompass a complete model of knowledge about the world; it only has to specify its connections with these other systems. Similarly, the operations of the pragmatic model do not have to describe how all inferences are made or how non-deductive inference operates in general; they only have to describe the operations of inference that occur within the boundaries of certain types of contextual information. In this way, the development of the pragmatic model answers Hornstein's criticisms by describing pragmatic ability in terms of highly constrained operations and representations.

Hornstein's criticisms of pragmatics, that pragmatics does not seem to be autonomous with respect to information about the world and that it lacks an explicit account of its internal operations, raise the larger theoretical issues of autonomy and modularity. A generative grammar is autonomous with respect to external information as described in §1.1; it also is modular in terms of its interaction with other systems. Newmeyer defines this aspect of modularity as follows:

[A] distinguishing feature of transformational generative grammar is its *modular* approach to explaining complex linguistic phenomena — an approach based on the hypothesis that not just formal grammar, but *all* human systems (or at least all those at work in language) are autonomous "modules," each governed by its particular set of general principles. In this view, the superficial complexity of language is a consequence of the *interaction* of such modules. . . .[A]ny explanation of a linguistic phenomenon that exploits the interaction of the formal grammar module with other modular systems [is] a "modular account" of that phenomenon. (1983: 2-3; author's emphasis)

Newmeyer cites several examples of modular interaction between grammar and other systems: one example, following earlier discussions by Chomsky and Miller (1963) and Chomsky (1965), is the explanation of center-embedded constructions like *The rat [$_S$ the cat [$_S$ the dog chased] ate] died.* An autonomous grammar freely generates sentences with any number of center embeddings; the sentence is confusing or difficult to understand, though, because of a principle within a sentence processing system: from left-to-right, the processing of a sentence can only be interrupted once, but the example violates this principle by interrupting the processing mechanism twice. Newmeyer points out that the explanation of the unacceptability of the sentence is the result of the interaction of two modular systems: part of the explanation comes from a grammatical component, and part of the explanation comes from a processing component (1983: 29-30).

Within a Government-Binding framework, the modularity of a generative grammar has two aspects: the first is modularity with respect to interaction with other systems, as described by Newmeyer above; another aspect is modularity within the internal organization of the grammar itself, as described by van Riemsdijk and Williams:

The rules and principles of grammar . . . account for grammatical phenomena in an essentially modular way in that they constitute autonomous subparts of the grammar that interact with each other in determining the properties of syntactic representations. (1986: xv)

Under this view, a grammar is organized into submodules whose internal principles and rules are autonomous, or independent, with respect to each other. Explanations of grammatical phenomena are the result of interaction among modules: the properties of D-structure, for example, are the result of the interaction of modules of X-bar theory and θ-theory.[3]

The issues of autonomy and modularity raise several questions about the nature of a pragmatic model. First, is the interaction of a competence model of grammar and a pragmatic model of interpretation a modular interaction? Second, is a pragmatic model itself an autonomous module; in other words, is it closed to information from other systems beyond itself? And third, is the internal organization of a pragmatic model modular; in other words, does a pragmatic model have internal submodules with independent principles, operations, and representations? Within the theory of nonsentential constituents, I claim that the interaction between a competence model of the grammar of constituent structures and a pragmatic model of the interpretation of constituent utterances is a modular interaction. I also claim that the pragmatic model is partially autonomous with respect to information from other systems and partially modular in its internal organization.

Chomsky has suggested the following view of the relationship between grammar and other systems:

> It is reasonable to suppose that the representations PF [Phonetic Form] and LF [Logical Form] stand at the interface of grammatical competence, one mentally represented system, and other systems: the conceptual systems, systems of belief, of pragmatic competence, . . . and so on. (1981: 18)

Following this view, one output of a competence model, Logical Form representation, is the input to a pragmatic model.

This interaction between a competence model of the grammar of constituent structures and a pragmatic model of the interpretation of constituent utterances is modular for two reasons. First, the interaction is characteristically modular in that the output of one component, the LF representation of the competence model, becomes the input to the second component, the pragmatic model. This version of modular interaction is a fairly standard one, conforming to what Zwicky calls "show[ing] one face" from a feeding component to a fed component (1984: 367-368); in other words, the interaction between the competence model and the pragmatic model takes place by means of the interface representation of Logical Form. The second reason the interaction between the competence model and the pragmatic model is modular is that the models combine in order to provide a theoretical explanation of some aspect of language, in this case, the meaning of nonsentential constituents. Even though a competence model is prohibited by the constraint of autonomy from using pragmatic information, the operation of a pragmatic model crucially depends upon information from a competence model, in particular the semantic representation provided by the Logical Form component of the grammar. The input to a pragmatic model is meaning narrowly defined as Logical Form representation; the output of a pragmatic model is meaning broadly defined as interpretation in context. Together, then, the interacting models provide an explanation for the semantic as well as pragmatic aspects of the meaning of nonsentential constituents.

Sadock (1983) explores some of the theoretical principles associated the general concept of modularity. He adopts an autonomy hypothesis in which different modules contribute to a native speaker's knowledge of his or her language; these modules include semantic ability, syntactic ability, lexical ability, and pragmatic ability. A strong autonomy hypothesis adds or assumes conditions concerning the independence and interactions of these modules. Sadock lists five subhypotheses about modularity: Formal Distinctness states that the elements and the principles of components are unique to each separate module; Sharpness of Boundaries establishes clearly distinct borders between modules; Interactional Simplicity describes interactions between modules that are limited to interface representations along the lines that Zwicky (1984) suggests; Submodularity assumes that the internal structure of each module consists of independent submodules; and finally, Nonredundancy of Function suggests that a module accounts for some aspect of linguistic knowledge without any duplication — in other words, a particular aspect of language receives its explanation within one and only one module. Sadock presents some non-linguistic counterexamples to each of the subhypotheses of modularity,[4] and using examples from different languages, he argues at length against the subhypothesis of Nonredundancy of Function, pointing out that many aspects of language are redundantly specified, especially within the syntactic and semantic components but also within the syntactic and pragmatic components. Sadock suggests that this redundancy actually is an argument supporting modularity because redundancy aids speaker communication, by giving more than one way to convey information; it aids hearer comprehension as well, by allowing more than one way to recover information.

Most of the subhypotheses that make up Sadock's description of modularity could, in principle, be gradient rather than binary conditions describing modular systems of different types. In fact, Sadock's main point in his discussion of Nonredundancy of Function is that a strong version of this condition is not necessary for the description of a modular grammar. Working with gradient versions of Sadock's subhypotheses of Formal Distinctness, Sharpness of Boundaries, and Interactional Simplicity, Zwicky (1984) makes further distinctions between strong and weak autonomy and between a sharply autonomous and a fuzzily autonomous interaction of components. Components are strongly autonomous if they do not interact at all; Zwicky cites the lack of interaction between the semantic and phonological components as strongly autonomous.[5] Components are weakly autonomous if they interact in a limited way through an interface representation (Sadock's Sharpness of Boundaries and Interactional Simplicity). An interface interaction between components is sharply autonomous if no principles in two components share any elements or properties; an interaction is fuzzily autonomous if any principles in two components share some properties (in a weak sense of Sadock's Formal Distinctness). Zwicky cites the interaction between the syntactic and phonological components as an example of interaction that is weakly and fuzzily autonomous.

The pragmatic model of the context-based interpretation of independent constituent utterances consists of two submodules of linguistic context and conversational context (cf. the illustration of the model in Figure 1 of the Introduction). The nature of this pragmatic model is partially autonomous and partially modular, in general satisfying a weaker version of the principles of Formal Distinctness, Sharpness of Boundaries, Interactional Simplicity, and Submodularity. Using Zwicky's terms, the interaction of the pragmatic model with a competence model is both weakly and fuzzily autonomous. A competence model and a pragmatic model interact through the interface representation of Logical Form, which makes the components weakly autonomous. Further, the interaction is fuzzily autonomous because the pragmatic model is not completely distinct from the competence model in formal elements since it crucially depends upon information from its input representation of Logical Form; both models share the use of certain formal elements, such as syntactic categories like NP and thematic roles like Agent. In addition, the pragmatic model is only weakly autonomous in terms of its interactions with other systems besides the competence model because it crucially depends upon information from other systems, such as background knowledge or knowledge about the world, although this interaction is highly constrained to interface points of contact between the pragmatic model and other systems. Finally, the internal structure of the pragmatic model is only partially modular: there are two submodules within the model, but they do not satisfy a strict version of Sadock's principles of Submodularity or Formal Distinctness because the central operation of Gricean inference takes place within both submodules. This partial autonomy and partial modularity of the pragmatic model reflects the diversity as well as the unity of pragmatic interpretation: the diversity arises from the many different contexts in which pragmatic interpretation takes place; the unity arises from the operation of pragmatic inference within these contexts. It is only by incorporating such diversity and unity that the pragmatic model can explain indeterminacy as a characteristic feature of pragmatic interpretation.

The organization of the pragmatic model into two submodules also reflects its partially autonomous and partially modular nature. The interactions throughout the model are weakly autonomous because the input to each submodule is the output of the previous one: the output of the grammar is the input to the submodule of linguistic context; the output of the submodule of linguistic context is the input to the submodule of conversational context. The interactions within the pragmatic model are fuzzily autonomous as well because properties within the representation of Logical Form are crucial to interpretation within the submodule of linguistic context; properties within the representation of linguistic context, in turn, are crucial to interpretation within the submodule of conversational context. The internal structure of the pragmatic model is only partially modular; both submodules have the same constructs: a principle creating a structure of context, an operation of inference elaborating that structure, and an acceptability condition governing the elaborated representation. The principle creating the structure of context within each submodule, though, draws upon a different kind of contextual information, and once that information has been incorporated within one submodule, it is not utilized again; in other words once information from the linguistic context has figured in interpretation within the first submodule of the pragmatic model, it does not figure in the interpretation within the second submodule of conversational context, nor does information from the conversational context figure in interpretation within the first submodule of linguistic context. The operations of inference within each submodule also are distinct types: within the submodule of linguistic context, the operation of discourse inference is generalized, describing discourse-based interpretation only; within the submodule of conversational context, in contrast, the operation of cooperative inference is particularized, describing information-based interpretation in specific contexts.

One way to motivate the claim that the two submodules of the pragmatic model incorporate different types of inference based on different kinds of contextual information is to consider some examples. The distinction between the submodule of linguistic context and the submodule of conversational context corresponds roughly to the difference in interpretive processes across the examples in (3) and (4):

(3a) P: Who grants immunity? The judges?
(3b) HP: He is apt to blast us all publicly.
P: Sirica?
(*Transcripts* 1974: 210, 520)

(4a) D: Criminal charge, that is a little different. That would be dynamite to try to defend that.
P: Use the Flanigan analogy?
(4b) D: Maybe we could invite the Committee down to the Roosevelt Room or the Blair House.
H: Maintain informality.
(*Transcripts* 1974: 114, 164)

In (3), information from the linguistic context is the basis for interpreting the NP in (3a) as a potential answer to the question by assigning it a discourse function as an Agent for the predicate *grant*; information from the linguistic context also is the basis for interpreting the NP in (3b) as a specification of the pronoun *he* by assigning it a discourse function as a Theme. Within the submodule of linguistic context, the generalized operation of discourse inference fits the NPs into the context of the previous utterances, describing the discourse-based interaction of utterances.

In contrast, in the examples of (4), the information to interpret the VPs comes from beyond the linguistic context. To interpret the VP *use the Flanigan analogy* in (4a), a discourse participant has to know that the Flanigan [sic] case established a precedent of executive privilege; a hearer can use this information to arrive at a possible interpretation of the VP as a suggestion offering one way to structure a defense for a Watergate defendant charged with a criminal offense. Similarly, in (4b), to interpret the VP *maintain informality* in the context of a discussion about members of the Executive staff appearing before the Senate Watergate Committee, a discourse participant must know that the Roosevelt Room is a room in the White House and that the Blair House is the residence for guests of the President; a hearer also might know or figure out that moving the Watergate Committee out of its Senate hearing rooms into a room under the jurisdiction of the Executive branch would strip it of most of its authority.

This information could be the basis for arriving at a possible interpretation of the VP as a proposal suggesting that informality is a desirable way for the Executive staff to interact with the Committee. Within the submodule of conversational context, the particularized operation of cooperative inference, working from the assumption that a constituent utterance is a cooperative contribution to the conversation, generates hypotheses about the possible relevance of the constituent utterances based on knowledge of the topic of the conversation as well as shared background knowledge of the participants and/or their general knowledge about the world. The submodule of conversational context describes the interaction of a possible interpretation with such information from a specific conversational context.

The generalization here is that discourse participants utilize different kinds of contextual information and different types of inference to interpret the utterances in (3) as opposed to (4); my claim is that a pragmatic model with two submodules captures this generalization.

Another way to motivate the modularity of the pragmatic model and its two submodules is to describe their distinct theoretical domains. The input to the pragmatic model is Logical Form representation with a domain defined as semantic meaning. Semantic meaning is the core of structural meaning that is common to all native speakers; in other words, it is determinate meaning because it is generated by the derivation of a structure within a grammar. The Logical Form representation of the determinate meaning of a structure out of context, while vital to understanding, is extremely limited, and the domain of determinate meaning of Logical Form is in distinct contrast to the domain of indeterminate meaning represented by the pragmatic model.

The domain of Logical Form representation is limited to a single structure, which is another of its distinguishing characteristics with respect to the representation of implicated meaning in the pragmatic model, particularly the first submodule of linguistic context. In contrast to the single structure bounds of a Logical Form representation, the domain of the submodule of linguistic context encompasses interactions among utterances. Consider the interpretations of the sequences in (3) again: the operation of discourse inference generates an interpretation in which the NP constituent utterances function in the discourse roles of Agent in (3a) and Theme in (3b). This discourse-based interpretation is the result of interactions among utterances within the submodule of linguistic context.

The domain of the submodule of linguistic context is restricted to discourse-based interpretation, which is its distinguishing characteristic with respect to the submodule of conversational context. The domain of the submodule of conversational context encompasses the interaction of constituent utterances with information and knowledge from beyond the linguistic context. Consider the interpretations of the sequences in (4) again: to arrive at a possible interpretation of the VP constituent utterances, the operation of cooperative inference utilizes a variety of information. In contrast to the discourse-based domain of the submodule of linguistic context, the defining characteristic of the domain of the submodule of conversational context is its incorporation of a large number of sources of information, including knowledge of the physical context of situation, the topic of conversation, the shared background knowledge of the interlocutors, and their general knowledge about the world.

The development of a partially autonomous and partially modular pragmatic model is intended to serve as a general argument supporting the use of the theoretical concepts of autonomy and modularity in work in pragmatics, responding to researchers who reject the notion that pragmatics has these features. Wilson and Sperber, for instance, argue against the application of modularity to pragmatics: "There are no special-purpose pragmatic principles, maxims, strategies or rules. . . .Modular grammatical processes offer little direct insight into the nature of non-modular pragmatic processes" (1986: 67). They also object to indeterminacy as characteristic of pragmatic interpretation: while agreeing that a variety of possible interpretations usually is available for an utterance, they claim that a pragmatic theory has to pick out "not just some arbitrary interpretation, but the interpretation intended by the speaker: this is the only interpretation it is worth the hearer's effort to recover" (1986: 67). This is a view of interpretation as determinate with a theoretical goal that is closely connected to the general aims of psychology: Wilson and Sperber wish their theory to predict the ability to formulate a single interpretation as a specific instance of behavior. In contrast, my goal is more connected to the general aims of linguistic theory: the pragmatic model has to be able to describe a variety of interpretations, reflecting the ability of a native speaker to do the same. It must incorporate the ability of a native speaker to formulate multiple hypotheses, to change, elaborate, or reject hypotheses, and to perform many other interpretive operations. To offer an analogy, just as a model of grammar has to provide a way to have more than one structural description of an ambiguous syntactic structure, so a model of pragmatics has to provide a way to have more than one interpretive representation of the indeterminate meaning of an utterance.

The account of the interpretation of independent constituent utterances proposed here is a pragmatic one; a competing account of the interpretation of nonsentential constituents is a semantic one based on an ellipsis theory like Morgan's (1973), which assumes that the meaning of an independent major category is dependent upon the semantic representation of its full sentence source, which is found somewhere in discourse. An ellipsis theory easily explains question and answer sequences as in the examples of (3): by looking to discourse, the grammar constructs a semantic representation describing the interpretation of the independent major lexical categories:

(5a) P: Who grants immunity? The judges?
(Do) the judges (grant immunity)?
(5b) HP: He is apt to blast us all publicly.
P: Sirica?
Sirica (is apt to blast us all publicly).

An ellipsis theory of the interpretation of independent major lexical categories accounts for approximately the same range of data as the submodule of linguistic context in the pragmatic model of the interpretation of constituent utterances.

There is, however, at least one empirical argument against an ellipsis theory of the interpretation of nonsentential major lexical categories, which is an extension of an argument previously mentioned in the Introduction. An ellipsis analysis cannot provide a determinate semantic representation for every nonsentential major lexical category, a familiar problem since an ellipsis analysis could not provide a determinate syntactic representation for independent major lexical category structures that occurred without a controller to trigger deletion rules (cf. the discussion of the examples in (4) in the Introduction). While an ellipsis analysis works smoothly on question and answer sequences, it breaks down in attempts to interpret independent major lexical categories that do not occur within a determinate linguistic context as in the examples of (4) in this section: there is no recoverable source to provide a full sentence semantic representation for the VPs *use the Flanigan analogy* and *maintain informality*. Furthermore, an indefinite number of possible sources exist, so an ellipsis theory would have to predict indeterminacy in the semantic representation for these major categories, an undesirable consequence within a determinate grammar. An ellipsis theory thus is empirically and theoretically inadequate to account for the semantic interpretation of all independent major lexical categories. The pragmatic model of the interpretation of constituent utterances, however, claims that the examples in (4) are ones that are interpreted within the submodule of conversational context through background knowledge and/or knowledge about the world.

The account of the meaning of nonsentential constituent utterances presented here respects the autonomy of grammar and explicitly shifts the explanation of interpretation to pragmatics; within the pragmatic model, it also makes a modular distinction between independent constituents that are interpreted within a discourse context and independent constituents that are interpreted within a larger context of conversation. In an overall sense, I claim that the theory of nonsentential constituents provides a theoretically satisfying division of interpretive labor with respect to the meaning of non-sentential constituents.

2. Motivating a Nonsentential Constituent Structure Analysis

2.0 Introduction

In this chapter, I begin developing the theory of nonsentential constituents by motivating its central claim that nonsentential constituent structures derive from major lexical categories as initial nodes, arguing against the standard ellipsis analysis in the traditional and generative grammar literature, which assumes that nonsentential major lexical categories derive from a sentential source truncated by the operation of deletion rules. In §2.1, I briefly discuss the place of deletion in research on generative grammar and then review the ellipsis analyses that extend a deletion framework to account for the structure of independent major lexical categories, paying particular attention to the work of Morgan (1973). I also review previous work in generative grammar which suggests the idea of a nonsentential analysis of independent major lexical categories, discussing the work of Yanofsky (1978), Brame (1979), and Napoli (1982). In §2.2, I consider these two competing analyses and systematically motivate the nonsentential constituent structure analysis of independent major lexical categories by presenting arguments which demonstrate the empirical and theoretical inadequacy of any ellipsis analysis.

2.1 Deletion and ellipsis in generative grammar

The standard explanation of fragments is that they derive from full sentence sources truncated by the operation of ellipsis. The following definition of ellipsis is a representative one from traditional and descriptive grammar:

> Ellipsis means the omission from a sentence of words needed to complete the construction or the sense. (Fowler 1926: 152)

Examples of constructions that fit under this definition include sentences with ellipted phrases as well as elliptical comments and answers to questions:

(1a) The evil consequences of excess of these beverages is much greater than alcohol.
The evil consequences of excess of these beverages is much greater than (the evil consequences of excess of) alcohol.

(1b) So it will be a miracle if we get our restoration.
Undoubtedly.
(So it will) undoubtedly (be a miracle if we get our restoration).

(1c) How often does it happen?
Once a month.
(It happens) once a month.
(Fowler 1926: 152-154, 674-675, 591)

The traditional/descriptive definition allows ellipsis to operate both within and across sentences.

In the 1960s, generative grammarians adopted and formalized a structural definition of ellipsis, formulating intrasentential deletion rules constrained by a Condition of Recoverability as described by Chomsky:

> We are proposing the following convention to guarantee recoverability of deletion: a deletion operation can eliminate only . . . a formative explicitly mentioned in the structure index . . . or the designated representative of a category . . . or an element that is otherwise represented in the sentence in a fixed position. (1965: 144-145)

Each of the three options for deleting lexical items within sentences is commonly associated with a particular transformational rule in Standard Theory:[1]

(2a) You will stop → Stop!
(2b) I know *wh*-someone with a scar →
Who do I know with a scar?
(2c) John will fire his staff, and Mary will fire her staff, too →
John will fire his staff, and Mary will, too.

In (2a), an operation of Imperative Deletion deletes the formatives *you will*, which are explicitly mentioned in the structural index of the transformation; in (2b), an Interrogative Transformation deletes the singular indefinite pronoun *someone* as the designated representative of the NP category; and in (2c), a Verb Phrase Deletion transformation deletes a VP element otherwise represented in the first clause of the sentence. This last case is deletion under identity, which operates in a number of Standard Theory transformations besides VP Deletion, including Equi, Gapping, Coordinate Deletion, Conjunction Reduction, and others (cf. Akmajian and Heny 1975; Green and Morgan 1979).

In addition to formulating specific deletion rules like the ones above, researchers working in Standard Theory also explored the nature of the Condition of Recoverability as a constraint on deletion under identity. Chomsky describes the requirement of identity:[2]

> We have mentioned in several places that deletion must be recoverable, and have suggested that this condition can be formalized by the following convention relating to what we called "erasure transformations": an erasure transformation can use a term X of its proper analysis to erase a term Y of the proper analysis only if X and Y are identical. (1965: 177)

Researchers developed both formal and empirical arguments in support of the Condition of Recoverability as a constraint on deletion. The formal arguments state that a grammar requires a Condition of Recoverability in order to prohibit free deletion and generate a decidable set of sentences (Lees 1960; Matthews, G. 1961; but cf. Peters and Ritchie 1971, 1973, who showed that such a recoverability condition cannot in and of itself ensure decidability). The empirical arguments demonstrate that numerous transformations, including VP Deletion, Equi, and others, require a Condition of Recoverability in order to generate well-formed sentences (Chomsky 1964, 1965).[3]

Some of the details of deletion operations changed significantly during the development of transformational grammar from the 1960s to the 1980s. The most significant change was the proposal that deletion rules apply after the derivation of S-structure. In Standard Theory, deletion rules were assumed to be transformations operating in the derivation of a D-structure to an S-structure (cf. the discussion of the examples in (2) above). Sag (1976), however, argued that deletion rules operate on S-structures because they require identity at Logical Form to trigger their operation.[4] As a result, in Extended Standard Theory, the place of deletion rules in the grammar changed:

D-structure representation

$\downarrow$ transformational rules

S-structure representation $\longrightarrow$ Logical Form

$\downarrow$ deletion rules

surface structure representation

In current work in Government-Binding, deletion rules are considered a part of the phonological component when that component is broadly defined (van Riemsdijk and Williams 1986: 176, 188; Zwicky 1984: 374). Napoli (1982) presents specific arguments supporting this placement of deletion rules into the phonological component; her work is discussed below.

Another change in deletion during the development of transformational grammar was that the multiplicity of specific deletion rules in Standard Theory merged into more general statements regarding deletion across different types of categories in different constructions. Rather than separate rules for VP Deletion, *Wh*-Deletion, and so on, the current view of the deletion component of the grammar is that it seems to consist of a minimum number of general rules, or perhaps even a single rule like 'Delete constituents freely up to recoverability' (van Riemsdijk and Williams 1986: 160-161, 176; Radford 1981: 271, 274).[5] Yet in spite of changes in the form, operation, and placement of deletion rules, the Condition of Recoverability has remained an important constraint on generative grammars. Even in the most recent formulations of Government-Binding theory, Chomsky (1981, 1986a,b) and others assume that such a condition constrains deletion under identity.

Most generative grammarians assume that this framework of intrasentential deletion under identity extends across sentences to account for the creation of fragments. In the classic article within this framework, Morgan (1973) suggests two alternatives for deriving independent major lexical categories like the examples in (3):

(3a)   What does Mitchell have in his head?
       Hydrogen sulfide.
(3b)   What does he want to do to the press?
       Suppress it.
(3c)   How fast does Hubert's mind change?
       Very fast.

(3d) Just how strange are Schlesinger's ideas?
      Very strange.
      (1973: 720, 722)

One alternative, Morgan explains, is "[enlarging] the inventory of initial symbols in the grammar to include at least S, NP, VP, AdjP, Adv, and probably several others" (1973: 723), a suggestion which is the basis of the nonsentential constituent structure analysis I motivate in the following section of this chapter. Morgan rejects this alternative, however, in favor of an ellipsis analysis which derives all fragments from full sentence sources with the initial node of S, remarking that such an analysis "reflects the common-sense judgment that [fragments] are the remnants of full sentences" (1973: 721). The sentential source for a fragment is found in discourse; thus, Morgan proposes a rule of General Ellipsis, which deletes "indefinitely large" portions of a sentence to produce a fragment; the rule operates under a discourse version of the Condition of Recoverability:

> In its structural change GE [General Ellipsis] is a deletion rule. . . .In context the deleted elements are recoverable. In other words, the deletion is deletion under identity. But the identity holds between the sentence to which the rule applies and another sentence in the discourse. (1973: 730-731)

Morgan also claims that the semantic interpretation of fragments depends upon the semantic representation of their full sentence source, adding that "fragments have the semantic import (in context) of full sentences" (1973: 723).

Morgan claims that fragments require a full sentence source because the representation of this sentential source will contain "syntactic properties of full sentences [that] will bear directly on the well-formedness and interpretation of fragments" (1973: 724). In support of this claim that the syntactic derivation of fragments requires full sentence sources, Morgan offers several arguments, including ones based on the backwards anaphora constraint, the distribution of reflexives, and the choice of complementizers; in each case below, a well-formed sentential source predicts a well-formed fragment, and an ill-formed source predicts an ill-formed fragment:

(4a) What does John$_i$ think?
      *John$_i$ thinks that the bastard$_i$ is being spied on →
      *That the bastard$_i$ is being spied on
(4b) John$_i$ thinks that the bastard$_j$ is being spied on →
      That the bastard$_j$ is being spied on.

(5a) Who does John want to shave?

*John$_i$ wants to shave him$_i$ →

*Him$_i$

(5b) John$_i$ wants to shave himself$_i$ →

Himself$_i$.

(6a) What does John think?

*John thinks that Tricia's having given birth to a 7-pound chin →

*Tricia's having given birth to a 7-pound chin

(6b) *John thinks for Tricia to have given birth to a 7-pound chin →

*For Tricia to have given birth to a 7-pound chin

(6c) John thinks that Tricia has given birth to a 7-pound chin →

That Tricia has given birth to a 7-pound chin.

(1973: 725-726)

In the case of (4), the ill-formed sentence in (4a) violates the backward anaphora constraint because the epithet *the bastard* is c-commanded by its coreferential antecedent *John* (under a strong definition of c-command; cf. §3.1.1 and note 1 there for a brief discussion of c-command); the well-formed sentence in (4b) does not violate the constraint because the NPs *the bastard* and *John* are not coreferential (cf. Reinhart 1981, *inter alia* for an explanation of c-command in backward anaphora; cf. Bolinger 1972, *inter alia* for an explanation of the application of pronominal constraints on epithets). In (5), the ill-formed sentence in (5a) violates the distribution pattern of reflexives and pronominals because the pronoun *him* is ill-formed when it is coreferential with *John*; the reflexive *himself* in (5b) is the well-formed coreferential NP that produces a well-formed fragment. In (6), the ill-formed sentences in (6a) and (6b) violate the choice of complementizer for the verb *think*; in (6c), however, with the well-formed selection of a *that*-complementizer in the sentential source, the corresponding fragment is well-formed. To explain these and other cases, Morgan concludes that the application of constraints to full sentence sources is the only possible explanation for the corresponding well-formedness or ill-formedness of fragments.

Morgan also offers a second series of arguments in support of his claim that the derivation of a fragment necessarily requires a full sentence source. In each example below, Morgan argues that a transformation has applied to the sentential source before General Ellipsis has operated to produce a fragment:

(7a) A: Who was John killed by?
    B: By the FBI.
        The FBI killed John →
        John was killed by the FBI →
        By the FBI.
(7b) A: Who did the boys see?
    B: Each other.
        Each of the boys saw the other →
        The boys saw each other →
        Each other.
(7c) A: What has John just done?
    B: Broken the vase.
        John Pres - have - en - broke the vase →
        John has broken the vase →
        Broken the vase.
        (1973: 727-729)

In (7a), the source of the fragment is a sentence which has undergone Passive; in (7b), the full sentence source has undergone Each Other formation before ellipsis to a fragment; and in (7c), the transformation of Affix Hopping has created the form of the verb phrase before the operation of ellipsis.[6] As in the previous argument, Morgan concludes that positing full sentence sources is the only way to explain the structure of fragments.

The rule of General Ellipsis operates under a condition that a fragment must remain a constituent after the application of the ellipsis rule; in the case of NPs and VPs, Morgan adds: "nouns and verbs can be fragments only if they constitute a full NP or VP, respectively" (1973: 736), citing the examples in (8) as evidence for his proposed constituent condition:

(8a) A: Does Wolf like the soprano?
    B: *No, tenor
    B: No, the tenor.
(8b) A: Does John want to kiss Martha?
    B: No, (to) hit her.
    B: *No (to) hit
    (1973: 736)

In short, Morgan's rule of General Ellipsis creates fragments which are constituents remaining from full sentence sources.

In a similar extension of the framework of deletion under identity across sentences to create fragments, Sag (1976) claims that his theory of deletion based on identity at Logical Form automatically accounts for fragments. Sag proposes the following ellipsis rule:

> For instance, the ellipsis rule that produces short answers to questions might be formulated simply as:
> W - X - Z
> ∅   ∅
> General considerations of logical form will then account for most of the restrictions on the application of this rule. (1976: 300)

The crucial general consideration here must be that identity at Logical Form can hold across sentences within a discourse and trigger the operation of the ellipsis rule.

In sum, the standard explanations of fragments in generative grammar, whether syntactic like Morgan's or semantic like Sag's, suggest that identity is the crucial factor in the creation of a fragment by triggering the operation of ellipsis. The proposed ellipsis rules operate across sentence boundaries to create fragments from full sentence sources.

In spite of the widespread adherence to an ellipsis analysis, some generative grammarians have noticed that certain nonsentential fragment-type structures (e.g., questions like *Coffee*?) do not seem to derive in a straightforward manner from an analysis consisting of discourse-based ellipsis rules. Hankamer and Sag, for example, basically support an ellipsis analysis: "[E]llipsis processes . . . can be controlled syntactically across a speaker boundary from a discourse antecedent" (1976: 411). They also, however, point out some interesting exceptions, such as the seemingly ellipted VPs in exclamations like *Don't! Please don't!* said when someone approaches the speaker brandishing a weapon (1976: 409). In an attempt to account for such counterexamples, Sag and Hankamer suggest the concept of pragmatic deletion, in which an extra-linguistic event provides a sufficient context for a recoverable deletion: "Once an event or situation has been observed long enough in silence, it becomes part of a tacit discourse between the observers" (1977: 134). Such a pragmatic controller, they suggest, is like a discourse controller, providing enough identity to trigger deletion rules. Hankamer and Sag admit, however, that the concept of pragmatic deletion is not very well defined or understood.

Like some traditional and descriptive grammarians (cf. the brief discussion in §1.0 of Fowler 1926; Curme 1931; and Jespersen 1924, 1933,

1949), a few generative grammarians have suggested that deletion or ellipsis rules do not operate in the creation of all nonsentential structures. The first systematic challenge to an ellipsis analysis came from Yanofsky (1978), who considered noun phrases that initiate a discourse or a topic:

(9a) Teamwork.   (after winning tennis doubles)
(9b) Your move.   (during a game of Monopoly)
(9c) The time[?]   (at a bus stop to a stranger)
(9d) Thief! Thief!   (as a mugger is running away)
      (1978: 491-492)

Since these NP utterances occur initially, Yanofsky argues, they cannot derive from full sentence sources because there is no previous linguistic context to trigger a deletion rule nor is there any mutual pragmatic controller to guarantee recoverable deletion. Yanofsky, however, does not arrive at any explanation of the grammatical status of these initial NPs. She is correct when she points out that initial NPs have "no motivation for positing any deletion rule at all," but she begs the question of the origin and derivation of these NPs by stating, "I am led to posit that the SS [surface structure] is all there is" (1978: 493). Yanofsky then devotes the majority of her article to a taxonomy of the functions of these NPs, concluding that the general function of a NPU is to call immediate attention to its content (1978: 493).

Yanofsky's article is devoted to NPs; the work of Brame, however, suggests that the phenomenon of nonsentential structures may not be limited to NPs alone. In a short article, he offers a set of examples that are all well-formed structures of English even though they are not all sentences:

(10a) met Mary
(10b) with a knife
(10c) these interesting proposals
(10d) that John met Mary
(10e) John met Mary
      (1979: 384)

Brame criticizes the emphasis on S in linguistic research, which, he claims, concentrates solely on examples like (10e) and fails to account for examples like those listed in (10a)-(10d): "Transformational grammar is a theory of sentence grammar; what is desired is a theory of grammar, a theory of phrasal types, all of which are on a par with respect to syntactic phrasal type characterizations, S' and S being simply two of the available types" (1979:

385). Brame does not, though, suggest any specific way of incorporating a theory of alternative phrasal types into current theories of syntax.

In a recent article, Napoli (1982) synthesizes a number of trends in research on deletion and its relation to nonsentential structures. She considers sentences with missing material at the beginning:

(11a) Wish Tom were here. (I wish . . .)
(11b) You seen Tom?   (Have you . . .)
(11c) Paper boy's here.   (The paper . . .)
(11d) Cat got your tongue? (Has the cat . . .)
          (1982: 85)

Napoli observes that the missing material is neither a single constituent nor a grammatical category like the subject of a sentence; in (11a), the subject NP is missing, but in (11b) the missing material is a moved auxiliary verb; in (11c), a determiner; and in (11d), the missing material is a combination of auxiliary plus determiner. Napoli develops a parallel analysis of these sentences and words with missing initial material:

(12a) 'fessor   (professor)
(12b) 'sgusting   (disgusting)
(12c) 'splains   (explains)
          (1982: 85)

Both the words and the sentences have deleted material that is unstressed. Napoli proposes a phonological rule that deletes unstressed initial material in sentences to account for examples like (11):

> [I]f we adopt the 'hat pattern' approach to intonation and divide the intonation còntour of a sentence into the prehead (the part preceding the first main accent), the head (from the first main accent to the last main accent), and the post-head (the falling part after the last main accent), we could say that this rule deletes the prehead. (1982: 99)

The correlation between stress and deletion has been noticed in the literature (Sag 1976: 293-294; Quirk et al. 1972: 545) and has served as one general motivation for the placement of deletion rules in the phonological component of the grammar. Napoli's work, however, provides specific argumentation to adopt a phonological approach to deletion in the creation of certain sentence fragments, specifically those with missing initial material.

In a brief section in her article, Napoli points out that these particular sentence fragments with missing initial material contrast with structures like

Yanofsky's initial NPs. She further suggests that Yanofsky's arguments against deletion provide evidence to adopt a nonsentential analysis of all independent major lexical categories:

> Since NP utterances can occur in discourse initial position, there is no reasonable linguistic or pragmatic controller for many such utterances. Given that these utterances then demand a base generated analysis, this same analysis can account for all NP utterances. [These] arguments hold equally as well for other single category utterances, such as APs and PPs. (1982: 87-88)

Napoli also points out that generating constituents directly automatically incorporates a constituent condition like that proposed by Morgan (1973), noting, "Certainly base generating these utterances as single nodes not dominated by S is more insightful than requiring an *ad hoc* condition on the result of general ellipsis" (1982: 88). Napoli improves upon Yanofsky's work by suggesting the hypothesis that nonsentential constituents may derive from major lexical category initial nodes; like Yanofsky, though, Napoli does not explore the origin and derivation of nonsentential major category structures in any detail, nor does she discuss any examples of structures dominated by major lexical category initial nodes.[7]

In spite of their shortcomings, Yanofsky's examination of initial NPs, Brame's comments on the bias towards S in research, and Napoli's study of phonological deletion indicate a promising direction in the study of nonsentential major lexical category structures within the framework of generative grammar. Yanofsky's examples of initial NPs and her arguments against deletion suggest that an ellipsis analysis like the ones proposed by Morgan (1973) and Sag (1976) cannot account for all nonsentential structures. Napoli's related suggestion, the alternative rejected by Morgan, that independent constituents may be derived under major lexical category initial nodes, is the basis of the nonsentential constituent structure analysis that I develop in this work, an analysis which incorporates Brame's suggestion about alternative category types by postulating that S, S', and the set of major lexical categories all function as initial nodes in a generative grammar.

2.2 Competing analyses: an ellipsis analysis vs. a nonsentential constituent structure analysis

The claim of an ellipsis analysis is that independent major lexical category structures are necessarily related to full sentence sources through ellipsis rules operating under the Condition of Recoverability. The claim of a nonsentential constituent structure analysis, in contrast, is that independent major lexical category structures are generated under the initial nodes of NP, VP, ADJP, ADVP, and PP.[8]

Empirically and theoretically, one class of data provides the crucial evidence to motivate the nonsentential constituent structure analysis. The data consist of independent major lexical category structures that cannot be the result of ellipsis rules because there is no discourse or pragmatic controller providing the identity that is necessary to trigger their operation and to guarantee recoverability. Yanofsky (1978) originally suggested these arguments in her discussion of discourse initial NPs, and Napoli (1982) pointed out that they support an analysis of nonsentential constituents generated under major lexical category initial nodes; neither Yanofsky nor Napoli, however, systematically motivates this hypothesis. In this section, I extend Yanofsky's arguments by applying them to all major lexical categories within discourse and by demonstrating that the arguments support the claim that independent major lexical categories are generated as nonsentential constituent structures. Extending Yanofsky's arguments to major lexical category structures within discourse is necessary for two reasons: first, it eliminates the possible counterclaim that discourse initial NPs are a special set of utterances with pragmatic qualities that allow them to appear alone; and second, it provides evidence for adopting a nonsentential constituent structure analysis for all independent major lexical category structures.

In many cases, an ellipsis analysis and a nonsentential constituent structure analysis predict the same results. Consider the examples of (13):

(13a) A: What happened in 1974?
       B: A scandal in the White House.
(13b) A: What did President Nixon and his Executive staff try to do?
       B: Obstruct justice.
(13c) A: When was Nixon elected President?
       B: In 1968 and 1972.
(13d) A: How did he feel when he was forced to resign?
       B: Very angry.

(13e) A: Has a U.S. President resigned before?
      B: Never.

Either analysis describes straightforward answers to questions.

An ellipsis analysis claims that each answer in (13) is necessarily related to a representation of a full sentence source:

(14a) A scandal in the White House (happened in 1974).
(14b) (President Nixon and his Executive staff tried to) obstruct justice.
(14c) (Nixon was elected President) in 1968 and 1972.
(14d) (He felt) very angry (when he was forced to resign).
(14e) (A U.S. President) never (has resigned before).

Within Morgan's (1973) syntactic framework, a deletion rule of General Ellipsis would delete the portions of the syntactic representations of the answers that are structurally identical to the syntactic representations of the questions. Within Sag's (1976) logical framework, an ellipsis rule would delete the portions of the S-structure representations of the answers that are semantically identical to the Logical Form representations of the questions.[9]

A nonsentential constituent structure analysis, in contrast, claims that each answer in (13) is dominated by a major lexical category initial node:[10]

(15a) $[_{NP} [_{DET}$ a$] [_N$ scandal$] [_{PP}$ in the White House$]]$
(15b) $[_{VP} [_V$ obstruct$] [_{NP}$ justice$]]$
(15c) $[_{PP} [_P$ in$] [_{NP}$ 1968 and 1972$]]$
(15d) $[_{ADJP} [_{ADVP}$ very$] [_{ADJ}$ angry$]]$
(15e) $[_{ADVP} [_{ADV}$ never$]]$

The nonformal definition of a well-formed nonsentential constituent structure is that it conforms to the expansion properties of the lexical structure of its head; these properties include the selection of obligatory complements as well as the occurrence of optional specifiers and modifiers.[11] The major lexical category structures in (15) are well-formed in terms of the lexical structure of their heads: in (15a), the N head of the NP *a scandal in the White House* occurs with a determiner as a specifier and a prepositional phrase as a modifier; in (15b), the V head of the VP *obstruct justice* selects a NP as a Patient; in (15c), the P head of the PP *in 1968 and 1972* selects a NP as a complement; in (15d), the ADJ head of the ADJP *very angry* occurs with an optional ADVP as a specifier; and in (15e), the ADV head of the ADVP *never* stands alone.

Within a nonsentential constituent structure analysis, expansion properties of lexical structure predict the well-formedness or ill-formedness of nonsentential constituent structures in a general way. In contrast to the well-formed examples in (15), the following examples are ill-formed because they violate expansion properties of their heads:

(16a) *scandal in the White House obstruct

$*[_{NP} [_N$ scandal] $[_{PP}$ in the White House] $[_{VP}$ obstruct]]

(16b) *the obstruct justice

$*[_{VP} [_{DET}$ the] $[_V$ obstruct] $[_{NP}$ justice]]

In (16a), a head N does not select a VP as a complement nor does it occur with a verb as some kind of modifier; in (16b), a head V does not occur with a determiner as a specifier.

So far, I have not presented any syntactic evidence to choose between an ellipsis analysis or a nonsentential constituent structure analysis of independent major lexical category structures. Since an ellipsis analysis operates within a grammar with a lexicon, it can predict the same range of expansion properties to account for the internal well-formedness or ill-formedness of independent major lexical categories. But a nonsentential constituent structure analysis does predict one class of data that an ellipsis analysis cannot account for, namely, the occurrence of well-formed major lexical category structures that have no discourse or pragmatic controller to trigger recoverable deletion under identity. In question and answer sequences, identity and recoverability usually are not a problem because the question almost always provides a discourse controller within the linguistic context. But other independent major lexical category structures, ones that are themselves questions or comments within a discourse, may not have a controller to trigger ellipsis rules. Consider the following sequences:[12]

(17a) A: The White House staff doesn't visit Tip O'Neill in his Congressional office.

B: Old grudge.

(17b) A: John doesn't know what the best defense against criminal charges would be.

B: Ask any lawyer.

(17c) A: They always put cash campaign contributions in a passbook savings account.

B: Cautious.

(17d) A: The President suggested forming a permanent Council on Ethics in Government.

B: Not with my tax money!

(17e) A: John probably would be involved in criminal activity if he carries too much money out of the country on his vacations.

B: Really?

Within a nonsentential constituent structure analysis, these examples are dominated by major lexical category initial nodes:

(18a) $[_{NP} [_{ADJP} \text{ old}] [_N \text{ grudge}]]$
(18b) $[_{VP} [_V \text{ ask}] [_{NP} \text{ any lawyer}]]$
(18c) $[_{ADJP} [_{ADJ} \text{ cautious}]]$
(18d) $[_{PP} [_{ADVP} \text{ not}] [_P \text{ with}] [_{NP} \text{ my tax money}]]$
(18e) $[_{ADVP} [_{ADV} \text{ really}]]$

Each nonsentential constituent structure is well-formed in terms of expansion properties of the lexical structure of its head.[13]

An ellipsis analysis, however, cannot predict that the major lexical category structures of (17) are well-formed within their respective discourse sequences because they do not occur with a controller to trigger deletion under identity. None of the major lexical category structures of (17) can occur at the beginning, in the middle, or at the end of the previous sentence within the discourse to indicate that a well-formed full sentence representation has created a linguistic context with a discourse controller for ellipsis. Consider, for example, the sequence of (17a):

(19a) *Old grudge the White House staff doesn't visit Tip O'Neill in his Congressional office

(19b) *The White House staff doesn't, old grudge, visit Tip O'Neill in his Congressional office

(19c) *The White House staff doesn't visit old grudge Tip O'Neill in his Congressional office

(19d) *The White House staff doesn't visit Tip O'Neill in his Congressional office old grudge

Without a discourse controller for identity, there is no well-formed syntactic or Logical Form representation to trigger ellipsis rules. Morgan's General Ellipsis rule requires a full sentence syntactic representation, but one does not exist for the NP *old grudge*. Sag's ellipsis rule requires a full sentence Logical Form representation; again, one does not exist for this NP.

The same argument holds for the other major lexical category structures in (17b) through (17e).

In addition to the fact that there is no discourse controller, there is no obvious pragmatic controller to trigger deletion or ellipsis in the sequences of (17). Hankamer and Sag (1976) define a pragmatic controller as discourse participants paying common attention to an extra-linguistic situation or event in context; each of the sequences in (17), however, could occur as a part of a telephone conversation in the absence of any common situational context, which indicates that pragmatic deletion is not a viable explanation.

In short, an ellipsis analysis would have to predict incorrectly that the major lexical category structures in (17) are ill-formed within their respective discourse sequences because it has no way of deriving the structures; thus, any ellipsis analysis is empirically inadequate because it cannot account for the entire range of independent major lexical categories within discourse.

Any ellipsis analysis with deletion rules also is theoretically inadequate because it is not able to maintain the Condition of Recoverability. It is possible to construct a variety of possible full sentence sources for each major lexical category structure in (17); again, consider the NP *old grudge* in (17a) as an example:

(20a) That's because of an old grudge.
(20b) The White House staff has an old grudge against Tip O'Neill.
(20c) Tip O'Neill has an old grudge against the White House staff.
(20d) He never forgave them for an old grudge.
(20e) They never forgave him for an old grudge.
(20f) There's an old grudge between them.

Since syntactic and Logical Form representations are different for each possible source, ellipsis rules would be operating on an indeterminate full sentence source. The source could be one of an indefinite number of possible sources, and any deletion would be free. Generating these independent major lexical category structures with ellipsis rules would have the undesirable consequence of free deletion creating undecidability within the grammar, just the consequence that the Condition of Recoverability protects against. Since the Condition of Recoverability is such a well-motivated constraint on generative grammars, any ellipsis analysis which cannot maintain it is theoretically undesirable.

The assumptions of an ellipsis analysis within generative grammar are summed up here by Hankamer:

> The basic fact to be accounted for is that every elliptical sentence is a truncated version of some well-formed non-elliptical sentence. . . .If the elliptical clauses . . . are generated directly by the base rules, this generalization is lost. (1973: 24)

The arguments above, however, demonstrate that an ellipsis analysis is inadequate because Hankamer's generalization about the extension of the deletion framework incorporates a hidden assumption that there is always a unique and recoverable one-to-one correspondence between a nonsentential structure and a full sentence source. The lack of such a source as shown in the examples of (19) and the variety of possible sources as shown in the examples of (20) demonstrate that this automatic and predictable correspondence does not always occur.

In sum, an ellipsis analysis is empirically and theoretically inadequate for two main reasons: first, it cannot describe independent major lexical category structures for which there is no controller to trigger deletion under identity; and second, any deletion creating such major lexical categories would be unrecoverable because a full sentence source is indeterminate, which violates the Condition of Recoverability. A nonsentential constituent structure analysis, in contrast, automatically predicts well-formed independent major lexical category structures without a controller for identity. Further, it does not violate the Condition of Recoverability because it does not postulate any deletion. It is the best-motivated analysis to account for all independent major lexical category structures because it accounts for the examples of (13) as well as those of (17).

One possible objection to the nonsentential constituent structure analysis motivated here is that it crucially depends upon examples that some native speakers regard as awkward. A few speakers point out that the examples of (17) could be considered awkward even though they admit that they seem to be grammatically well-formed. Many such independent major lexical category structures, though, do occur quite regularly in natural language. Consider the following examples taken from *The Presidential Transcripts*:

(21a) P: Apparently, she [Mrs. Hunt] was the pillar of strength in that family before [her] death.

　　 H: Great sadness.

(21b) P: The point would be to date it back on Saturday, so it is that
           day.
      D: Continuous.
(21c) E: This grand jury started focusing on the aftermath and he
           might be involved.
      H: Exactly.
(21d) D: Hunt and Libby were in his office.
      H: In Colson's office?
(21e) D: Maybe we could invite the Committee down to the
           Roosevelt Room or the Blair House.
      H: Maintain informality.
      (*Transcripts* 1974: 109, 65, 232, 124, 164)

Each of these independent major lexical categories could serve as a crucial
example in the argumentation motivating a nonsentential constituent structure analysis because each one occurs without a controller to trigger recoverable deletion. The VP in (21e), for example, cannot occur at any point in
the previous sentence to create a linguistic context for ellipsis:

(22a) *Maintain informality maybe we could invite the Committee
      down to the Roosevelt Room or the Blair House
(22b) *Maybe we could invite the Committee maintain informality
      down to the Roosevelt Room or the Blair House
(22c) *Maybe we could invite the Committee down to the Roosevelt
      Room or the Blair House maintain informality

In addition, any deletion creating the VP would violate the Condition of
Recoverability because of the variety of possible full sentence sources:

(23a) H: Perhaps we could maintain informality there.
(23b) H: We could maintain informality if we were in the Roosevelt
           Room or the Blair House.
(23c) H: Inviting the Committee there would allow us to maintain
           informality.

Nor is there any obvious pragmatic controller for the examples in (21) since
none refers to a simultaneous event.

The examples in (21) are representative of the structure and style of
nonsentential constituents as a part of conversational discourse in natural
language, and thereby serve as a check on the validity of the constructed
examples presented in (17). In response to the problem of awkward exam-

ples, I attempt to provide clear and stylistically acceptable examples of independent major lexical categories in this work. Not all of the examples will be well-regarded by all native speakers; nevertheless, there should be enough noncontroversial examples to support the basic points of the argumentation and analysis.

2.3 Conclusion

As the first step in the development of a theory of nonsentential constituents, this chapter presented arguments motivating the claim that nonsentential constituent structures are dominated by major lexical categories as initial nodes. This nonsentential constituent structure analysis is intended to replace previous ellipsis analyses, which assume that deletion rules operate across sentence boundaries to create fragments. Although it is easy to see why an ellipsis analysis seems intuitively obvious, it is important to realize why such an analysis is misleading on both empirical and theoretical grounds. This chapter has shown that ellipsis analyses are empirically inadequate because they cannot account for the entire range of independent major category structures. I suspect that ellipsis analyses suffered from this inadequacy because of a flaw in the data under consideration: the only examples of independent major category structures considered were answers to questions. Sag specifically states that his ellipsis rule is intended to account for answers to questions (1976: 300). Morgan says that his ellipsis rule is intended to account for "replies to questions, orders, statements, etc. of a sort commonly referred to as 'sentence fragments' " (1973: 720). His data, however, consist entirely of question and answer sequences. Yanofsky's most important insight was her identification of a class of data, initial NPs, which, when considered carefully, challenge the assumptions of an ellipsis analysis. Once data beyond answers to questions are considered, the empirical problems of an ellipsis analysis become more obvious. This chapter also has shown that ellipsis analyses are theoretically inadequate because they cannot maintain the Condition of Recoverability as a general condition on deletion. I believe that ellipsis analyses suffered from this inadequacy because of a certain carelessness with regard to the definition of the autonomous boundaries of syntax, which technically restrict grammatical operations such as deletion to an intrasentential role. Once the constraint of autonomy is considered seriously, the theoretical problems of an ellipsis analysis become more clear.

In this chapter, I have motivated a nonsentential constituent structure analysis by showing how it accounts for the entire range of independent major lexical categories without violating the Condition of Recoverability. In the next chapter, I show how a competence model of nonsentential constituent structures accounts for the syntactic properties of independent major lexical categories within the bounds of an autonomous grammar.

3. A Competence Model of the Grammar of Nonsentential Constituent Structures

3.0 Introduction

This chapter develops a competence model of the grammar of nonsentential constituent structures dominated by major category initial nodes using the Government-Binding (GB) theory of Chomsky (1981, 1982, 1986a,b):[1] §3.1 describes the D-structure representation of nonsentential constituent structures; §3.2 describes their S-structure representation; and §3.3 describes their representation at Logical Form. Each section also considers the implications of this research in terms of general issues within research on the theory of GB.

At D-structure, describing the grammar of nonsentential constituent structures requires integrating a generalization within X-bar theory, namely, the statement that the initial node of a generative grammar is X^{max}. Generalizing the initial node to X^{max} correctly describes all of the categories generated by a grammar, including sentence structures from the initial node of INFL" and major lexical category constituent structures from the set of initial nodes represented by X". This proposal has general implications for certain issues within research on X-bar theory: it provides evidence that the category of sentence is integrated into X-bar theory as the maximal projection of INFL rather than V; it also supports a constraint limiting the participating categories in X-bar theory to the set of major syntactic categories.

At S-structure, describing the grammar of nonsentential constituent structures requires an extension of the principles of Case theory in order to describe well-formed independent NPs. The extension of Case theory is presented in the form of a rule assigning Case to nouns and pronouns generated under the major lexical category of NP as their initial node.

At Logical Form, describing the grammar of nonsentential constituent structures requires the formulation of a marked principle of Binding theory in order to describe well-formed independent NPs, in particular, reflexives and reciprocals in or as nonsentential constituent structures. The description of the Logical Form representation of nonsentential constituent structures also illustrates the implications of the constraint of autonomy: if the semantic representation of constituent structures is limited to properties of Logical Form determined by the grammar, then the burden of accounting for the interpretation of independent constituents is shifted from semantics to pragmatics.

3.1 The D-structure representation of nonsentential constituent structures

This section of Chapter Three works out the effects of generalizing the initial node of the grammar to X^{max}. In this section, I first provide some background information on the theory of GB and the submodule of X-bar theory in §3.1.1 and describe well-formed nonsentential constituent structures at the level of D-structure in §3.1.2; I then consider the implications of this research in terms of general issues within research on X-bar theory in §3.1.3.

3.1.1 *Background*

The theory of GB is a development of Chomsky's continuing work on constraining the number and form of possible generative grammars; such work began with his early distinction between describing the generative grammars of particular languages and describing linguistic theory, which "specifies the form of the grammar of a possible human language" (1965: 25). The Condition of Recoverability on Deletion is an early example of a constraint within linguistic theory: it restricts the operation of all deletion rules in individual grammars, so no grammar can include a deletion rule that violates recoverability; furthermore, because the Condition is stated as a generalization within linguistic theory, it need not be repeated in the grammars of individual languages. Linguistic theory describes Universal Grammar, the set of basic elements and the set of generalizations and restrictions that apply to all generative grammars of individual languages, thereby specifying crucial aspects of the form of a possible grammar. GB is a theory of Universal Grammar, and research in GB concentrates upon investigating the principles that constrain rules and representations within the components of generative grammars describing individual languages.

Figure 2

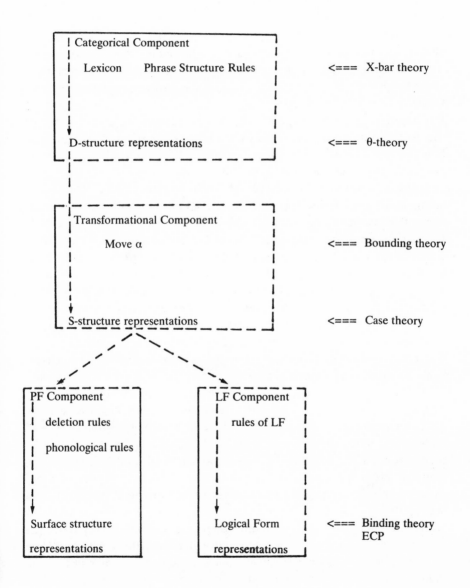

Figure 2 illustrates the components of a generative grammar and their connections to the modules of GB. The double arrows indicate that the modules of GB on the right constrain the associated rules and representations in the grammar: the principles of X-bar theory constrain the form of phrase structure rules in the categorical component; the principles of θ-theory constrain the form of D-structure representations; the principles of Bounding theory constrain the operation of the movement rule in the transformational component; the principles of Case theory constrain the form of S-structure representations; and the principles of Binding theory constrain the form of Logical Form representations, in particular the relations between anaphors and antecedents, and the ECP (Empty Category Principle) governs interpretation of empty categories.

The organization of the theory of GB into modules is an extension of strong autonomy: as discussed in Chapter One, the constraint of autonomy treats the grammar as a whole as a module by restricting it to internally defined elements and independent operation; the condition of modularity defines each subsystem of principles within GB as an autonomous module; in other words, the principles of X-bar theory or Case theory, for example, are defined and formulated internally to that module, and the internal operation of each module is independent of other modules. The interaction of principles within different modules within GB functions to explain many structural properties of the representations generated by a grammar.

Each module of GB theory contains a small number of principles, some of which are formulated in terms of parametric variation with binary values that are determined through the interaction of Universal Grammar with the grammar of an individual language. Within the categorical component, for example, languages vary with respect to the position of a head with respect to its complements: English, for instance, is head-left (complements within a VP, for example, follow the head verb); other languages, in contrast, are head-right (e.g., Japanese, Amharic). A principle of X-bar theory offers this parameter of head-left or head-right to languages, and setting this parameter in a generative grammar accounts for word order within the phrase structure of an individual language. Once the parameters of Universal Grammar are set in a particular way, the result is a Core Grammar of an individual language. The generative grammar of an individual language consists of a Core Grammar plus a periphery, which includes such additions as irregular morphology, dialectal variation, and other marked rules and constructions.

In addition to the principles within subsystems, in GB there are general principles which Chomsky calls "overriding principles"; these include the Projection Principle, the Predication Principle, and the Principle of Full Interpretation (1986a: 93, 102). The Projection Principle specifies that D-structure, S-structure, and Logical Form representations must preserve lexical structure. The Projection Principle ensures, for example, that a verb marked as transitive in the lexicon occurs with a NP argument functioning as a direct object in D-structure and that this lexical structure of the VP is preserved through the derivation of the syntactic structure to S-structure and Logical Form. The idea here is that given lexical representation, syntactic representation follows, and the Projection Principle ensures this relationship. The Predication Principle ensures that a VP predicate has a NP subject within a sentence structure (Williams 1980). The Projection Principle and the Predication Principle apply to all of the levels of syntactic derivation within the grammar, D-structure, S-structure, and Logical Form. The Principle of Full Interpretation, in contrast, applies only to the interpretive representations at Phonetic Form and Logical Form; it specifies that each element within a PF or LF structure generated by the grammar must be licensed for the structure to be well-formed. Licensing means that each element in a structure must be there by virtue of some other element: for example, an anaphor is licensed by its antecedent; each complement within a VP is licensed by the head V; a NP subject is licensed by its VP predicate.[2]

Many of the principles in GB are defined and formulated in terms of government, which is essentially the relationship between the head of a category and the categories that are dependent upon it. Government is based on the notion of c-command, which Sells defines as follows:

(1)   α c-commands β iff every branching node dominating α dominates β
      (1985: 39)

Structural configurations can be analyzed in terms of c-command:

(2) $[_{V''} [_{V'} [_V] [_{N''}]] [_{P''}]]$

In this V" configuration, for example, V c-commands N" because the branching node V', which dominates V, also dominates N". In this configuration, V does not c-command P" because V' does not dominate P".[3] Sells also provides a definition of government:

(3)   α governs β iff:
    (a)   α c-commands β, and
    (b)   α is an X^0, i.e., {N, V, P, A, INFL}, and
    (c)   every maximal projection dominating β dominates α
    (1985: 40)

In the V" configuration in (2), V governs N" in the prototypical case of government, which is a head verb governing its complements within a VP. Government is the basic relationship within GB theory, and several modules, including θ-theory, Case theory, and Binding theory, have principles defined in terms of government and c-command.[4]

Within the development of GB as a description of a restrictive theory of Universal Grammar, research on the theory of phrase structure has progressed towards the goal of constraining the number and form of possible types of phrase structure rules within the categorical component of individual grammars. The general direction of this work has been to eliminate the type of phrase structure rules that linguists proposed while working within the framework of Standard Theory. In the 1960s, Standard Theory rewriting rules detailed the expansion of each different syntactic category in a language:

(4a)   S → NP AUX VP
(4b)   VP → V NP
(4c)   NP → DET N
    (Chomsky 1965: 68)

This type of rewriting rule, however, soon proved inadequate because it is essentially unconstrained (cf. Radford 1981, who summarizes Lyons' (1968) argument against Standard Theory rewriting rules, which is their lack of a constrained connection between a lexical head and a phrasal category; in other words, no constraint eliminates rules like VP → AP NP in Standard Theory). In the 1970s, Chomsky (1970) and others (in particular, Jackendoff 1977a,b) began to develop the theory of phrase structure called X-bar theory, which, acting like other modules of linguistic theory, defines the set of basic elements in phrases and establishes a set of general restrictions on the form of phrase structure in individual grammars.

Van Riemsdijk and Williams (1986) note that a theory of phrase structure has to account for two generalizations. The first generalization is that the head of a category projects to a matching phrasal category: N, for example, projects to the major lexical category of NP, or N^{max}; V projects to VP, or V^{max}; and so on. The second generalization is that complements occur in certain orders within major lexical categories; in the expansion of VP in English, for instance, the verb is followed by its set of complements, within which the NP precedes any other elements:

(5a) John put the bug in the Democratic party headquarters.
(5b) *John the bug in the Democratic party headquarters put
(5c) *John put in the Democratic party headquarters the bug

X-bar theory incorporates these generalizations concerning hierarchical structure and internal order by specifying abstract principles that describe *all* well-formed phrases generated by a grammar. For example, by making X stand for any lexical category X^0, and X^{max} (or XP) stand for the phrasal category of X, the generalization that lexical heads are identical to their phrasal projections as major lexical categories is incorporated into the grammar. X as a variable stands for all lexical and phrasal categories, so the generalization holds for the hierarchical structure of well-formed NPs, VPs, and so on. To account for the order of a head with respect to its set of complements, a parameterized principle within X-bar theory is set for head-left in the generative grammar of English.

To explain the internal order of elements within phrases, particularly the order of the set of complements within a VP, current research explores the relationship of X-bar theory to other principles in modules of GB in an effort to see whether interaction among principles accounts for any of these properties of phrase structure. In one example of interaction, Stowell (1981) points out that an Adjacency Principle within Case theory accounts for the NP-first order of complements within the expansion of a VP by requiring a NP to be next to its governing V in order to receive Case. In the most significant example of interaction, Chomsky (1981, 1986a,b) points out that the combination of the principles of X-bar theory and the Projection Principle makes all Standard Theory rewriting rules redundant and therefore eliminatable. The lexical entry for each verb, for example, specifies its selection properties, so there is no need for any special rewriting rule to describe the expansion of VP in English: in (5), for instance, the lexical entry for the verb *put* specifies the type of complements that must follow it (NP, PP), and the Projection Principle ensures that this structure of complements is preserved throughout the levels of representation in the grammar. Since each lexical item specifies its selection properties, the interaction among principles in GB functions to eliminate the need for traditional phrase structure rules in the categorical component of a generative grammar.[5]

Following Stowell (1981, 1983) and others (Koopman 1984; Travis 1984; Kayne 1984), Chomsky suggests that the following schema constitutes X-bar theory:

(6a) X" → X"* X'
(6b) X' → X X"*
      (Chomsky 1986b: 3)

The rule for X" in (6a) states that a major lexical category expands to a set (0 or more) of specifiers plus an intermediate category; the rule for X' in (6b) states that an intermediate category expands to a lexical category plus a set (0 or more) of complements. Theoretically, the order of X"* and the head X is irrelevant, and a specific order is parameterized within the grammars of individual languages; the order above reflects the order of English. In this schema, X"* represents zero or more occurrences of any maximal projection, so both specifiers and complements are themselves major lexical categories.[6]

Stowell articulates the principles of X-bar theory represented in this schema:

(7a) [i]   Every phrase is endocentric.
(7b) [ii]   Specifiers appear at the X" level; subcategorized complements appear within X'.
(7c) [iii] The head always appears adjacent to one of the boundaries of X'.
(7d) [iv]   The head term is one bar-level lower than the immediately dominating phrasal node.
(7e) [v]   Only maximal projections may appear as non-head terms within a phrase.
      (1981: 70; (i) - (v))

Principle (7a), Stowell's (i), ensures that each phrase has matching phrasal and lexical heads: N" → N; V" → V; and so on. Stowell's principle (ii) describes the structure of the specifiers and complements within phrases: specifiers occur at the X" level; complements occur at the X' level because they are subcategorized. Principle (iii) describes the one parameter within the principles of X-bar theory: languages vary as to the position of the head with respect to its set of complements, and the Core Grammar of a particular language describes the left or right setting of this head parameter. Principle (iv) describes the hierarchical structure of phrases as X" → X' → X, and principle (v) specifies that only maximal projections can occur as the specifier or complement of a head.

Stowell's major contribution to research on phrase structure is to suggest that these principles of X-bar theory are category neutral because they describe all major lexical categories — NP, VP, ADJP, and so on. Like Chomsky, Stowell concludes that there are no specific rewriting rules in the categorical component of individual grammars; he proposes, in fact, that the phrase structure portion of the categorical component be completely eliminated, claiming that the principles of X-bar theory in combination with other principles are sufficient to describe the structure of all types of well-formed phrases at D-structure.

Rizzi (1987) supports Stowell's conclusion by pointing out that an informal description of the rules within X-bar theory states that any maximal projection can occur as a specifier or as a complement with any head, which captures a generalization that the internal structure of phrases is homogeneous, especially for the set of complements (in general, heads in English can take NP, PP, and embedded S complements). One consequence of eliminating phrase structure rules, though, is the generation of certain ill-formed structures:

(8a)   *The scandal exist Mary
(8b)   *John is fond money
(8c)   *The destruction the evidence

The interaction of principles within the theory of GB, however, explains the ill-formedness of these structures. A violation of the Projection Principle explains (8a): the verb *exist* is intransitive, so it is ill-formed within a transitive structure; this structure would be ruled out at D-structure. A violation of a principle of Case theory would rule out (8b) and (8c) at S-structure: NPs require Case, but do not receive it from adjectives such as *fond* or nouns such as *destruction*; a preposition, on the other hand, can assign Case in the contrasting well-formed S-structures *fond of money* and *the destruction of the evidence*. Rizzi cites the explanation of these structures as one illustration of the interaction of principles functioning to eliminate ill-formed structures within the framework of GB.

In his most recent work, Chomsky extends the X-bar framework to sentential and clausal categories by proposing the following rules for two categories stipulated as major non-lexical categories, where I = INFL (formerly AUX in Standard Theory) and C = COMP (complementizer):

(9a) $S = I" = [_{NP} [_{I'} I [_{VP} V \ldots]]]$
(9b) $S' = C" = [\ldots [_{C'} C I"]]$
(1986b: 3)

He suggests that these rules fall under the principles of X-bar theory because the structures of sentences or clauses conform to the general rules expanding X" to specifiers, heads, and complements. In (9a), a sentence is considered the maximal projection of its head of INFL, which is the node dominating Tense, Modal, and certain other auxiliary-type features like negation; NP is the specifier of INFL and VP is its complement. In (9b), Complementizer is considered a head which selects a sentence (INFL") as its complement. The two rules account for the following structures:

(10a) Mary will implicate John.
$[_{I"} [_{N"} Mary] [_{I'} [_I [_M will]] [_{V"} [_{V'} [_V implicate] [_{N"} John]]]]]$
(10b) for Mary to implicate John
$[_{C"} [_{C'} [_C for] [_{I"} Mary to implicate John]]]$
(10c) that Mary implicated John
$[_{C"} [_{C'} [_C that] [_{I"} Mary implicated John]]]$

Example (10a) is a matrix sentence; (10b) and (10c) are examples of sentential complements. Under the extension of X-bar theory in (9), sentences (I") and clauses (C") are major non-lexical categories, and phrases (X") are major lexical categories.[7]

Rizzi (1987) points out that extending the X-bar framework to clausal structures solves at least two interesting theoretical problems. First, it allows a simple structural definition of the notion subject as [NP, XP]: in sentences, for example, the subject is the NP immediately dominated by the maximal projection of INFL"; in NPs, the subject is the N" immediately dominated by the maximal projection of N". A unified definition of subject accounts naturally for the parallel subjects in sentences and noun phrases:

(11a) John will destroy the evidence.
$[_{INFL"} [_{N"} John] [_{INFL'} [_I [_M will]]$
$[_{V"} [_{V'} [_V destroy] [_{N"} the evidence]]]]]$
(11b) John's destruction of the evidence
$[_{N"} [_{N"} John's] [_{N'} [_N destruction] [_{P"} of the evidence]]]$

Second, Rizzi also points out that extending the X-bar framework to clausal structures allows a more unified statement about movement, namely, that movement is to the specifier position. Consider the following examples:

(12a) John may have been implicated t.

$[_{INFL''} [_{N''}$ John$] [_{INFL'} [_{INFL} [_M$ may$]]$
$[_{V''}$ [have] [been] $[_{V'} [_V$ implicated$] t]]]]$

(12b) John may be likely to succeed.

$[_{INFL''} [_{N''}$ John$] [_{INFL'} [_{INFL} [_M$ may$]] [_{V''} [_{V'} [_V$ be$] [_{ADJ''}$ likely$]$
$[_{S'}$ for $[_S t [_{V''} [_{V'} [_V$ to succeed$]]]]]]]]]$

(12c) the city's destruction (by the enemy)

$[_{N''} [_{N''}$ the city's$] [_{N'} [_N$ destruction$] [_{P''}$ by the enemy$]]]$

(12d) Who might see John?

$[_{C''}$ who $[_{C'} [_C] [_{INFL''} t [_{INFL'} [_{INFL} [_M$ might$]]$
$[_{V''} [_{V'} [_V$ see$] [_{N''}$ John$]]]]]]]$

In examples (12a) - (12c), movement is to the NP specifier position: in (12a) and (12b), the NP is the specifier of the sentence; in (12c), the NP is specifier of a NP. In example (12d), *Wh*-movement is to the specifier position for a *wh*-element in COMP. Based on these and other arguments, Rizzi's conclusion is that extending the X-bar framework to sentential and clausal structures has significant theoretical advantages.

3.1.2 *Describing nonsentential constituent structures*

Integrating the generalization that major lexical categories can function as initial nodes within a generative grammar does not involve a change in the schema of X-bar theory; in fact, the principles of X-bar theory govern the well-formedness of constituents whether they are generated independently or internally within sentences. It does, however, involve a generalization in the definition of the initial node in a grammar. In his work in Standard Theory, following work in mathematical and computational linguistics which defined S as a start symbol, Chomsky designates S as the initial node of a grammar: "S is the designated *initial symbol* of the grammar (representing the category 'Sentence')" (1965: 66; author's emphasis). Research within a Chomskyan framework has operated under this assumption of a single sentential initial node ever since. What is proposed here, in contrast, is that the initial node of X-bar theory is X^{max}. Generalizing the initial node to X^{max} describes *all* of the structures generated by a grammar: the maximal projection of Inflection (INFL") generates sentence structures; the maximal projection of Complementizer (C") generates clausal structures; and the maximal projection of a lexical category (X") generates nonsentential major lexical category constituent structures.[8] All together, INFL", C", and X" constitute the set of major syntactic categories represented by the term X^{max} within the version of X-bar theory adopted here: INFL" and C" represent the major non-lexical categories, and X" represents the set of major lexical categories.[9] The generalization concerning X^{max} as an initial node is a part of X-bar theory, and, ultimately, Universal Grammar, although the discussion here will focus upon the effects of incorporating this generalization into the generative grammar describing English.

X^{max} as the initial node in X-bar theory interacts with general and specific licensing principles in GB in order to describe well-formed sentence structures and nonsentential constituent structures. The general licensing principles that are particularly relevant for a consideration of sentence structures and nonsentential constituent structures at the level of D-structure are the Projection Principle and the Predication Principle because the two classes of structures generated by the grammar contrast in terms of their interaction with them. Well-formed sentence structures are licensed by a combination of the Projection Principle and the Predication Principle, which ensures that their D-structure, S-structure, and Logical Form representations preserve not only the lexical structure of the internal constituents but also the predication structure of the sentence, which includes a subject as the external argument of the VP. Well-formed nonsentential constituent structures, in contrast, are licensed by the Projection Principle alone, which ensures that their D-structure, S-structure, and Logical Form representations preserve the lexical structure of their heads.

The licensing of well-formed nonsentential constituent structures at D-structure crucially depends upon the Projection Principle. The Projection Principle reflects speakers' knowledge of the structure of specific lexical items; in other words, given a lexical representation of an item, a verb, for example, its syntactic representation necessarily preserves its lexical representation as a transitive verb or a verb with an obligatory PP complement. Within syntactic structures, the Projection Principle formally preserves lexical structure, which is defined as the θ-marked arguments associated with any particular lexical head. θ-marked arguments are thematic roles such as Agent, Experiencer, Theme, Patient, Source, Goal, Location, and Instrument.[10] A lexical entry selects and marks a subset of θ-roles in a relationship entitled s-selection (semantic selection). θ-roles, in turn, are associated with syntactic categories through a relationship of Canonical Structural Realization: in English, the θ-role of Patient, for example, has a canonical structural realization as a NP; the θ-role of Location has a canonical structural realization as a NP within a PP with a locative preposition; and so on. θ-marking entails syntactic subcategorization, so lexical structure also includes the subcategorization frame for the head of a phrase; a subcategorization frame consists of a set of categories in a relationship entitled c-selection (category selection). Chomsky describes the Projection Principle as follows:

> [The Projection Principle] states informally that the θ-marking properties of each lexical item must be represented categorially at each syntactic level: at LF, S-structure, and D-structure. . . .Properly formulated, the Projection Principle extends the θ-Criterion from LF to S-structure and D-structure. (1982: 8-9)

Van Riemsdijk and Williams define the θ-Criterion and use it in a statement of the Projection Principle:

> θ-Criterion
> Every NP must be taken as the argument of some predicate; furthermore, it must be so taken at most once. (1986: 243)

> Projection Principle
> The θ-Criterion holds at D-structure, S-structure, and LF. (1986: 145)

Rizzi (1987) characterizes the level of D-structure in the grammar as the syntactic representation that immediately reflects lexical properties: there is a direct correspondence between θ-roles and their recipients because the NP recipients of θ-roles are in the positions to which θ-roles are assigned. The extension of the θ-Criterion through the Projection Principle ensures the preservation of this fundamental argument structure through S-structure and Logical Form.

The following examples illustrate the licensing action of the Projection Principle for two nonsentential constituent structure VPs:

(13a) A: John did something stupid, but I'm not sure what.
       B: Put the bug in the Democratic party headquarters.
           $[_{V''} [_{V'} [_V \text{ put}] [_{N''} \text{ the bug}] [_{P''} \text{ in the Democratic party head-}$
           quarters]]]   PATIENT   LOCATION

(13b) B: *Put the bug the camera in the Democratic party headquarters
           $*[_{V''} [_{V'} [_V \text{ put}] [_{N''} \text{ the bug}] [_{N''} \text{ the camera}]$
           $[_{P''} \text{ in the Democratic party headquarters}]]]$

The lexical entry for the verb *put* s-selects a Patient argument and a Location argument; the Patient argument entails the c-selection of its canonical structural realization as a NP, and the Location argument entails the c-selection of its canonical structural realization as a NP within a locative PP. Both θ-marking and subcategorization are satisfied under government, which has the effect of limiting selection to the relationship between a head and the categories that it selects within its own maximal projection (cf. §3.1.1 for a definition of government). A nonsentential constituent structure VP that conforms to these selection properties is well-formed because it preserves the θ-Criterion and satisfies the Projection Principle at D-structure. In the VP in (13a), for example, each NP, the NP *the bug* and the NP within the PP *in the Democratic party headquarters*, is selected once and only once as an argument: *the bug* functions as a Patient argument, and *the Democratic party headquarters* functions as a Location argument (an NP within a PP receives its θ-role compositionally from the verb and the preposition). A nonsentential constituent structure VP that violates selection properties of its lexical head is ill-formed because it violates the θ-Criterion at D-structure: within the VP in (13b), for example, there are three NPs but only two possible arguments, which violates the required one-to-one correspondence between NPs and argument roles required by the θ-Criterion and the Projection Principle.[11]

Licensing nonsentential constituent structures via an interaction of X-bar theory and the Projection Principle accounts for the well-formedness or ill-formedness of their D-structure representations in a general way. Nonsentential constituent structures are well-formed if they conform to the expansion properties of their heads; conversely, nonsentential constituent structures are ill-formed if they violate the expansion properties of their heads. Consider the examples in the following sequences:

(14a) A: The White House staff doesn't visit Tip O'Neill in his Congressional office.

     B: Old grudge.

(14b) A: John doesn't know what the best defense against criminal charges would be.

     B: Ask any lawyer.

The syntactic representations of the nonsentential constituent structures in (14) indicate their major lexical category initial nodes:

(15a) [$_{N''}$ [$_{N'}$ [$_{ADJ''}$ old] [$_N$ grudge]]]
(15b) [$_{V''}$ [$_{V'}$ [$_V$ ask] [$_{N''}$ any lawyer]]]
PATIENT

These nonsentential constituent structures are well-formed because they conform to the expansion properties of their heads: in (15a), the head noun *grudge* occurs with an ADJP modifier, and in (15b), the head verb *ask* selects a Patient, and the NP *any lawyer* canonically functions as that argument. This method of licensing thus accounts automatically for the properties of D-structure representation, which Chomsky describes as a structure conforming to the principles of X-bar theory along with a "pure" representation of θ-role assignment (1986a: 100).

In contrast to the well-formed examples in (14) and (15), consider the following representations:

(16a) *grudge ask
  *[$_{N''}$ [$_{N'}$ [$_N$ grudge] [$_{V''}$ ask]]]
  *[$_{N''}$ [$_{N'}$ [$_N$ grudge]] [$_{V''}$ ask]]
(16b) *any lawyer ask
  *[$_{V''}$ [$_{N''}$ any lawyer] [$_{V'}$ [$_V$ ask]]]

These examples violate the expansion and ordering properties of their heads: in (16a), the head noun *grudge* does not select a VP as a single-bar complement, nor does it occur with a VP as a double-bar modifier. In (16b), the head verb *obstruct* does not select a NP as a specifier; the NP is uninterpretable as an argument, so the structure violates the θ-Criterion. Both nonsentential constituent structures are ill-formed (or not licensed as well-formed) at D-structure because they violate the Projection Principle by not conforming to the lexical structure of their heads.

In his work developing GB, Chomsky points out in several places that small changes in the principles of GB have complex consequences throughout the theory, and generalizing the initial node of X-bar theory to X^{max} does indeed have a significant consequence, namely, the generation and description of nonsentential constituent structures within the grammar. Yet at the same time, Chomsky warns, echoing Bresnan (1976a), that a proposed change in the theory is "no contribution . . . if it is matched or exceeded by proliferation elsewhere" (1981: 13). The proposed initial node of X^{max} as a method of generating nonsentential constituent structures and the proposed method of licensing their well-formedness at D-structure, however, does not require any new mechanisms, rules, or principles within the grammar because most of the grammatical properties of well-formed nonsentential constituent structures at D-structure fall out from the licensing interaction of X-bar theory and the Projection Principle.

Although the Projection Principle applies to all of the structures generated by the grammar, nonsentential constituent structures dominated by a major lexical category as a manifestation of the initial node of X" contrast with sentences generated under the initial node of INFL". The distinguishing feature of this contrast is the presence or the absence of the category INFL: nonsentential constituent structures, including VP, do not have any INFL node; sentence and clausal structures, however, do. What INFL triggers in the grammar is the Predication Principle as a licensing principle. The Predication Principle captures the compositional relationship between a predicate and a subject within a sentence. It describes the unique characteristic of a sentence, which is a structure that associates a subject with a verb phrase through the mediation of INFL.[12]

The contrast between sentences and nonsentential constituents is particularly clear in terms of the contrast between verbal and sentential structures. V" as an initial node generates a nonsentential constituent structure; C" as an initial node generates a clausal structure, possibly a subordinate clause (cf. note 8); and INFL" as an initial node generates a sentence structure:

(17a) A: John doesn't know what the best defense against criminal charges would be.

      B: Ask any lawyer.

      $[_{V"} [_{V'} [_V \text{ ask}] [_{N"} \text{ any lawyer}]]]$

(17b) A: John doesn't know what the best defense against criminal charges would be.

      B: Whether he asks a lawyer or not.

      $[_{C"} [_{C'} [_C \text{ whether}] [_{INFL"} \text{ he asks a lawyer or not}]]]$

(17c) A: John doesn't know what the best defense against criminal charges would be.

      B: He could ask any lawyer.

      $[_{INFL"} [_{N"} \text{ he}] [_{INFL'} [_{INFL} [_M \text{ could}]]$
      $[_{V"} [_{V'} [_V \text{ ask}] [_{N"} \text{ any lawyer}]]]]]]$

The contrast between the examples illustrates the ability of a grammar with X^{max} as its initial node to generate all of these types of structures: in (17a), the initial node is V"; in (17b), the initial node is (possibly) C"; and in (17c), the initial node is INFL".

A paradigm of sentential and verbal structures illustrates the necessity for a grammar that distinguishes between sentences and nonsentential VP constituent structures:

(18a) It seems that John won't resign gracefully.
(18b) Seems that John won't resign gracefully.
(18c) John, resign gracefully.
(18d) John will resign gracefully, and Mary will, too.
(18e) John will resign his position, and Mary hers.
(18f) A: John refuses to do something.
     B: Resign gracefully.

Examples (18a) - (18e) are sentential structures deriving from INFL'': (18a) is a full sentence structure; (18b) is a sentence structure with deletion of unstressed initial material as described by Napoli (1982) (cf. §2.1); (18c) is an imperative; (18d) is a sentence structure with a deleted VP in the second clause; and (18e) is a sentence structure with a gapped construction across clauses. What (18a) - (18e) have in common is the grammatical features of tense and agreement as well as the predication feature of an external argument as subject, even though the subject has been deleted in (18b) and the subject plus auxiliary have been deleted in (18c).[13] These examples contrast with (18f), which is a nonsentential constituent structure deriving from V'': the base form of the verb *resign* does not exhibit tense or agreement and the VP has no external argument. The contrast between INFL'' and V'' as initial nodes thus correctly distinguishes between sentential structures and non-sentential VP constituent structures.

The contrast between INFL'' and X'' as initial nodes allows deletion in the grammar to be limited to an intrasentential domain. Deletion rules, operating under identity, create truncated sentence structures with missing material that is recoverable in a predictable way. These intrasentential deletion rules may be phonological in nature as Napoli (1982) and others (e.g., Zwicky 1983; van Riemsdijk and Williams 1986) suggest. The structures in (18b) - (18e), with deletion of unstressed initial material, deletion of an identical VP, deletion to an imperative, and deletion to a gapped construction, illustrate types of recoverable deletion within full sentences. The result of deletion operations, though, is a truncated *sentence*, which indicates that the structure was generated from an initial node of INFL''. In contrast, the structure in (18f), which is a nonsentential VP, does not involve any deletion at all.[14]

3.1.3 *Implications*

Chomsky points out that theoretical proposals within the framework of GB should have far-reaching effects (1986a: 148), and the generalization that X^{max} is the initial node of X-bar theory has effects in at least two areas: first, it generates and describes well-formed nonsentential constituent structures, and second, it has implications in terms of issues in research on X-bar theory. In this section, I first review some of the automatic predictions of the analysis of X^{max} as the initial node of the grammar, arguing that this generalization correctly constrains the grammar to generating just those syntactic structures that are well-formed sentences, clauses, and nonsentential constituents, and no others. I then discuss the implications of this research in terms of issues within the literature on X-bar theory.

The analysis of X^{max} as the initial node of the grammar defines the set of initial nodes to INFL", C", and the set of major categories represented by X". The restriction to major lexical categories dominated at their X" level automatically accounts for a number of properties of nonsentential constituent structures. First, it predicts exactly which single lexical items are well-formed as nonsentential constituent structures. Well-formed single lexical items are ones which do not select any obligatory complements within their bar projections as nonsentential constituent structures:

> (19a) A: John plays for a minor league baseball team in Washington D.C.
>   B: Outfielder.
> $[_{N''} [_{N'} [_{N} \text{outfielder}]]]$
> (19b) A: He's a left-handed batter.
>   B: Right-handed.
> $[_{ADJ''} [_{ADJ'} [_{ADJ} \text{right-handed}]]]$
> (19c) A: He might be moving up to the major leagues soon.
>   B: Never.
> $[_{ADV''} [_{ADV'} [_{ADV} \text{never}]]]$
> (19d) A: Was John's batting average over .200 last year?
>   B: Under.
> $[_{P''} [_{P'} [_{P} \text{under}]]]$
> (19e) A: John is upset about his newest contract.
>   B: Renegotiate.
> $[_{V''} [_{V'} [_{V} \text{renegotiate}]]]$

Single lexical items that are ill-formed as nonsentential constituent structures are ones which do not appear with their obligatorily selected complements:

(20a) A: John did something stupid, but I don't know what.
      B: *Put

           $*[_{V''} [_{V'} [_V \text{put}]]]$

(20b) A: Why does John spend so much time at the Washington zoo?
      B: *Fond

           $*[_{ADJ''} [_{ADJ'} [_{ADJ} \text{fond}]]]$

(20c) A: John's reading an interesting manuscript.
      B: *Part

           $*[_{N''} [_{N'} [_N \text{part}]]]$

In (20a), the single verb *put* is ill-formed because it occurs without its obligatory complements. In (20b) and (20c), the single adjective *fond* and the single noun *part* are ill-formed because they occur without their obligatory NP complements. These lexical items are only well-formed when they occur with their obligatory complements as in the following examples:

(21a) A: John did something stupid, but I don't know what.
      B: Put the bug in the Democratic party headquarters.

           $[_{V''} [_{V'} [_V \text{put}] [_{N''} \text{the bug}] [_{P''} \text{in the Democratic party head-}$
           quarters]]]

(21b) A: Why does John spend so much time at the Washington zoo?
      B: Fond of clandestine meetings there.

           $[_{ADJ''} [_{ADJ'} [_{ADJ} \text{fond}] [_{P''} \text{of clandestine meetings}]]$
           $[_{ADV''} \text{there}]]$

(21c) A: John's reading an interesting manuscript.
      B: Part of Nixon's memoirs.

           $[_{N''} [_{N'} [_N \text{part}] [_{P''} \text{of Nixon's memoirs}]]]$

An analysis which generates nonsentential major lexical categories under X" and licenses them via the Projection Principle automatically ensures the selection of obligatory complements at the single-bar level.

Defining the initial node of nonsentential constituent structures at the X" level also correctly predicts that they occur with their optional specifiers and modifiers at the double-bar level. The examples below are nonsentential constituent structures with optional specifiers:

(22a) A: The Attorney General will not promote John.
     B: The old grudge.

$[_{N''} [_{DET}$ the$] [_{N'} [_{ADJ''}$ old$] [_N$ grudge$]]]$

(22b) A: Experienced newspaper reporters give everyone the same advice about interpersonal relations in politics.
     B: Never gossip.

$[_{V''} [_{ADV''}$ never$] [_{V'} [_V$ gossip$]]]$

(22c) A: How did John feel about his boss's request for his time reports?
     B: Quite angry.

$[_{ADJ''} [_{ADV''}$ quite$] [_{ADJ'} [_{ADJ}$ angry$]]]$

(22d) A: Where does John live?
     B: Really near the office.

$[_{P''} [_{ADV''}$ really$] [_{P'} [_P$ near$] [_{N''}$ the office$]]]$

(22e) A: When will he be home?
     B: Very quickly.

$[_{ADV''} [_{ADV''}$ very$] [_{ADV'} [_{ADV}$ quickly$]]]$

In example (22a), the NP occurs with a determiner as a specifier. In examples (22b) - (22e), the VP, ADJP, PP, and ADVP constituent structures occur with ADVPs as specifiers. Nonsentential constituent structures also occur with optional modifiers at the double-bar level:

(23a) A: I know why the Attorney General will not promote John.
     B: The old grudge, which everybody knew about anyway.

$[_{N''} [_{DET}$ the$] [_{N'} [_{ADJ''}$ old$] [_N$ grudge$]]$
$[_{S'}$ which everybody knew about anyway$]]$

(23b) A: Experienced newspaper reporters give everyone the same advice about interpersonal relations in politics.
     B: Never gossip because people will believe that you are indiscreet.

$[_{V''} [_{ADV''}$ never$] [_{V'} [_V$ gossip$]]$
$[_{S'}$ because people will believe that you are indiscreet$]]$

(23c) A: Why did John slam his door?
     B: Angry, since his boss has never asked for time reports before.

$[_{ADJ''} [_{ADJ'} [_{ADJ}$ angry$]]$
$[_{S'}$ since his boss has never asked for time reports before$]]$

In each example above, the nonsentential constituent structure occurs with an optional S' modifier at the double-bar level.

Finally, an initial node of X" also predicts that some nonsentential constituent structures are free of certain sentential-type restrictions when they occur independently. In English, for example, certain adjectives are exclusively predicative; in a sentence, these predicative adjectives occur only within a VP:

(24a) John is ready.
(24b) *ready John
(24c) John is ill.
(24d) *Ill John
(24e) Mary feels faint.
(24f) *Faint Mary

As an independent major category, though, such an adjective can occur without the predicate structure of a VP:

(25a) A: Does John know we're leaving?
      J: Ready. (running into the room putting his jacket on)
          $[_{ADJ''} [_{ADJ'} [_{ADJ} ready]]]$
(25b) A: Why isn't John here?
      B: Ill.
          $[_{ADJ''} [_{ADJ'} [_{ADJ} ill]]]$
(25c) A: Mary looks funny.
      B: Faint.
          $[_{ADJ''} [_{ADJ'} [_{ADJ} faint]]]$

The analysis of X" as an initial node for nonsentential constituent structures, which includes ADJP as one initial node within the set of major lexical categories, correctly predicts that any adjective, whether attributive or predicative, can occur as a nonsentential constituent structure.

The analysis of X" as the one node of the grammar restricts the set of nonsentential constituent structures to the set of major lexical categories under their X" projections, a restriction which automatically accounts for many of the similarities between nonsentential constituents and constituents generated within sentences. This restriction, however, is not equivalent to the claim that constituents within sentences and nonsentential constituents are always identical, as shown by the examples of independent ADJPs in (25).

The most controversial example of a difference between constituents in sentences and nonsentential constituents concerns the presence or absence of a determiner within a NP. Singular count nouns like *thief*, *grudge*, and *tenor* require a determiner when they occur within sentences:

(26a) A/The thief left the door open.

(26b) *Thief left the door open

(26c) An/The/Some old grudge between Tip O'Neill and the White House staff keeps them apart.

(26d) *Old grudge between Tip O'Neill and the White House staff keeps them apart

(26e) A/The/Any tenor sings beautifully.

(26f) *Tenor sings beautifully

Within an ellipsis analysis, independent NPs retain their structure as a constituent internal to a sentence; in other words, singular count nouns must occur with a determiner. Morgan (1973) cites the following examples as evidence supporting such a constituent condition on NPs:

(27) Does Wolf like the soprano?
      *No, tenor
      No, the tenor.
      (1973: 736)

Yanofsky, though, points out that singular count NPs, which require a determiner when they occur as a constituent within a sentence, can occur without one when they initiate a discourse, citing the example of *Thief!* (1978: 492). The nonsentential constituent structure NP *old grudge* is another example that violates Morgan's condition on NPs by occurring without a determiner. Even Morgan's own examples can occur as independent NPs without determiners as in the following sequences, in which the NPs contradict the previous statement:

(28a) A: Mary is an/the alto.
      B: Soprano.

(28b) A: John is a/the bass.
      B: Tenor.

Morgan's examples include the word *no* as an overt contradictory element, and NPs without determiners occur in this construction as well:[15]

(29) A: Does Mary want to become an alto?
      B: No, soprano.

This seems to be a general phenomenon: as far as I can tell, any singular count noun can occur without a determiner when it is generated as a nonsentential constituent structure NP:

(30a) A: John is superstitious enough to write with only one kind of writing implement.

   B: Yellow pencil/Black pen/Felt marker/Special-order pen with invisible ink/Computer.

(30b) A: Someone implicated John.

   B: Butler/Wife/Handyman/Plumber/Old friend.

(30c) A: The legislature has been called into emergency session.

   B: Budget crisis/War/Death of the president.

(30d) A: John is someplace, but I don't know where.

   B: Office/Home/House/Committee meeting.

A constituent condition as incorporated into Morgan's ellipsis analysis is unable to predict this feature of the internal structure of independent NPs because it claims that constituents within sentences and nonsentential constituents are necessarily identical.[16]

In contrast, a nonsentential constituent structure analysis in which X" represents the set of major lexical category initial nodes automatically accounts for the internal feature of independent NPs without determiners because the licensing conditions for D-structure well-formedness consist of an interaction of X-bar theory and the Projection Principle. These licensing conditions predict that a singular count noun can occur without a determiner because determiners are an optional specifier possibility for the category of NP at D-structure. In an important way, the form of nonsentential constituent structure NPs is similar to that of plural NPs and non-count NPs, both of which can occur without determiners:

(31a) Thieves look for open doors.

(31b) Grudges often keep groups apart unnecessarily.

(31c) Tenors sing beautifully.

(31d) Death often serves the cause of political expediency.

The crucial point is that at D-structure the schema of X-bar theory and the Projection Principle allow nonsentential constituent structure NPs to occur without a determiner because the expansion of X" to a specifier (X"*, where * indicates zero or more) plus X' indicates that specifiers are optional, not obligatory, in the expansion of any category. The rules of X-bar theory and the Projection Principle in and of themselves do not require

that NPs occur with determiners; instead, the rule expanding N" (N" →
X"* N') describes a nonsentential constituent structure NP like *old grudge*
as well as a plural NP like *grudges* or a non-count NP like *death* as well-
formed: in each case, the specifier slot is unfilled.[17]

James McCawley (personal communication) disputes this analysis that
old grudge is a N" without a specifier; he suggests that the reason it occurs
without a determiner is that it may be generated simply as N'. This suggestion raises the possibility that the analysis presented above, in which nonsentential constituents are dominated by an initial node at the X" level, is
too restrictive, and suggests the counteranalysis that categories dominated
by a single-bar projection (X') or even lexical items dominated by a lexical
category (X⁰) can be initial nodes. I disagree with the claim that *old grudge*
is dominated by N' as an initial node because of the empirical and theoretical inadequacies of this counteranalysis.

First, an analysis which allows lexical categories (X⁰) to be initial nodes
clearly is empirically inadequate; such an analysis incorrectly predicts that
single lexical items without their obligatory complements are well-formed:

(32a) A: John did something stupid, but I don't know what.
      B: *Put
(32b) A: Why does John spend so much time at the Washington zoo?
      B: *Fond
(32c) A: John's reading an interesting manuscript.
      B: *Part

An analysis in which a nonsentential constituent structure is dominated at
its X" level, though, automatically predicts that heads must occur with their
obligatory complements and limits the occurrence of single lexical items to
just those which do not have any obligatory complements (cf. the discussion
of these examples as (20) - (21) above).

An analysis allowing initial nodes at the X' level, however, also
automatically accounts for the ill-formedness of examples like (32) since
obligatory complements occur at the single-bar level. An empirical argument ruling out an initial node of X' requires a consideration of some contrasts between sentence structures and nonsentential VP constituent structures. VP as an initial node generates nonsentential constituent structures
in the base form of the verb as in the following set of examples:

(33a) A: What does John do for a living?
      B: Play baseball for a minor league team in Washington D.C.
           [$_{V''}$ [$_{V'}$ [$_V$ play] [$_{N''}$ baseball]]
           [$_{P''}$ for a minor league team in Washington D.C.]]
(33b) A: Will he go to spring training this year?
      B: Be leaving any day now.
           [$_{V''}$ [be] [$_{V'}$ [$_V$ leaving]] [$_{ADV''}$ any day now]]
(33c) A: I wonder whether he'll make the big leagues this year.
      B: Have been wondering about that lately.
           [$_{V''}$ [have] [been] [$_{V'}$ [$_V$ wondering]] [$_{P''}$ about that]
           [$_{ADV''}$ lately]]

The first verb in a nonsentential VP has to be in its base form because there
is no INFL to mediate tense and agreement between a subject and a verb:
in (33a), the verb *play* is in its base form; in (33b) and (33c), aspectual *be*
and *have* are in their base forms.[18]

Consider, however, the possibility of a construction consisting of a
tensed aspectual verb plus a VP, which would be dominated by the structure INFL'; these constructions are not well-formed:

(34a) A: What does John do for a living?
      B: *Is playing baseball
           *[$_{INFL'}$ [$_{INFL}$ [Pres be]] [$_{V''}$ [$_{V'}$ [$_V$ playing] [$_{N''}$ baseball]]]]
(34b) A: Will he go to spring training this year?
      B: *Is leaving any day now
           *[$_{INFL'}$ [$_{INFL}$ [Pres be]] [$_{V''}$ [$_{V'}$ [$_V$ leaving]] [$_{ADV''}$ any day now]]]
(34c) A: I wonder whether he'll make the big leagues this year.
      B: *Has been wondering about that lately
           *[$_{INFL'}$ [$_{INFL}$ [Pres have]] [$_{V''}$ [been] [$_{V'}$ [$_V$ wondering]]
           [$_{P''}$ about that] [$_{ADV''}$ lately]]]

These examples are ill-formed whether they are in the third person singular
present, as above, or whether they are in any other combination of person,
number, and tense:

(35a) A: What does John do for a living?
      B: *Am playing baseball
      B: *Are playing baseball
      B: *Was playing baseball
      B: *Were playing baseball

(35b) A: Will he go to spring training this year?
      B: *Am leaving any day now
      B: *Are leaving any day now
      B: *Was leaving any day now
      B: *Were leaving any day now
(35c) A: I wonder whether he'll make the big leagues this year.
      B: *Had been wondering about that lately

An analysis which restricts initial nodes to the set of major lexical categories dominated by their X" projections correctly predicts that the structures in (34) and (35) are ill-formed because a construction consisting of INFL' is not dominated by a major category initial node at the X" level.[19]

At first, some constructions consisting of a modal plus a VP may seem like counterexamples to the argument above since the following well-formed structures could be analyzed as INFL':

(36a) A: What does John do for a living?
      B: Might play baseball.
(36b) A: Will he go to spring training this year?
      B: Could be leaving any day now.
(36c) A: I wonder whether he'll make the big leagues this year.
      B: Would have been wondering that (if you hadn't asked).

In addition, there are single modals that are well-formed in English, especially in sequences that mimic laconic speech:

(37a) A: Do you think John will play baseball in the major leagues?
      B: Could.
(37b) A: It could be a source of pride for the whole community.
      B: Would (indeed).
(37c) A: Will John make it to the big leagues this year?
      B: Might.

A closer consideration of the features of the category of modals, however, provides evidence that these constructions actually derive from an initial node of S and have a surface form that has to be the result of phonological deletion of an unstressed subject (cf. the discussion of Napoli (1982) in §2.1). Most modals, including *might*, *could*, and *would*, do not display inflections for tense and agreement, so it is impossible to tell whether the examples in (36) and (37) are generated as INFL' structures or as sentence structures that have undergone deletion. The modal *do*, however, does display inflections for tense and agreement, features that it must acquire through the presence of a subject in a sentence structure:[20]

(38a) John$_i$ did$_i$ play baseball.
(38b) John$_i$ does$_i$ play baseball.
(38c) John and Tom$_i$ do$_i$ play baseball.

In (38a), the modal is in the past tense form common to all persons and numbers; in (38b), the well-formed modal is in the third person singular present tense form because it is coindexed with a third person singular subject; and in (38c), the modal is in the plural form because it is coindexed with a compound subject. A well-formed sentential structure like (38a) - (38c) can then undergo phonological deletion to a surface structure consisting of a modal plus a VP:

(39a) A: What does John do for a living?
      B: Did play baseball.
(39b) A: Doesn't John do anything to earn a living?
      B: Does play baseball.
(39c) A: What do John and Tom do for a living?
      B: ?Do play baseball.

The point here is that it is the well-formedness or ill-formedness of its sentential structure which predicts whether a surface structure with the modal *do* plus VP is well-formed. Whenever a construction with *do* plus a VP occurs, its well-formedness or ill-formedness depends upon features it must have acquired via coindexing with a subject at some point in a sentential derivation. Bare modals, or modals with VPs, then, must be the result of phonological deletion of an unstressed subject, whether that subject affects the form of the modal, as it does for *do*, or whether the subject does not affect the form of the modal, as it does not for *might, could,* or others. What holds for *do*, in short, holds for the entire category of modals. The generalization concerning examples (34) - (35) still stands: an analysis with X" representing the set of major lexical categories that can function as initial nodes of the grammar correctly predicts that certain structures not dominated by a major category initial node, in particular structures dominated at the X' level, are ill-formed.

Although the argument above rules out X' as an initial node in general, there is no confirming empirical argument for ruling out a single-bar projection of N' as an initial node. A theoretical argument, though, suggests that

constraining the initial node of nonsentential constituent structures to X"
has at least the value of a unified explanation. The analysis of *old grudge*
predicted by the nonsentential constituent structure analysis presented
above is that it is simply an instance of a NP without a determiner, which is
one of a variety of possible forms of a nonsentential NP:

(40a) A: The White House staff doesn't visit Tip O'Neill in his Con-
           gressional office.
       B: Grudge?
(40b) B: Old grudge.
(40c) B: An/The/Some grudge.
(40d) B: An/The/Some old grudge about partisan politics.

An analysis limiting the initial node of nonsentential constituent structures
to X" categories automatically predicts the unity of the above cases of nonsentential constituent structure NPs manifesting different structural possibilities of N": in (40a), the NP consists of a single lexical head noun; in
(40b), the head noun occurs with an adjective modifier; in (40c), the head
noun occurs with a determiner as a specifier; and in (40d), the head noun
occurs with a determiner specifier and adjective and prepositional modifiers. An analysis in which lexical items as in (40a), single-bar projections
as in (40b) and double-bar projections as in (40c) - (40d) are all dominated
by different initial nodes fails to capture the unity of (40a) - (40d) as different structural possibilities of the same initial node. Either analysis, X" as an
initial node, or X" and X' as initial nodes, predicts the correct facts about
the NPs in (40a) - (40d). Only an analysis with a single initial node of X",
though, automatically unifies all of the cases as nonsentential constituent
structure NPs deriving from the initial node of N". In sum, the empirical
and theoretical evidence presented above favors an analysis in which an initial node at the X" level, and not the levels of X' or X^0, correctly constrains
the grammar to generating well-formed major lexical categories as nonsentential constituent structures.

The analysis of X^{max} as the initial node of a generative grammar captures the unity and diversity of sentences, clauses, and nonsentential constituents as the major syntactic structures generated by the grammar. This
generalization, though, also has implications in terms of general issues
within current research on X-bar theory. Newmeyer points to a number of
unresolved issues within the X-bar literature, including the relationship of
X-bar theory to the notion of sentence, the number of bar projections

within X-bar theory, the relationship of X-bar theory to a feature system describing syntactic categories, the description of configurational vs. nonconfigurational languages, and the relationship of major and minor categories within X-bar theory (1986: 153-154). This research on nonsentential constituent structures has implications concerning the first and final issues from this list. First, it supports the view that sentence is integrated as a category within the set of major syntactic categories in X-bar theory; it also provides specific evidence that the category of sentence should be integrated as a non-lexical projection of INFL rather than as a lexical projection of V. Second, it illustrates the need for a clarification of the relationship between major categories and minor categories in terms of their participation in X-bar theory, one which correlates with the ability of a category to function as an initial node in the derivation of a nonsentential constituent structure.

As I have pointed out previously, in research from Standard Theory through GB, the notion of sentence has occupied a particularly privileged position. In *Aspects*, for example, Chomsky equates the symbol S with all other symbols that occupy the left-hand side of phrase structure rules, calling them "category symbols" (1965: 65). The category S, though, has the special position of initial node of the grammar (cf. Chomsky's remarks quoted in §3.1.2 above). In the course of research developing grammars within a Chomskyan framework, this privileged position for S and the associated notion that a generative grammar generates sentences and nothing else has been largely unchallenged until this work (although cf. the discussion of Yanofsky (1978), Brame (1979), and Napoli (1982) in §2.1). But by focusing on the notion of structures generated by the grammar, including sentences, clauses, and nonsentential constituents, not only is the definition of initial node generalized to all major syntactic categories (X^{max}), but the status of the category of sentence within X-bar theory is not privileged in any way.

There have been arguments for and against the integration of the category sentence into X-bar theory: the unresolved question is whether the schema for X and its projections also applies to S and its projections (cf. §3.1.1). In Chomsky's original discussion, S was a separate category, not integrated into X-bar theory (1970: 210). Some researchers (e.g., Hornstein 1977; Bresnan 1982; McCloskey 1983) continue to support the position that S should not be integrated into X-bar theory. Other researchers (most notably, Jackendoff 1977a,b, but also Bresnan 1976b; van Riemsdijk 1978;

Koster 1978; Marantz 1980; Gazdar 1982; Borsley 1983) argue that the description of the structure of a sentence can be formulated in terms of projections of V within X-bar theory, although the details of their treatments vary considerably.[21] Most researchers whose work does not force them to take a position regarding this controversy do not do so. As people have used labels like NP and VP in order to avoid taking a position with regard to the appropriate number of bars in a projection of a lexical category, so people use the labels S and S' while explicitly stating that they are not taking a position on the status of S with regard to X-bar theory. Chomsky himself has begged this question in the past, sidestepping the issue in a footnote: "It remains an open question whether VP is a maximal projection (as I will assume below) or whether the S-system is a further projection of [the category] V" (1981: 138).

More recently, however, following Stowell (1981, 1983), Chomsky has taken the position that integrating the structure of sentence into X-bar theory is a desirable option:

> Does this system [X-bar theory] extend to the non-lexical categories as well? Evidently, the optimal hypothesis is that it does. Let us assume this to be correct. Then the clausal categories conventionally labeled S and S' might be I" and C" respectively. (1986b: 3)

Rizzi (1987) points out that Chomsky's extension of X-bar theory to clausal and sentential structures has the effect of conceptualizing S as a non-unique structure. In the version of X-bar theory presented here, the non-uniqueness of S (INFL") as one category among the set of major syntactic categories is formally captured by the proposed generalization that X^{max} is the initial node of X-bar theory: within this generalization INFL" is exactly equivalent to the other major non-lexical category, C", as well as to the major lexical categories represented by X", in that all of these categories are subject to the restrictions of the X-bar schema.

A consideration of nonsentential constituent structures also provides evidence to consider the category of INFL" as a distinct category within the set of major syntactic categories in X-bar theory; in other words, the argument I develop here is that S is not equivalent to a maximal projection of V. The idea that a sentence actually may be the maximal projection of V is most closely associated with the work of Jackendoff (1977a,b), who explicitly claims that "S and S' are instances of V'" " (1977a: 261). One of Jackendoff's arguments for V'" as the initial node for a sentence is that it allows a parallel definition of subjects across NPs and sentences. This same parallelism, however, can be obtained by defining INFL" as the initial node for a sentence as already noted in §3.1.1 (cf. the examples in (11) above). Another of Jackendoff's arguments for V"' as a sentence node is that it maintains his "three level hypothesis" and describes a parallel system of category expansions.[22] X' expansions are those that are strictly subcategorized for lexical items: the V *put*, for example, strictly subcategorizes NP plus PP complements, and the N *part* strictly subcategorizes a NP complement. X" expansions are restrictive modifiers, such as restrictive relative clauses for N" and adverbial phrases for V". X"' expansions are nonrestrictive modifiers and auxiliary assertions, such as sentence tags or other appositive clauses for V"' and nonrestrictive appositives for N"'. Jackendoff claims that the parallelism of expansions provides evidence for his theory of phrase structure, including the claim that the initial node for a sentence is V"':

> We see therefore that there are three distinct kinds of [expansions] in both sentences [V"'] and NPs, corresponding to the three levels predicted by the phrase structure rule schema. Furthermore, the parallels in structure and function across the two categories S [V"'] and NP are clear and confirm the view of grammatical parallelism we have advocated here. (1977a: 269)

An examination of the expansion system of nonsentential NP and VP constituent structures, however, reveals that they, too, occur with the same range of complements and modifiers, which poses a problem for Jackendoff's claim that the initial node for a sentence structure is a maximal projection of V.

Nonsentential NP constituent structures must occur with obligatory complements and can occur with restrictive and nonrestrictive modifiers:[23]

(41a) A: John's reading an interesting manuscript.
      B: Part of Nixon's memoirs.
        *Part of
(41b) A: John's scared of somebody in this room.
      B: The man who is lurking in the corner.
(41c) A: Yesterday Mary left when she saw somebody come into the room.
      B: The man that is lurking in the corner, who is dangerous.

Nonsentential VP constituent structures, too, must occur with their obligatory complements and can occur with restrictive and nonrestrictive modifiers:

(42a) A: John did something stupid, but I don't know what.
     B: Put a bug in Democratic party headquarters.
       *Put a bug
       *Put in Democratic party headquarters
(42b) A: John has to place this bug behind a picture on a plaster wall.
     B: Press the adhesive firmly.
(42c) A: John has to place this bug behind a picture on a plaster wall.
     B: Press the adhesive firmly, of course.
(42d) A: John got advice from Tom about how to place this bug
       behind a picture on a plaster wall.
     B: Press the adhesive firmly, which anybody should know.

Because they are dominated by their XP projections, both NP and VP constituent structures can occur with the entire system of expansions as described by Jackendoff.

The conclusion to be drawn from the paradigm of nonsentential VP constituent structures is that a maximal projection of V does not necessarily describe a sentence structure. Jackendoff tries to establish a distinction between sentences and verb phrases contrasting V''' and V'' and arguing that V''' expansions are "auxiliary assertions" connected to sentences (1977b: 62). As already noted, though, nonsentential constituent structure VPs freely occur with such nonrestrictive modifiers:

(43a) A: John did something stupid, but I don't know what.
     B: Put a bug behind a picture on a plaster wall, which he usually does without any trouble.
(43b) A: John doesn't know what the best defense against criminal charges would be.
     B: Ask a lawyer, I suppose.

The presence of nonrestrictive modifiers thus does not characterize the maximal projection of V as a sentence node.

In X-bar theory within the GB framework, especially as modified with the generalization that X^{max} is the initial node, a maximal projection of V cannot be an initial node for a sentence derivation because it would be impossible to distinguish a sentence structure from a nonsentential VP constituent structure, and these two structures are in distinct contrast. The main semantic characteristic of a sentence is its argument-predicate structure, which corresponds with the syntactic selection of a subject by a VP, and this compositional structure is mediated by the syntactic category of

INFL. The category of INFL also determines other syntactic features of a sentence, notably its tense and agreement. In contrast, the maximal projection of V describes a nonsentential VP constituent structure. One semantic characteristic of a nonsentential VP constituent structure is its lack of structural predication, which corresponds to its lack of a subject. This lack of compositional structure is indicated by the absence of the syntactic category of INFL, which also determines other syntactic features of a VP constituent structure, notably its lack of tense and agreement. VP as an initial node generates a nonsentential constituent structure in the base form of the verb. The contrast between sentence structures and nonsentential VP constituent structures is reflected formally by the contrast in their conditions for well-formedness: the condition describing a well-formed nonsentential VP constituent structure is the Projection Principle; the conditions describing a well-formed sentence structure include the Projection Principle and the Predication Principle.

A grammar must be capable of generating both sentential and nonsentential verbal structures. The following sequence is from a commercial featuring the championship tennis player Jimmy Connors recommending a financial brokerage house:

(44)   What am I supposed to do? Open up a Paine Webber account?

The first question is a full predication within a tensed sentence; the second question is an VP constituent structure in the base form of the verb. The important point is that the nonsentential VP would be judged ill-formed according to any rule for sentence, whether with S or V''' as an initial node. Consider, for example, Jackendoff's rule for a sentence:

(45)   V''' → N''' - M''' - V'' (1977a: 264)

Consider, too, a rule for sentence from earlier work by Chomsky:

(46)   S → NP INFL VP (1981: 52)

With either of these rules, the VP structure *Open up a Paine Webber account?* would be ill-formed as a sentence because there is no subject and because it is not an imperative (imperatives do not occur with question intonation; cf. note 14). Within the analysis suggested here, though, in which any maximal projection can be an initial node, the distinction between a nonsentential VP constituent structure and an INFL'' sentence structure is possible, and both sentences and independent VPs are accounted for.

In summary, evidence from a consideration of nonsentential constituent structures has interesting implications regarding the issue of integrating S into X-bar theory. The generalization of the initial node of X-bar theory to X^{max}, which is independently motivated by the grammar of nonsentential constituent structures, offers a formal way to reflect the nonunique status of sentence (INFL") as one category within the set of major syntactic categories of a language. Within this set of major syntactic categories, the contrast between the major lexical category of V", which generates a nonsentential constituent structure when it functions as an initial node, and the major non-lexical category of INFL", which generates a sentence structure when it functions as an initial node, offers evidence that the category of INFL" is indeed a sentential one rather than a verbal one, which argues against any equation of S with a maximal projection of V.

A second implication of this research is the illustration of the need for a clarification of the status of major and minor categories within X-bar theory. Throughout these chapters, I have included examples of nonsentential ADVP constituent structures in parallel with examples of NP, VP, ADJP, and PP constituent structures, tacitly implying that the category of ADVP has major category status, at least with respect to the set of nonsentential constituent structures. Yet the category of ADVP generally has been regarded as a minor category in the literature (cf. Jackendoff 1977a,b; Emonds 1985; van Riemsdijk and Williams 1986). The unclear status of ADVP raises the larger question of exactly which categories participate in X-bar theory.

The terms 'major category' and 'minor category' have occurred sporadically throughout the literature, but they have not been defined in a consistent way. In Standard Theory research, Chomsky once offered a category-based definition:

> A category that appears on the left in a lexical [insertion] rule we shall call a *lexical category*; a lexical category or a category that dominates a string . . . X . . ., where X is a lexical category, we shall call a *major category*. Thus in the grammar, the categories N, V, and M are lexical categories, and all categories except Det (and possibly M and Aux) are major categories. (1965: 74; author's emphasis)

In work introducing X-bar theory, though, Chomsky (1970) suggests that syntactic categories are defined in terms of features.

The feature-based definition of major categories developed by Jackendoff (1977a,b) generally has been regarded as characterizing the set of major lexical categories in the generative grammar literature (e.g., Chomsky 1986b: 2; van Riemsdijk and Williams 1986: 42; Sells 1985: 30 all cite a feature system based on Jackendoff). In Jackendoff's feature matrix, Noun = [+N, -V]; Verb = [-N, +V]; Adj = [+N, +V]; and P = [-N, -V] (1977b: 31-33). Jackendoff, though, defines major and minor categories differently at different times: in his summary article (1977a), he suggests that nouns and verbs are major categories and all other categories are minor ones; in his book (1977b), he suggests that the major categories are the ones defined by a feature matrix, namely, the categories of NP, VP, ADJP, and PP. According to his application of a syntactic feature matrix to the notion major category, the crucial feature for distinguishing a major category from a minor category is the ability of the category to occur with a complement:

> We will also use the feature [[-]comp] to describe other minor lexical categories in the language. (1977b: 32)

Nouns, verbs, adjectives, and prepositions can occur with complements; thus, NP, VP, ADJP, and PP are the proposed major categories of English. Minor categories, which Jackendoff lists as adverbs, degree adverbs, particles, modals, articles, and quantifiers, cannot occur with complements.

In spite of the fact that ADVP is not one of the major categories of English according to any of Jackendoff's feature-based definitions, it seems to occur as an initial node in the derivation of nonsentential constituent structures. There are several different approaches towards explaining this occurrence of ADVP in a major category role. One way is to conflate the category of adverb with another major category, the category of adjective. This is the approach taken by Emonds:

> Traditional and generative grammar agree that central among the categories of syntax are the "major lexical categories": nouns (N), verbs (V), and adjectives (A). The characteristic of major lexical categories is that in English and in most languages they contain usually upwards of a thousand members listed in a lexicon. (1985: 13)

In a footnote, Emonds accounts for adverbs by calling them "adjectives with an ending" (1985: 13), referring, no doubt, to -ly adverbs. Conflating the categories of adverb and adjective would explain why nonsentential ADVP as well as ADJP constituent structures occur; Emonds' definition does not, however, account for the large number of words traditionally described as adverbs which do not derive from adjectives, including forms like *ever, never, almost, well, so, too, rather, really, quite, very, here, there, yet, always, perhaps, nevertheless,* and others. This definition has another problem as well, which is the rather obvious fact that adjectives and adverbs do not simply conflate into one category, at least not a category with any integrity according to distribution, coordination, or any other standard criteria; adjectives and adverbs clearly are different in many of their grammatical properties.

Another way to account for the occurrence of nonsentential ADVP constituent structures is to claim that they are an exception to the generalization that major categories function as initial nodes; in other words, ADV is a minor category, but it is a minor category that can function as an initial node. Aside from the obvious *ad hoc* nature of this proposal, it ignores the evidence that ADVPs seem to have most of the characteristics of major categories, although in a rather limited way. Jackendoff suggests that ADVP is a minor category because adverbs do not select complements; this generalization, however, is not completely accurate. Although most adverbs, including all *-ly* forms, do not select sentential complements, a subset of lexical adverbs do. Adverbs like *enough* and *now*, for instance, regularly select *that*-complements:

> (47a) A: John's making an effort to improve his performance on the job.
>
> B: Now that it's too late.
>
> $[_{ADV''} [_{ADV'} [_{ADV}$ now] $[_{C''}$ that it's too late]]]
>
> (47b) A: He has some credibility left.
>
> B: Enough that he'll be able to get another position.
>
> $[_{ADV''} [_{ADV'} [_{ADV}$ enough] $[_{C''}$ that he'll be able to get another position]]]

The presence of the *that* complementizer indicates that these structures can be analyzed as adverbs with sentential complements. Also, certain adverbs select prepositional complements as in the following examples:[24]

> (48a) A: Does John discuss campaign contributions in connection with ethical campaign practices?
>
> B: Independently from any ethical issue.
>
> $[_{ADV''} [_{ADV'} [_{ADV}$ independently] $[_{P''}$ from any ethical issue]]]
>
> (48b) A: Does John discuss campaign contributions and ethical campaign practices?
>
> B: Differently from every one else.
>
> $[_{ADV''} [_{ADV'} [_{ADV}$ differently] $[_{P''}$ from anyone else]]]

These structures are not examples of an adverb specifier for a PP because the adverb clearly governs the choice of the preposition: *independently* and *differently* cannot occur with any preposition, only the preposition they select as a complement, namely, *from*.

ADVP, in short, seems to be on the borderline between major and minor category, so another way to account for the properties of ADVP, including its size as a large class of lexical items, some of which are capable of occurring ̪with a complement, as well as its ability to occur as the initial node in a nonsentential constituent structure, is to claim that ADVP is, in fact, a major category. This inclusion of ADVP into the set of major categories correctly predicts a number of facts not only about the specific category of ADVP but also about the general distribution and properties of major and minor categories.[25]

Consider once more Chomsky's schema for X-bar theory in (6) as well as Stowell's explication of the principles constituting X-bar theory in (7). The schema is formulated in terms of major categories (X''), and Stowell's principle (v) specifically states that non-head terms in an expansion, that is, specifiers, modifiers, and complements, are major categories. Together, Chomsky's schema and Stowell's principle (v) suggest a constraint restricting the participating categories in X-bar theory to major categories, but there is a significant contradiction between this constraint and the distribution of ADVP. If ADVP is a minor category, then it cannot participate in the general distribution of major categories as heads, specifiers, complements, modifiers, and initial nodes. The proposal that ADVP is included in the set of major categories, though, does predict that ADVP, along with NP, VP, ADJP, and PP, can be specifiers, complements, modifiers, and initial nodes in the derivation of nonsentential constituent structures. Assigning ADVP the status of major category automatically explains its occurrence as an initial node in the derivation of a nonsentential constituent structure; it also automatically explains the occurrence of ADVP as a complement and modifier of various major categories (VPs in particular). The proposed major category status of ADVP, however, also captures another generalization: only by assigning to ADVP the status of major category can the schema for X-bar theory preserve the general claim that specifiers are themselves major categories (condition (v) of Stowell).

ADVPs are specifiers *par excellence*; they function as specifiers for every major category, including themselves:

(49a) A: They are giving up their jobs as Congressional aides.
      B: Such fools.
           $[_{N''} [_{ADV''} \text{ such}] [_{N'} [_N \text{ fools}]]]$
(49b) A: John thinks he will protest political corruption by resigning.
      B: Rather foolish.
           $[_{ADJ''} [_{ADV''} \text{ rather}] [_{ADJ'} [_{ADJ} \text{ foolish}]]]$
(49c) A: He's worried about the effect on his career.
      B: Directly off the fast track.
           $[_{P''} [_{ADV''} \text{ directly}] [_{P'} [_P \text{ off}] [_{N''} \text{ the fast track}]]]$
(49d) A: Mary has some good advice for John.
      B: Never act so hastily.
           $[_{V''} [_{ADV''} \text{ never}] [_{V'} [_V \text{ act}]] [_{ADV''} \text{ so hastily}]]$
(49e) A: John may regret his resignation someday.
      B: Very quickly.
           $[_{ADV''} [_{ADV''} \text{ very}] [_{ADV'} [_{ADV} \text{ quickly}]]]$

ADVPs also function as specifiers for the major non-lexical categories of
sentence and clause:

(50a) A: Certainly Tom acted foolishly by resigning so suddenly.
           $[_{INFL''} [_{ADV''} \text{ certainly}] [_{N''} \text{ Tom}] [_{INFL'} [_{V''} \text{ acted foolishly by}$
           resigning so suddenly]]]
(50b) A: Do you think that his boss might accept an apology from
           Tom?
      B: Only if he acts quickly.
           $[_{C''} [_{ADV''} \text{ only}] [_{C'} [_C \text{ if}] [_{INFL''} \text{ he acts quickly}]]]$

Assigning to ADVP the status of major category correctly predicts its general ability to function as a specifier in addition to its ability to function as
a complement, modifier, and initial node. This consideration of ADVPs
also provides evidence in support of a constraint restricting the participating
categories in X-bar theory to major categories.[26]

Although such a constraint limiting the participating categories in X-
bar theory to just major categories correctly predicts certain facts about the
set of major categories necessarily including ADVPs, it also predicts that
minor categories, such as determiners, for instance, are theoretically distinct from major categories in their properties and their distribution.[27] In
particular, the constraint correctly predicts that minor categories cannot be
initial nodes in the derivation of nonsentential constituent structures, which
is shown to be true in the following examples:[28]

(51a) A: John has something for Mary.

   B: *A

        *[$_{DET}$ a]

(51b) A: John has a job in the White House.

   B: *The

        *[$_{DET}$ the]

(51c) A: John has an appointment with the President soon.

   B: *This

        *[$_{DET}$ this]

(51d) A: John lost something.

   B: *These

        *[$_{DET}$ these]

Each of these determiners, though, could occur as a specifier for a NP:

(52a) A: John has something for Mary.

   B: A new assignment.

        [$_{N''}$ [$_{DET}$ a] [$_{N'}$ [$_{ADJ''}$ new] [$_{N}$ assignment]]]

(52b) A: John has a job in the White House.

   B: The position on the Executive staff?

        [$_{N''}$ [$_{DET}$ the] [$_{N'}$ [$_{N}$ position] [$_{P''}$ on the Executive staff]]]

(52c) A: John has an appointment with the President soon.

   B: This Thursday.

        [$_{N''}$ [$_{DET}$ this] [$_{N'}$ [$_{N}$ Thursday]]]

(52d) A: John lost something.

   B: These briefing papers?

        [$_{N''}$ [$_{DET}$ these] [$_{N'}$ [$_{ADJ''}$ briefing] [$_{N}$ papers]]]

Unlike the major category of ADVP, though, which can function as a specifier for any category, the minor category of Determiner functions as a specifier only in a restricted way, specifically as a specifier for the category NP. Determiners cannot function as specifiers for other major categories:

(53a) A: John doesn't know what the best defense against criminal charges would be.

   B: *The ask any lawyer

        *[$_{V''}$ [$_{DET}$ the] [$_{V'}$ [$_{V}$ ask] [$_{N''}$ any lawyer]]]

(53b) A: He also could tell his story.

   B: *This to the investigating committee

        *[$_{P''}$ [$_{DET}$ this] [$_{P'}$ [$_{P}$ to] [$_{N''}$ the investigating committee]]]

(53c) A: Why is John delaying his testimony to the Grand Jury?
       B: *A cautious
            *[$_{ADJ''}$ [$_{DET}$ a] [$_{ADJ'}$ [$_{ADJ}$ cautious]]]
(53d) A: How soon should he ask for immunity?
       B: *These quickly
            *[$_{ADV''}$ [$_{DET}$ these] [$_{ADV'}$ [$_{ADV}$ quickly]]]

This specificity suggests that major lexical categories occur with specific minor categories preceding them. These specific minor categories may be selected in the lexicon, a possibility briefly suggested by Chomsky (1986b: 91); in other words, what is proposed here is that minor categories are not selected by virtue of X-bar theory. Such lexically-selected minor categories like Determiners could then occur at the X^0 level without X-bar projections, which would eliminate a frequent criticism of Jackendoff's analysis of minor categories with full bar projections: Newmeyer points out that no rules ever apply to the bar projections of minor categories (1986: 153); within the analysis proposed here, in which minor categories do not participate in X-bar theory and are selected within the lexicon at the X^0 level only, such superfluous structure does not exist.

Although this brief analysis is speculative, it does seek to capture some generalizations about differences between major and minor categories by supporting a constraint within X-bar theory that restricts participating categories to major ones and eliminates minor categories from the X-bar system. First, it correctly predicts the generality of major lexical categories, including ADVPs, as complements, modifiers, specifiers, and initial nodes. Second, it also correctly predicts the lack of generality associated with minor categories as specifiers; it also accounts for their lack of head-like hierarchical structure. Finally, the constraint explains the contrast in the abilities of the categories to serve as the initial node in the derivation of nonsentential constituent structures: major categories can function as initial nodes because they participate in the X-bar system as a manifestation of X'', but minor categories cannot function as initial nodes because they do not participate in the X-bar system.

The generalization that X^{max} is the initial node of the grammar is one which could be incorporated into a number of contemporary syntactic theories; the work above describes its integration into the version of X-bar theory current in research within the GB framework. There is also a great deal of interesting work on X-bar theory within the framework of Generalized Phrase Structure Grammar developed in the work of Gazdar,

Klein, Pullum, and Sag (1985). Although it is beyond the scope of this volume to work out a full account of nonsentential constituents within GPSG, I would like to consider the work presented here with respect to a part of Pullum's (1985) review of X-bar theory.[29]

Pullum discusses six defining conditions associated with formulations of X-bar theory: Lexicality, Succession, Uniformity, Optionality, Maximality, and Centrality. Lexicality, which Pullum suggests is the most strict condition on X-bar theory, has both strong and weak versions: the strong version stipulates that all categorical bar projections are projected from lexical categories; the weak version states that only some subset of the set of maximal projections is projected from lexical categories. The condition of Succession incorporates the hierarchical structure of phrases as $X^n \rightarrow \ldots X^{n-1}$ $\rightarrow \ldots X^0$; in other words, succession ensures that the head of a constituent matches its phrasal category; it also ensures that the bar projections build up from the lexical category in increments of 1. Pullum points out that most X-bar analyses violate the second aspect of succession by allowing a category to dominate a category of the same bar level (e.g., N' $\rightarrow$ N' PP), a type of recursion recommended by Pullum in the form of a condition of weak Succession in which X^n may dominate X^{n-1} or X^n. The condition of Uniformity states that the maximum number of bar levels is the same for every category, a condition associated with the Uniform Three Level Hypothesis of Jackendoff (1977a,b), where the maximum projection of any lexical category is three bars. Pullum points out that most of the debate over Uniformity centers not on the condition itself but on the number of bar projections allowed in an X-bar system. The condition of Optionality states that every non-head projection in an expansion is optional, which does not establish any clear relationship between obligatory complements and optional modifiers, raising doubts, in Pullum's mind at least, about the legitimacy of Optionality as a legitimate condition on X-bar theory. The condition of Maximality, in its strong form, states that every non-head projection in an expansion must be a maximal projection. Pullum points out, however, that Jackendoff's adherence to a strict version of Maximality leads to superfluous structures, especially for minor categories as, for example, in the projection $Art^3 \rightarrow Art^2 \rightarrow Art^1 \rightarrow Art \rightarrow the$. Finally, the condition of Centrality states that the starting symbol for a derivation must be a maximal projection of a lexical category. The actual use of Centrality, though, as Pullum points out, either has violated Centrality by positing S as a unique symbol for an initial node, or has preserved Centrality by incor-

porating the assumption that a maximal projection of V is the unique starting symbol for a derivation as in Jackendoff 1977a,b *inter alia* (cf. note 21).

As presented above, the version of X-bar theory within a GB framework follows Chomsky (1986b) and Stowell (1981) (cf. (6) and (7) above),
modifying the definition of the initial node of the system by generalizing it
to X^{max} and constraining the participating categories in X-bar theory to the
set of major syntactic categories, which consists of the set of major lexical
categories at the X" level plus the major non-lexical categories of INFL and
COMP. In terms of Pullum's conditions, such a version of X-bar theory
satisfies weak Lexicality because some categories, notably INFL and
COMP, are projected from non-lexical categories. This version of X-bar
theory satisfies strict Succession by defining the hierarchical structure of
phrases as X" → X' → X without direct recursion of the head (although cf.
note 6). It satisfies a strict version of Uniformity in which the maximal projection for any major category is two bars. It also follows a condition of
Maximality, incorporated as condition (v) of Stowell and strengthened by
the evidence discussed above which supports this constraint restricting the
participating categories in the X-bar system to major categories. Finally, by
defining the initial node of the grammar as X^{max}, the version of X-bar
theory presented here satisfies a strict version of Centrality.

Pullum's discussion of Centrality is most relevant to the modification of
X-bar theory presented here. He suggests dropping the notion of S as a
unique start symbol, which is exactly in line with the work presented here.
My position, though, is even more specific: I have argued that the
privileged status of S as the single initial node is an historical accident, not
a legitimate condition on grammars; I also have argued that the correct constraint on the initial symbol of a derivation is that it is a major syntactic category, with S (or INFL") simply as one of the possibilities of X^{max}. These
arguments actually suggest preserving a strict version of Centrality as a condition on X-bar theory because the generalization of the initial node of the
grammar to X^{max}, which is the maximal projection of the set of major syntactic categories, ensures Centrality by specifying that the starting symbol is
the maximal projection of a lexical or non-lexical category. Although my
arguments for this position support a generalization of the initial node of a
grammar to X^{max} within a GB framework, I suspect that the arguments also
support the same revision of X-bar theory within a GPSG framework as
described by Pullum (1985).

3.2 The S-structure representation of nonsentential constituent structures

The previous section of this chapter showed that generalizing the initial node of X-bar theory to X^{max} accounts for all of the major syntactic structures generated by a grammar, including sentence structures and nonsentential constituent structures. In a consideration of the representation of nonsentential constituents at the level of D-structure, the section showed that licensing through an interaction of X-bar theory and the Projection Principle accounts for their well-formedness in a general way without adding any additional principles or rules to the grammar.

Although all of the initial nodes of a grammar are unified within the X-bar theory construct of X^{max}, they also contrast in terms of the different structures each one generates as an initial node in a derivation, the relevant contrast being between INFL" generating a sentence structure and a manifestation of X" generating a nonsentential constituent structure. One function of this contrast between X" and INFL" is that it allows a distinction between some principles and rules that apply specifically to nonsentential constituent structures and other principles and rules that apply identically to both nonsentential constituent structures and sentence structures. The majority of principles and rules apply in the same fashion to both classes of structures generated by the grammar. The description of each component of the grammar, however, must include specific principles or rules that describe nonsentential constituent structures only. This section of Chapter Three considers the S-structure representation of nonsentential constituent structures, demonstrating that adding a rule to the grammar is necessary to describe their well-formedness. The additional rule is an extension of Case theory, the subsystem of GB which constrains representations at the S-structure, representations generated by the transformational component of the grammar. In this section, I briefly discuss movement within nonsentential constituent structures; I then describe the marked aspects of Case for NP constituent structures at S-structure.

S-structure representations are generated by the transformational component of the grammar, which consists of one rule: Move α, where α is any category; the effect of such a general movement rule is to allow any category to move anywhere. The operation of the movement rule is highly constrained by the principles of Bounding theory. The most important of these principles, Subjacency, regulates this relationship between a moved element and its trace, ensuring that the relationship does not cross more than one bounding node. In nonformal terms, Subjacency prohibits movement of a category across more than one bounding node, S (INFL") and NP being barriers to movement in English. Movement is mainly a sentential phenomenon, although it does occur within nonsentential constituent structures, especially those with embedded sentential complements.

When movement does occur within nonsentential constituent structures, the movement rule is constrained by the principles of Bounding theory in exactly the same ways as it is constrained in sentence structures. Consider the following examples:

(54a) A: John heard some gossip lately.
      B: The rumor that Nixon is likely to fire his entire staff.
(54b) B: *Nixon the rumor that is likely to fire his entire staff

The D-structure representation for both NP constituent structures is the same:[30]

(55) $[_{NP}$ the rumor $[_{S'}$ that $[_{S^1} [_{NP}$ e$] [_{VP}$ is likely $[_{S'}$ for $[_{S^2} [_{NP}$ Nixon$] [_{VP}$ to fire his entire staff$]]]]]]]$

The rule Move α can extract the NP *Nixon* across one bounding node S^2 into the empty NP in S^1 to generate the S-structure in (54a) with an antecedent-trace relationship that does not violate Subjacency since it crosses only one bounding node, S^2:

(56) $[_{NP}$ the rumor $[_{S'}$ that $[_{S^1} [_{NP}$ Nixon$] [_{VP}$ is likely $[_{S'}$ for $[_{S^2} t [_{VP}$ to fire his entire staff$]]]]]]]$

Further extraction of the NP *Nixon* is impossible because the resulting S-structure would violate Subjacency:

(57) *Nixon $[_{NP}$ the rumor $[_{S'}$ that $[_{S^1} t [_{VP}$ is likely $[_{S'}$ for $[_{S^2} t [_{VP}$ to fire his entire staff$]]]]]]]$

Extracting *Nixon* to the left of the entire NP would create an ill-formed antecedent-trace relationship across three barriers, NP, S^1, and S^2. In addition, there is no empty NP to function as a landing site for *Nixon* at the left of the NP. The principles of Bounding theory thus prohibit the ill-formed nonsentential constituent structure in (54b).

Nonsentential constituent structure NPs allow internal movement because NP is a cyclic node for movement, so the hypothesis that the principles of Bounding theory apply identically to the movement rule when it operates within sentences and nonsentential constituent structures should hold true for movement within NPs. Chomsky briefly discusses NP movement within derived nominals like *the destruction of the city by the enemy* (1970: 203). A GB analysis of a similar nonsentential NP would posit a base-generated *by*-phrase and an empty NP in the specifier:

(58) $[_{NP} [_{NP} e] [_N$ destruction] $[_{NP}$ the city] $[_{PP}$ by the enemy]]

The NP *the city* could move to the empty NP slot in the specifier and receive genitive Case:

(59a) $[_{NP} [_{NP}$ the city] $[_N$ destruction] $t [_{PP}$ by the enemy]]
(59b) the city's destruction t by the enemy

The relationship between the moved NP and its trace satisfies the principle of Subjacency in Bounding theory because the moved NP does not cross any bounding nodes.

The principles of Bounding theory operate identically whether movement takes place within sentence structures or within nonsentential constituent structures, which follows from the nature of the principles themselves: they are principles that constrain the operation of the movement rule within the transformational component of the grammar; if the rule applies in any structure, S or X", it is constrained by the principles of Bounding theory.

At S-structure, the principles and rules of Case theory are the major constraints upon representations generated by the transformational component of the grammar. A NP receives its abstract Case from its governor at S-structure (cf. §3.1.1 for a definition of government). In the rules of Case assignment for English, V and P assign objective Case; tensed INFL assigns nominative Case; and the structure [NP X'] assigns genitive Case (Chomsky 1981: 50). The following sentences illustrate Case assignment for English:

(60a) He warned me.
  $[_{INFL"} [_{N"}$ he] $[_{INFL'} [_{INFL}$ [Tense Past]] $[_{V"} [_{V'} [_V$ warn] $[_{N"}$ me]]]]]]
(60b) She gave the recordings to me.
  $[_{INFL"} [_{N"}$ she] $[_{INFL'} [_{INFL}$ [Tense Past]] $[_{V"} [_{V'} [_V$ give]
  $[_{N"}$ the recordings] $[_{P"} [_{P'} [_P$ to] $[_{N"}$ me]]]]]]]]
(60c) His recordings interested Mary.
  $[_{INFL"} [_{N"} [_{N"}$ his] $[_{N'} [_N$ recordings]]] $[_{INFL'} [_{INFL}$ [Tense Past]]
  $[_{V"} [_{V'} [_V$ interest] $[_{N"}$ Mary]]]]]

In (60a), tensed INFL assigns nominative Case to the pronoun *he*, and V assigns objective Case to the pronoun *me*. In (60b), tensed INFL assigns nominative Case to the pronoun *she*; V assigns objective Case to *the recordings*; and P assigns objective Case to the pronoun *me*. In (60c), the structure [N" N'] assigns genitive Case to the pronoun *his*; tensed INFL assigns nominative case to *recordings*; and V assigns objective case to *Mary*. Representations at S-structure are regulated by the Case Filter:

(61) Case Filter
      Every phonetically realized NP must be assigned (abstract) Case.
      (Chomsky 1986a: 74)

For an S-structure representation to be well-formed, every non-empty NP must receive abstract Case, even lexical NPs like *recordings* and *Mary* which, unlike pronominal NPs, do not overtly show any morphological realization of Case. Stowell (1981) suggests that Case theory also includes an Adjacency Principle stating that a NP must be next to its governor in order to receive Case; Adjacency accounts for the order of complements in VPs: direct object NPs must be next to the verb in order to receive Case and be well-formed.[31]

Within nonsentential constituent structures, the rules of Case theory assign Case to NPs with governors in a regular way. The Genitive Case Rule, for example, operates to assign genitive Case whenever the structure [N" X'] occurs within any nonsentential constituent structure:

(62a) A: John is reading an interesting manuscript.
      B: Nixon's memoirs.
           $[_{N''} [_{N''} \text{Nixon}] [_{N'} [_{N} \text{memoirs}]]]$
(62b) A: What's wrong with John?
      B: Angry about his salary.
           $[_{ADJ''} [_{ADJ'} [_{ADJ} \text{angry}]$
           $[_{P''} [_{P'} [_{P} \text{about}] [_{N''} [_{N''} \text{his}] [_{N'} [_{N} \text{salary}]]]]]]$
(62c) A: John doesn't know what the best defense against criminal
           charges would be.
      B: Ask his lawyer.
           $[_{V''} [_{V'} [_{V} \text{ask}] [_{N''} [_{N''} \text{his}] [_{N'} [_{N} \text{lawyer}]]]]]$

Each of the [N" N'] constructions, *Nixon's memoirs*, *his salary*, and *his lawyer*, triggers the Genitive Case Rule to assign genitive Case to the first NP. Similarly, if, within a nonsentential constituent structure, V governs a direct object NP, or if P governs a NP complement, then the rules of Case theory assign objective Case in a regular way:

(63a) A: John doesn't like children in the office.
      B: Keep them away.
           $[_{V''} [_{V'} [_V$ keep] $[_{N''}$ them]] $[_{ADV''}$ away]]
(63b) A: John is reading some interesting material.
      B: Books about politics.
           $[_{N''} [_{N'} [_N$ books]] $[_{P''} [_{P'} [_P$ about] $[_{N''}$ politics]]]]
(63c) A: John gave a book about Nixon to someone.
      B: To me.
           $[_{P''} [_{P'} [_P$ to] $[_{N''} [_{N'} [_N$ me]]]]]

In (63a), the V *keep* assigns objective Case to the pronoun *them*; in (63b), the P *about* assigns objective Case to the NP *politics*; and in (63c), the P *to* assigns objective Case to the pronoun *me*. When any nonsentential constituent structure includes a NP with a governor, the rules of Case operate in a regular way.

Nonsentential constituent structure NPs, however, have no INFL, V, or P governor to assign Case to them. Consider the following sequences:

(64a) A: John wants something special for Christmas.
      B: A book.
           $[_{N''} [_{DET}$ a] $[_{N'} [_N$ book]]]
(64b) B: A briefcase.
           $[_{N''} [_{DET}$ a] $[_{N'} [_N$ briefcase]]]
(64c) B: A recording.
           $[_{N''} [_{DET}$ a] $[_{N'} [_N$ recording]]]

The head Ns in these NPs are in technical violation of the Case Filter because they have phonetic content but no abstract Case.

An explanation of Case for NP constituent structures comes from an examination of pronouns, which, in English, exhibit morphological markings of their abstract Case. Pronouns are NPs, so the nonsentential constituent structure analysis predicts that they should be well-formed as independent structures. In English, independent pronouns in the objective case are always well-formed:

(65a) A: John gave a book to someone.
      B: Me.
(65b) B: You.
(65c) B: Him/Her.
(65d) B: Us.
(65e) B: Them.

Independent pronouns in the objective case are well-formed even if the pronoun is interpreted within discourse as an agent:

(66a) A: Someone gave a book to John.
     B: Me.
(66b) B: You.
(66c) B: Him/Her.
(66d) B: Us.
(66e) B: Them.

Some speakers, though, use an independent pronoun in the nominative case when the pronoun is interpreted within discourse as an agent:

(67a) A: Someone gave a book to John.
     B: I.
(67b) B: You.
(67c) B: He/She.
(67d) B: We.
(67e) B: They.

Speakers also use genitive pronouns independently:

(68a) A: That book is someone's.
     B: Mine.
(68b) B: Yours.
(68c) B: His.
(68d) B: Hers.
(68e) B: Ours.
(68f) B: Theirs.

Not all speakers accept all of the pronouns in (65) - (68) as well-formed; in general, native speakers' use of and judgments about independent pronouns are quite variable.[32]

What is significant about the examples in (65) - (68) is that judgments of well-formedness sometimes do not seem to depend upon any ellipsis analysis. Certain independent pronouns are judged to be well-formed or ill-formed without regard to their function in any putative full sentence source, which indicates that an ellipsis analysis cannot account for the distribution of well-formed independent pronominal structures. An ellipsis analysis would predict incorrect results, for example, with regard to the occurrence of independent objective pronouns, which are always well-formed since the objective case is the unmarked form for English. Consider the following sequence:

(69) A: Who gave a book to John?
B: Me.

An ellipsis analysis could not predict that the pronoun *me* is well-formed as an independent structure because it has no way of deriving an objective case for a subject pronoun. Since Case assignment takes place at S-structure, the following sentence would be ruled out:

(70) *Me gave a book to John

Because deletion takes place after S-structure, it never has access to a source sentence like (70), so an ellipsis analysis is unable to generate the independent pronoun in (69).

Rather than depending upon any sentential source, the judgments regarding the acceptability or unacceptability of independent pronouns seem to depend upon the possibility of an interpretation within a discourse context or a context of situation. Even though there is quite a bit of variation in the acceptability of independent pronominal NPs (cf. note 32), the grammar of nonsentential constituent structures still has to account for the fact that genitive, nominative, and objective pronouns regularly occur as independent constituent structures as in the sequences of (65) - (68). It also has to account for these nonsentential pronouns without appealing to an ellipsis analysis not only because an ellipsis analysis predicts incorrect results but also because generating nonsentential constituent structures dominated by a major category initial node in an autonomous grammar does not allow the grammar to depend upon external factors such as a discourse context. The best solution seems to be to allow an autonomous grammar to generate all of the possible independent pronoun structures and then depend on a pragmatic component to describe aspects of interpretation and acceptability that depend upon discourse factors.[33]

In order to account for well-formed genitive, nominative, and objective pronouns, then, the grammar must include an additional rule of Case theory to assign Case to nonsentential constituent structure NPs:

(71) Case Rule for NP Constituent Structures
If N" is the initial node, then assign any Case.

By specifically mentioning the initial node of N", the Case Rule applies in the derivation of NP constituent structures only. The rule allows the grammar to generate any pronoun in any Case.[34] It also accounts for NP constituent structures, whether lexical nouns or pronouns, not violating the Case Filter, which states that NPs must have Case to be well-formed. With the Case Rule assigning Case to constituent structures with N" as their initial node, all NPs have a Case and thus do not violate the Case Filter as it constrains S-structure representations. Accounting for the interpretation and acceptability of independent pronouns in or as constituent structures is then left to a pragmatic component (cf. Chapter Four, where I discuss the interpretation of independent pronouns in or as constituent utterances).

3.3 The logical form representation of nonsentential constituent structures

Chomsky often has stated that Logical Form as a component of a generative grammar is narrowly restricted:

> I will understand LF [Logical Form] to incorporate whatever features of sentence structure (1) enter directly into semantic interpretation of sentences and (2) are strictly determined by properties of (sentence-) grammar. (1977a: 165)

This restriction is a statement of the constraint of autonomy as it applies to the semantic component of a generative grammar: the semantic representation of a structure is limited to features that the grammar itself determines. These structurally-determined features of Logical Form, in current formulations of GB theory, are restricted to a representation of the distribution of θ-marked arguments as well as a description of the relations of anaphors and their antecedents, quantified expressions and their traces, and empty categories and their reference. In this section, I first describe the Logical Form representation of nonsentential constituent structures;[35] I then consider the consequences of an autonomous Logical Form component in terms of describing the meaning of nonsentential constituents.

Chomsky claims that the rules converting S-structure representations into semantic representations are simple and direct. Only a few elements, notably quantifiers such as *who* or *which*, require conversion to abstract notation in the Logical Form component (1981: 35). This conception of Logical Form representation is a consequence of the Projection Principle, which preserves an important semantic feature of lexical structure in all representations: D-structure is a pure representation of θ-role assignment; S-structure preserves this representation by indexing any movements that may have disrupted the original configuration; and Logical Form, too, represents the θ-role assignments of NPs functioning in the argument roles of Agent, Patient, Location, Instrument, Goal, and so on. Consequently, if a nonsentential NP or VP selects and θ-marks arguments, these appear at Logical Form as a result of the θ-Criterion within the Projection Principle:

(72a) A: John's reading an interesting manuscript.

     B: Part of Nixon's memoirs.

$[_{N''} [_{N'} [_N$ part $] [_{P''} [_{P'} [_P$ of$] [_{N''}$ Nixon's memoirs$]]]]]$
                                    THEME

(72b) A: John doesn't know where the Library of Congress is.

     B: Ask any police officer.

$[_{V''} [_{V'} [_V$ ask$] [_{N''}$ any police officer$]]]$
                         PATIENT

In (72a), the head N *part* obligatorily selects a Theme argument and the NP in the PP *of Nixon's memoirs* functions as an argument with that θ-role; in (72b), the head V *ask* obligatorily selects a Patient argument and the NP *any police officer* functions as that argument. The effect of the Projection Principle at Logical Form is the same for nonsentential constituents as well as constituents generated within sentence structures: lexical items, particularly predicates, select complements such as Patients and Locations, and this selection licenses NPs as well-formed within the LF representation of a structure. Sentences and nonsentential constituent structures, however, also contrast at Logical Form: whereas sentences require a predicate structure plus a subject argument as a result of the Predication Principle, nonsentential constituent structures, particularly VPs, are under no such constraint.

With respect to the interpretation of anaphors and antecedents which takes place at Logical Form, the operation of Binding theory also differs across sentence structures and nonsentential constituent structures, and the description of well-formed nonsentential constituent structures requires a marked formulation of one of the principles of Binding theory. At Logical Form, NPs appear with an index, either bound or free:

(73a) $NP_i \ldots NP_i$

(73b) $NP_i \ldots NP_j$

In (73a), the two NPs are bound because they have the coreferential index of i; in (73b), the two NPs are free because neither NP, NP_i or NP_j, is bound to a coreferential NP in the structure. Index assignment is free at S-structure according to a general rule that says 'Index NPs freely' (van

Riemsdijk and Williams 1986: 205). At LF, the principles of Binding theory then check the results of index assignment for well-formedness. Chomsky points out that the principles of the theory of Binding follow from the theory of government (cf. §3.1.1 for a definition of government):

> We define the *governing category* for α to be the minimal S or NP containing α and a governor of α. In terms of this notion, we can formulate the basic principles of the theory of Binding as follows:
> Principles of the Theory of Binding
> A. An anaphor is bound in its governing category.
> B. A pronominal is free in its governing category.
> C. An R-expression is free. (1982: 20)

Two of the principles of Binding, principles B and C, apply in exactly the same fashion to sentences and nonsentential constituent structures if a pronominal or a NP with reference occurs in or as a nonsentential constituent structure. The first principle of Binding, however, requires a marked formulation in order to describe the well-formed Logical Form representation of nonsentential constituent structures.

Rizzi (1987), Sells (1985), and van Riemsdijk and Williams (1986) all point out that defining the notion of governing category is one of the central issues within current GB research. A consideration of nonsentential constituent structures is quite interesting in this respect because it appears that a nonsentential constituent structure, such as a NP, for example, seems able to serve as a governing category for its contents, and the presence of a governor does not seem to be necessary in order to define the nonsentential constituent structure as a governing category. This may indicate that Binding theory requires a marked definition in order to describe nonsentential major lexical categories as governing categories; in the discussion below, however, I simply assume that a nonsentential constituent structure serves as its own governing category.

The second and third principles of Binding check for free reference of pronominals and for R-expressions, a category which includes referential nouns as well as *wh*-variables (Chomsky 1981: 101). These principles apply in a regular way to pronouns and NPs within nonsentential constituent structures as in the examples below:

(74a) A: Someone gave John a job.
B: The mayor.
$[_{N''} [_{DET} \text{ the}] [_{N'} [_{N} \text{ mayor}_i]]]$

(74b) A: Who gave John a job?
      B: Ask the Attorney General.
           $[_{V''} [_{V'} [_V$ ask] $[_{N''}$ the Attorney General$_i$]]]
(74c) A: John gave someone a job.
      B: Me.
           $[_{N''} [_{N'} [_N$ me$_i$]]]
(74d) A: Did John give someone a job?
      B: Ask her.
           $[_{V''} [_{V'} [_V$ ask] $[_{N''}$ her$_i$]]]

In examples (74a) and (74b), the NPs *the mayor* and *the Attorney General* are nominal R-expressions, so their free reference index i is in accord with the third principle of Binding that the reference of an R-expression is free within its governing category, which in (74a) is a nonsentential NP and in (74b) is a nonsentential VP. In examples (74c) and (74d), the NPs are pronominals, so their free reference is in accord with the second principle of Binding that the reference of a pronominal is free within its governing category, which again is a nonsentential NP in (74c) and a nonsentential VP in (74d).

The first principle of Binding theory, however, which states that reflexive and reciprocal anaphors must be bound within their governing category, requires a marked formulation to describe the well-formed indexing of anaphors within nonsentential constituent structures. Both reflexive and reciprocal anaphors can appear as NP constituent structures without an antecedent:

(75a) A: John hurt someone by revealing information.
      B: Himself.
(75b) A: Who are John and Mary exchanging information with?
      B: Each other.

Consider, too, the following examples:

(76a) A: Who will John and Mary exchange information with?
      B: With each other.
(76b) A: Why is John upset?
      B: Angry at himself.
(76c) A: What is Mary planning to do?
      B: Fire her entire staff by herself.

Reflexive and reciprocal anaphors without antecedents also appear within other nonsentential constituent structures such as the PP, ADJP, and VP above.

The fact that some anaphors violate the first principle of Binding by appearing without an antecedent within their governing category has not gone unnoticed. Chomsky himself notes that "Condition (A) is also sometimes overridden in colloquial speech. . . .[S]uch matters . . . raise interesting questions" (1986a: 216). Napoli, too, presents examples of anaphors with what she calls "pragmatic antecedents":

> (77a) Situation: Two parents look at each other as their daughter serves them the first dinner she's ever cooked alone. One says to the other,
>
> All by herself, too.
>
> [T]he reflexive pronoun, then, finds a pragmatic antecedent.
>
> (77b) Situation: Two parents hear their children bickering upstairs. One says to the other in despair,
>
> Always with each other — but never with their friends.
>
> Do you think it's inevitable?
>
> "[E]ach other" can find a pragmatic antecedent. (1982: 103-104)

What is particularly interesting about Napoli's examples is that they are nonsentential constituent structures. Within nonsentential constituent structures, then, it appears that reflexive and reciprocal anaphors can be either free or bound, and the grammar has to reflect this marked aspect of their well-formedness.[36]

Chomsky suggests that one of the characteristics of the periphery of the grammar is that it uses devices that have the effect of "relaxing certain conditions of core grammar" (1981: 8). Following this suggestion, a marked formulation of the first principle of Binding allows either bound or free reference for anaphors within nonsentential constituent structures:

> (78) Binding Theory for Nonsentential Constituent Structures
>
> Principle A. If X" is the initial node, then an anaphor in the structure may be free or bound.

By specifically mentioning X" as the initial node, the domain of the marked principle is limited to describing the set of nonsentential major lexical category constituent structures.

The following examples illustrate the explanation of anaphors according to the marked principle of Binding for nonsentential constituent structures:

(79a) A: The prosecutor wonders how to flatter John.
      B: Ask John$_i$ about himself$_i$
          [$_{V''}$ [$_{V'}$ [$_V$ ask] [$_{N''}$ John$_i$] [$_{P''}$ [$_{P'}$ [$_P$ about] [$_{N''}$ himself$_i$]]]]]
(79b) A: John hurt someone by releasing information.
      B: Himself$_i$.
          [$_{N''}$ [$_{N'}$ [$_N$ himself$_i$]]]
(79c) A: Who are John and Mary exchanging information with?
      B: Each other$_i$.
          [$_{N''}$ [$_{N'}$ [$_N$ each other$_i$]]]]

In the constituent structure VP in (79a), the reflexive pronoun *himself* finds an antecedent *John* within its minimal governing category of a constituent structure VP, so the marked principle of Binding describes the structure as well-formed because the anaphor has an antecedent and is bound to it through coindexing. In examples (79b) and (79c), the reflexive and reciprocal anaphors have no antecedents within their governing category of a nonsentential NP, and the marked principle of Binding also describes these structures as well-formed because the anaphors have a free index.

One consequence of the marked principle and conditions of Binding theory for nonsentential constituent structures is the generation of contrasting anaphors, some of which seem to function meaningfully within a discourse sequence and some of which do not (an explanation of the assignment of the notation # to signify pragmatic unacceptability is in the following chapter):

(80a) A: Who are John and Mary exchanging information with?
      B: Each other.
(80b) A: Who is John exchanging information with?
      B: #Each other
(80c) A: The Senators voted down a pay cut.
      B: For themselves?
(80d) B: #For himself?
(80e) A: John hurt someone by releasing information.
      B: Himself.
(80f) B: #Themselves

Grammatically well-formed nonsentential constituents that seem unacceptable within discourse sequences, however, are not limited to anaphors.

Other nonsentential constituents, including NPs, VPs, and so on, also seem unacceptable in certain discourse sequences:

(81a) A:　Someone will give John a job.
　　　 B:　The mayor.
(81b) B:　#The tree in front of his house
(81c) A:　John doesn't know where the Library of Congress is.
　　　 B:　Ask any police officer.
(81d) B:　#Ask the tree in front of his house

The grammar describes each of the nonsentential constituent structures in (80) - (81) as syntactically well-formed because they derive from a major lexical category and because they conform to the various conditions describing well-formed nonsentential structures generated by the grammar. And, indeed, each of the nonsentential constituent structures *is* well-formed within an autonomous grammar, especially within a grammar with an extremely restricted Logical Form component. The unacceptability of some of the examples above is not due to any of their grammatical features as nonsentential constituent structures. Instead, the contrast between the same independent constituent that is acceptable in some cases and unacceptable in others indicates that the issue here is not internal to a grammar; instead, the unacceptability results from constraints on the pragmatic interpretation of independent constituent utterances. It is within the context of a specific discourse sequence that some of the examples above fail to find an acceptable interpretation. It is not the domain of an autonomous grammar to account for the acceptability and unacceptability of the examples above within their specific discourse sequences; rather, the determination of acceptability or unacceptability as well as the description of interpretation has to take place within the domain of pragmatics because it is dependent upon discourse factors. The description of well-formed nonsentential constituent structures within an autonomous grammar is separate from the description of acceptable or unacceptable independent constituent utterances in their pragmatic contexts.

The constraint of autonomy severely limits the interpretive power of Logical Form in another way. As it cannot describe all aspects of acceptability, neither can an autonomous grammar describe all aspects of interpretation. It cannot predict, for example, the interpretation of the different functions of independent constituents in different discourse sequences. Consider the following examples:

(82a) A: Something blocks John's view of the Washington monument.

      B: The tree in front of his house.

(82b) A: John is cutting down something.

      B: The tree in front of his house.

(82c) A: John will hang the rubber tire swing somewhere.

      B: The tree in front of his house.

(82d) A: John wants fertilizer for something.

      B: The tree in front of his house.

(82e) A: John will break down the door with something.

      B: The tree in front of his house. (reading: use of tree as battering ram)

In (82a), the NP functions in discourse as an Agent; in (82b), as a Patient; in (82c), as a Location; in (82d), as a Goal; and in (82e), as an Instrument. No property of Logical Form can predict these different functions for an independent NP in discourse. All the grammar can do is describe each NP constituent structure as well-formed, leaving the interpretation of the NPs to a pragmatic component of the theory of nonsentential constituents.

The constraint of autonomy on Logical Form representations ensures that semantic representation in a generative grammar is limited to structural features determined by the grammar. This has turned out to be an extremely limited view of meaning: under this view, the sum total of meaning determined by the grammar is limited to a description of the semantic representation of anaphors, quantifiers, and empty categories plus a description of θ-role assignment. The description of the Logical Form representation of well-formed nonsentential constituent structures has to conform to this strict condition of autonomy; in practice, the Logical Form representation of nonsentential constituent structures consists mainly of a description of θ-roles, if there are any for a given structure, and a specification of indexing, which requires a marked principle of Binding theory. The consequence of the constraint of autonomy shifts the burden of accounting for interpretation and acceptability from semantics to pragmatics.

3.4 Conclusion

This chapter has developed a competence model of nonsentential constituent structures by describing their representation at each level of a generative grammar, D-structure, S-structure, and Logical Form. The main claim in the chapter is that generalizing the definition of the initial node of X-bar theory to X^{max} accounts for all of the major syntactic category structures generated by a grammar, including the major non-lexical categories of sentence and clause (represented by INFL'' and C'') as well as the set of nonsentential major lexical category constituent structures (represented by X''). For all structures, the description of well-formedness at the level of D-structure depends upon the licensing interaction of X-bar theory and the Projection Principle, although the well-formedness of sentential and clausal structures depends upon the combination of the Projection Principle and the Predication Principle, while the well-formedness of nonsentential constituent structures depends upon the Projection Principle alone. Most of the grammatical properties of nonsentential constituent structures fall out from the interaction of the Projection Principle with other principles of GB, although there are certain exceptions, particularly in the case of nonsentential constituent structure pronouns. At S-structure, an additional rule of Case theory accounts for well-formed nonsentential genitive, nominative, and objective pronouns as well as nonsentential lexical NP constituent structures that do not violate the Case Filter. At Logical Form, a marked principle within Binding theory accounts for the well-formed indexing of anaphors in or as nonsentential constituent structures. The grammar of nonsentential constituent structures, and especially the Logical Form representation of their meaning, is restricted by the constraint of autonomy, which has the consequence of a severely limited representation of meaning, one that does not account for most aspects of the interpretation and acceptability of independent constituents.

The analysis of nonsentential constituent structures presented in the previous two chapters is intended to replace an ellipsis analysis of independent major lexical categories, particularly the one proposed by Morgan (1973). In comparison to an ellipsis analysis, however, the nonsentential constituent structure analysis does not seem to predict the same range of phenomena associated with the interpretation and acceptability of independent major lexical categories. Morgan's ellipsis analysis correctly predicts that certain semantic features of independent major lexical categories seem predictable from full sentence sources, which could account for the interpretation of the examples I cited in §3.3 as illustrative of discourse-based interpretation:

(83a) A: Something blocks John's view of the Washington monument.
   B: The tree in front of his house.
       The tree in front of his house (blocks John's view of the Washington monument).
(83b) A: John is cutting down something.
   B: The tree in front of his house.
       (John is cutting down) the tree in front of his house.
(83c) A: John will hang the rubber tire swing somewhere.
   B: The tree in front of his house.
       (John will hang the rubber tire swing on) the tree in front of his house.
(83d) A: John wants fertilizer for something.
   B: The tree in front of his house.
       (John wants fertilizer for) the tree in front of his house.
(83e) A: John will break down the door with something.
   B: The tree in front of his house.
       (John will break down the door with) the tree in front of his house.

A full sentence source allows the grammar, and in particular, the Logical Form component, to assign different θ-roles to each NP: in (83a), the NP is in the configuration of Agent; in (83b), of Patient; in (83c), of Location; in (83d), of Goal; and in (83e), of Instrument. An ellipsis analysis thus predicts certain aspects of meaning that a nonsentential constituent analysis cannot.

Morgan's analysis also could account for all of the examples I cited in §3.3 as illustrative of discourse-based acceptability and unacceptability:

(84a) A: Who are John and Mary exchanging information with?
   B: Each other.
       (John and Mary are exchanging information with) each other.
(84b) A: Who is John exchanging information with?
   B: *Each other
       *(John is exchanging information with) each other
(84c) A: The Senators voted down a pay cut.
   B: For themselves?
       (The Senators voted down a pay cut) for themselves?

(84d) A: The Senators voted down a pay cut.
      B: *For himself?
           *(The Senators voted down a pay cut) for himself?
(84e) A: John hurt someone by releasing information.
      B: Himself.
           (John hurt) himself (by releasing information).
(84f) A: John hurt someone by releasing information.
      B: *Themselves
           *(John hurt) themselves (by releasing information)
(84g) A: Someone will give John a job.
      B: The mayor.
           The mayor (will give John a job).
(84h) A: Someone will give John a job.
      B: *The tree in front of his house
           *The tree in front of his house (will give John a job)
(84i) A: John doesn't know where the Library of Congress is.
      B: Ask any police officer.
           (John could/should) ask any police officer (where the
           Library of Congress is).
(84j) A: John doesn't know where the Library of Congress is.
      B: *Ask the tree in front of his house
           *(John could/should) ask the tree in front of his house
           (where the Library of Congress is)

Leaving small details aside, it seems that because Morgan's analysis predicts all of these aspects of interpretation and acceptability as a matter of
grammar, it would seem that an ellipsis analysis covers a range of empirical
data that a nonsentential constituent structure analysis cannot account for.
In particular, the distribution and interpretation of pronominals, reflexives
and reciprocals, which Morgan handles with a simple and independently
motivated rule system, I have to handle with a combination of an additional
rule of Case theory, a marked formulation of Binding theory as well as the
(as yet undelivered promise of a) discourse specification of the acceptability
or unacceptability of the interpretation of pronouns in or as nonsentential
constituent structures.

     Although the description of the syntax of nonsentential constituent
structure analysis presented here provides a well-motivated counteranalysis
to Morgan's ellipsis analysis, it is too soon, at this point in the explication of

the theory of nonsentential constituents, to judge the relative merits of the competing theories as they attempt to account for the meaning of independent major lexical categories. What Morgan handles in the grammar, I claim is better handled in a pragmatic component within a theory of independent constituents. In the following chapters, I offer support for this claim, arguing that the shift of accounting for interpretation and acceptability from semantics to pragmatics is both empirically and theoretically well-motivated. A full discussion of the validity of this position, however, has to take place during and after an explication of the pragmatic component shows exactly what it contributes to a theory of nonsentential constituents.

4. The Representation of Linguistic Context in the Pragmatic Model

4.0 Introduction

The pragmatic model of the interpretation of independent constituent utterances consists of the submodules of linguistic context and conversational context. This chapter describes the interpretation of independent constituent utterances within the submodule of linguistic context. The theoretical constructs within the submodule consist of a Principle of Linguistic Context along with its associated operation of Discourse Inference and Condition of Acceptability, all of which function together to describe the discourse-based interpretation of constituent utterances:

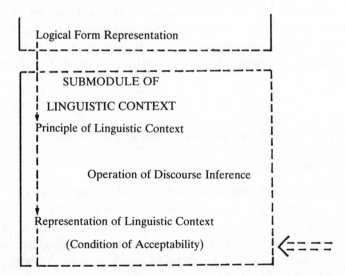

The Principle of Linguistic Context first creates a structure of linguistic context for each utterance within a discourse sequence; the operation of Discourse Inference then elaborates that structure by assigning a constituent utterance to a discourse function; and the Condition of Acceptability governs the resulting representation of linguistic context. Because discourse-based interpretation often (although not necessarily) is the initial hypothesis in the interpretation of many constituent utterances, the submodule of linguistic context is the first submodule in the pragmatic model.

Constituent utterances interpreted within the submodule of linguistic context function as answers to questions, specifications of pronouns, or expansions of previous elements in the linguistic context. A typical case of discourse-based interpretation is that of an independent constituent utterance functioning as an answer to a question:

(1a) P: Now what has changed their minds?
       D: Lack of [a] candidate or a body.
(1b) P: Where are you going to see him, here or there?
       E: In my office.
       (*Transcripts* 1974: 176, 208)

Through the operation of Discourse Inference, the constituent utterance NP in (1a) functions in the discourse role of Agent within an elaborated structure of linguistic context; similarly, the constituent utterance PP in (1b) functions in the discourse role of Location. Question and answer sequences, though, are not the only interpretations described within this submodule of the pragmatic model; the submodule also accounts for the interpretation of constituent utterances within sequences like the following examples:

(2a) E: I was just going to say, maybe if Rogers said it to him--
       P: Mitchell?
(2b) P: Yeah, in other words, you stay in the job.
       K: Until the trial.
       (*Transcripts* 1974: 195, 397)

In the elaborated structure of linguistic context for these examples, the constituent utterance NP in (2a) interrupts the previous utterance to function as a specification of the pronoun *him*; in (2b), the constituent utterance PP functions as a modifier of time for the predicate *stay*. The operation of Discourse Inference elaborates a structure of linguistic context by fitting constituent utterances in with previous utterances, and the linguistic context of a discourse sequence can grow quite complex as participants use independent constituent utterances to create multiple contradictions, elaborations, and expansions.

In the following sections of this chapter, I first describe interpretation within the submodule of linguistic context in §4.1; in §4.2, I present arguments supporting the claim that the submodule of linguistic context offers a theoretically satisfying description of the discourse-based interpretation of independent constituent utterances.

4.1 The submodule of linguistic context

In the following subsections, I first describe the Principle of Linguistic Context and the operation of Discourse Inference in §4.1.1 and present examples of interpretation within the submodule of linguistic context in §4.1.2; I then discuss the Condition of Acceptability governing the representation of linguistic context in §4.1.3.

4.1.1 *The principle of linguistic context and the operation of discourse inference*

Logical Form representation is the input to the submodule of linguistic context. In Zwicky's (1984) terms (cf. §1.2), this is a weakly autonomous interaction between the competence model and the pragmatic model because it takes place by means of the interface representation of Logical Form; it is fuzzily autonomous as well because certain properties of Logical Form representation, specifically the expansion possibilities of lexical items for selecting argument roles and occurring with modifiers, are relevant for pragmatic interpretation within the submodule of linguistic context. These expansion possibilities provide the basis for the discourse-based interaction that takes place within the submodule of linguistic context, an interaction which assigns a discourse function to an independent constituent utterance through a generalized operation of pragmatic inference.

One property of Logical Form that is crucial to pragmatic interpretation within the submodule of linguistic context is the representation of θ-roles. As far as I am aware, there is no generally accepted inventory of θ-roles in Government-Binding research. In several places, Chomsky (1981, 1982, 1986a,b) mentions Agent, Patient, and Instrument as examples of θ-roles, but nowhere does he describe a full set of θ-roles. Sells notes that there is neither a theory of possible θ-roles nor a set of tests for identifying particular θ-roles within a specific structure; he points out that working with θ-roles is right now a matter of "intuition" (1985: 35). In this work, I have loosely followed the work of Fillmore (1968, 1977), Chafe (1970), Jackendoff (1972), Foley and Van Valin (1984), and Marantz (1984) in order to arrive at Agent, Experiencer, Theme, Patient, Source, Goal (Beneficiary), Location, and Instrument as a working set of θ-roles.

Several features of this working set of θ-roles require brief comment. Because this is a fairly small set of θ-roles, each of the roles has a rather broad application. The role of Agent, for example, includes the traditional definition of an agent as an animate being who intentionally performs the action of the verb (e.g., *John* in *John revealed the information*); it also includes inanimate objects that perform the action of the verb (e.g., *the sun* in *the sun melted the film*). The role of Experiencer also includes animate beings and inanimate objects who (loosely speaking) experience the sense of the verb (e.g., *John* in *John knows a secret*; and *the committee* in *the committee needs information*). The role of Source also includes animate beings and inanimate objects (*John* in *John gave information to the committee* and *Washington* in *John went from Washington to New York*) as does the role of Goal (*John* in *The committee gave information to John* and *New York* in *John went from Washington to New York*); the role of Goal subsumes the concept of a beneficiary of the action of a verb (e.g., *John* in *He did a favor for John*). The roles of Theme and Patient require some differentiation: (roughly) following Marantz (1984: 32), Patient is the role that receives the action of a verb (e.g., *Tom* in *John fired Tom*); Theme is the relevant role occurring with a state or change of state verb (e.g., *the film* in *the film is overexposed, the film melted*, or *the sun melted the film*). Finally, in this work my assignment of θ-roles is intuitive, and readers may not agree with the exact interpretation for any given structure, although I hope that my decisions will be relatively uncontroversial.

The representation of θ-roles also requires brief comment. There does not seem to be a generally accepted form of representing the assignment of θ-roles in a Logical Form representation, so in this work I place the argument structure of a predicate underneath the verb using the following abbreviations: Agent (AG), Experiencer (EXP), Theme (TH), Patient (PT), Location (LOC), Source (SRC), Goal (GOAL), and Instrument (IN); in a representation, I also label each argument NP with its θ-role. The verb *give*, for example, receives the following representation in isolation and in sentence structures (optional θ-roles are in parentheses):[1]

(3a) $[_V$ give]
[SRC, PT, (GOAL)]

(3b) $[_S$ $[_{NP}$ John] $[_{VP}$ $[_V$ gave] $[_{NP}$ a donation]]]
    SOURCE   [SRC, PT, (GOAL)]   PATIENT

(3c) $[_S$ $[_{NP}$ John] $[_{VP}$ $[_V$ gave]
    SOURCE   [SRC, PT, GOAL]
$[_{NP}$ a donation] $[_{PP}$ to Nixon]]]
PATIENT   GOAL

The verb *give* has an optional θ-role of Goal as shown by the two contrasting examples in (3b) and (3c): in (3b) the θ-role is unrealized; in (3c), it is realized.

A crucial difference between θ-role assignment in sentences and in nonsentential VP constituent structures should be noted here. Sentences, which are licensed by the combination of the Projection Principle and the Predication Principle, almost always occur with verbs assigning a θ-role to the subject as an external argument as in examples (3b) and (3c); the only exceptions are the dummy subjects *it* and *there* which do not receive θ-roles. Nonsentential VP constituent structures, however, are licensed by the Projection Principle alone, which means that they do not select a subject argument. In order to represent this difference between verbs in sentences and verbs in nonsentential constituent structures, the external argument appears in curly brackets within the representation of a nonsentential VP constituent structure:

(4) A: What will John do with his tax refund?
    B: Give a donation to Nixon.

$[_{VP}$ $[_V$ give] $[_{NP}$ a donation] $[_{PP}$ to Nixon]]
[{SRC}, PT, GOAL] PATIENT   GOAL

The argument structure for the lexical entry *give* includes the θ-role of Source as its external argument, even though that argument is not selected in a nonsentential VP constituent structure.

In sentence structures, most NPs and some NPs within PPs have θ-roles; the Projection Principle, which governs Logical Form representations, ensures the one-to-one correspondence between selected arguments and the NPs that carry their θ-roles, as shown in the representations of sentences (3b) and (3c) above. In the representation of nonsentential constituent structures, however, independent NPs and NPs within PPs have no θ-roles because they are not derived in a configuration that assigns them. Consider the following discourse sequence, which contains one full sentence and two independent PP constituent utterances:

(5)   P: Mitchell has given a sworn statement, hasn't he?
      D: Yes, Sir.
      P: To the Jury?
      D: To the Grand Jury.
      (*Transcripts* 1974: 105)

The verb *give* obligatorily selects a Patient and a direct object NP canonically functions as this argument; the predicate selects a Source and a subject NP functions as this argument, so the Logical Form representation of the sentential structure in the discourse is well-formed:

(6) $[_S [_{NP}$ Mitchell$] [_{VP} [_V$ has given$]$ $[_{NP}$ a sworn statement$]]$
          SOURCE   [SRC, PT, (GOAL)]   PATIENT
      $[_{S'}$ hasn't he$]]$

The verb *give* also optionally selects and θ-marks as a Goal either an indirect object NP or a NP in a *to*-prepositional phrase, but neither of these options is realized within this particular sentence.

In (5), the independent PP constituent utterances are derived without any θ-role for their NPs. Intuitively, within the discourse sequence the NPs within the PPs seem to function in the role of Goal for the predicate *give*. But an autonomous grammar cannot assign any specific role to the independent constituents because it is limited to describing single structures. Assigning a discourse role to the PPs in order to represent the interpretation of their function within a discourse sequence must occur as an operation in the pragmatic model of the interpretation of independent constituent utterances.[2] The first submodule of the pragmatic model describes the interpretation that assigns a discourse function to an independent constituent utterance: a Principle of Linguistic Context first creates the structure of linguistic context for an utterance within a discourse sequence; an operation of Discourse Inference then describes the elaboration of this structure of linguistic context; and a Condition of Acceptability governs the elaborated representation of linguistic context.

In current work in linguistic theory, especially within a Chomskyan framework, principles can be structure-building or licensing (Rizzi 1987).[3] The first submodule of the pragmatic model has a structure-building Principle of Linguistic Context that creates a structure of linguistic context by associating the individual utterances within a discourse sequence together; such an association of utterances is a representation of the structure of linguistic context for each utterance within that sequence. To create a structure of linguistic context, the Principle of Linguistic Context builds upon the input representation of Logical Form:

(7) *Principle of Linguistic Context*
     In a discourse sequence, the Logical Form representation of each structure becomes the representation of each utterance within a structure of linguistic context.

Within the Principle, the term 'discourse sequence' is defined intuitively as a series of utterances that are somehow connected, perhaps by their contribution to a common topic of conversation.[4] To extend the symbol of the initial node of a grammar from X-bar theory, the Principle of Linguistic Context says that a discourse sequence consists of $(X^{max})^*$, where $X^{max} =$ X", C", or INFL" and * = an indefinite number; in other words, a discourse sequence consists of a collection of utterances that can be sentences, clauses, or independent constituents.

The Principle of Linguistic Context makes explicit the weakly autonomous interaction between the Logical Form component in the competence model and the submodule of linguistic context in the pragmatic model: a single structure generated by the grammar becomes one utterance in a developing structure of linguistic context. Merely applying the Principle of Linguistic Context to a discourse sequence does not create a representation that is different from the Logical Form representation for any individual utterance. But applying the Principle of Linguistic Context is necessary in order to begin discourse-based pragmatic interpretation because it creates a structure that goes beyond the single structure bounds of a grammar and brings utterances together, which creates the opportunity for inference-based interaction among utterances within the linguistic context.

To illustrate the operation of the Principle of Linguistic Context, consider the discourse sequence in (5). After applying the Principle of Linguistic Context, the utterances of this sequence are combined within a structure of linguistic context:[5]

(8) P: $[_S [_{NP}$ Mitchell] $[_{VP} [_V$ has given]
          SOURCE   [SRC, PT, (GOAL)]
          $[_{NP}$ a sworn statement]] $[_{S'}$ hasn't he]]
          PATIENT

D: $[_{ADVP}$ yes] $[_{NP}$ Sir]
P: $[_{PP} [_P$ to] $[_{NP}$ the Jury]]
D: $[_{PP} [_P$ to] $[_{NP}$ the Grand Jury]]

The Principle of Linguistic Context creates the structure that allows an independent constituent utterance to function in a discourse role, and assigning the PPs to function in the discourse role of Goal reflects an intuitive understanding of their function within this structure of linguistic context. The Principle of Linguistic Context, however, while it creates the structure for associating independent constituent utterances with other utterances within a sequence, cannot itself assign constituent utterances to function in a particular discourse role. Applying the Principle of Linguistic Context creates a structure that allows for the possibility for the interaction of utterances, but it does not describe the interaction itself. The Principle requires an associated operation to describe the inference that assigns an independent constituent utterance to function in a specific discourse role within a structure of linguistic context.

The operation that elaborates a structure of linguistic context by describing interaction among utterances is called Discourse Inference because it describes inferences that are based on knowledge of the structure of linguistic context. The actual operation of the inference is triggered by a match between an independent constituent utterance and an expansion possibility of a previous element within a structure of linguistic context:

(9) *Discourse Inference*
     If a discourse sequence includes an independent constituent utterance that potentially matches an expansion possibility of a previous element within the structure of linguistic context, then assign the constituent utterance to function as that expansion possibility in an elaboration of the structure of linguistic context.

In this statement, the term 'expansion possibility' is broadly defined to include the ability of a lexical item to select an argument role or to occur with a modifier. The operation of Discourse Inference describes interaction among utterances, specifically the discourse-based interaction of a constituent utterance functioning as a discourse role or a modifier in an elaboration of a structure of linguistic context.

To illustrate the operation of Discourse Inference, consider once more the representation of the structure of linguistic context in (8). The PP constituent utterances with the initial preposition *to* match the selection possibility of the predicate *give* for a Goal in a *to*-prepositional phrase, and on this basis the operation of Discourse Inference assigns the constituent utterances to function in that discourse role. The elaborated structure of linguistic context then represents the results of the operation of Discourse Inference by utilizing a formalization of solid arrows to describe the inferred match between an independent constituent utterance and its discourse function:

(10) P: [$_S$ [$_{NP}$ Mitchell] [$_{VP}$ [$_V$ has given]
        SOURCE   [SRC, PT, (GOAL)]
        [$_{NP}$ a sworn statement]]
        PATIENT
        [$_{S'}$ hasn't he]]

D: [$_{ADVP}$ yes] [$_{NP}$ Sir]

P: [$_{PP}$ [$_P$ to] [$_{NP}$ the Jury]]

D: [$_{PP}$ [$_P$ to] [$_{NP}$ the Grand Jury]]

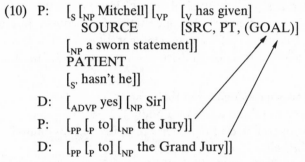

After the operation of Discourse Inference, the elaborated structure of linguistic context is defined as the representation of linguistic context.[6]

This overview of the Principle of Linguistic Context and operation of Discourse Inference describes only one type of interaction between independent constituent utterances and previous utterances in the linguistic context, an interaction in which a constituent utterance functions in a discourse role. Although this is a frequent type of discourse-based interaction described within the submodule of linguistic context, it is not the only type of interaction, and in §4.1.2, I discuss additional examples of independent constituent utterances functioning as discourse roles and modifiers. This overview also ignores the fact that the operation of Discourse Inference clearly has the potential to overgenerate interpretations based on possible matches in which an independent constituent utterance does not function meaningfully in a discourse sequence; this overgeneration is governed by the Condition of Acceptability, which is discussed in §4.1.3.

4.1.2 Interpretation within the submodule of linguistic context

After the Principle of Linguistic Context creates a structure of linguistic context for utterances within a discourse sequence, the operation of Discourse Inference describes the interaction between independent constituent utterances and other utterances when a constituent utterance functions as a discourse role or a modifier. In this subsection, I discuss several types of discourse-based interpretation within the submodule of linguistic context, including answers to questions, specifications of pronouns, and modifications of previous elements in the linguistic context. I also discuss some aspects of the interpretation of discourse-based anaphora within the submodule of linguistic context.

In what is perhaps the prototypical case of interpretation within the submodule of linguistic context, the operation of Discourse Inference describes the interpretation of independent constituent utterances that answer *wh*-questions and function in discourse roles. Consider the following sequences:

(11a) P: Now what has changed their minds?
     D: Lack of [a] candidate or a body.
(11b) K: Who else does Magruder implicate besides himself and Mitchell?
     E: Dean, LaRue, Mardian, Porter.
(11c) P: Where are you going to see him, here or there?
     E: In my office.
(*Transcripts* 1974: 176, 344, 208)

The representation of each question indicates its *wh*-pronoun θ-role:

(12a) $[_{S'} [_{ADVP}$ now]   [for which thing, x]
                                   AGENT

    $[_S$ x $[_{VP} [_V$ has changed] $[_{NP}$ their minds]]]]
       [AG, PT]   PATIENT

(12b) $[_{S'}$ [for which other persons, x] does $[_S [_{NP}$ Magruder]
        PATIENT   AGENT

    $[_{VP} [_V$ implicate] x $[_{PP}$ besides himself and Mitchell]]]]
       [AG, PT]

(12c) $[_{S'}$ [for which place, x] are $[_S [_{NP}$ you] $[_{VP} [_V$ going]
        LOCATION   AGENT   [AG]

    $[_{S'} [_S$ PRO $[_{VP} [_V$ to see] $[_{NP}$ him] x
       EXPERIENCER   [EXP, PT, LOC] PATIENT

    $[_{ADVP}$ here or there]]]]]]]

Within a structure of linguistic context, a constituent utterance NP or PP can match the *wh*-pronoun: in these examples, constituent utterance NPs in (12a) and (12b) match the *wh*-pronouns *what* and *who*, and a constituent utterance PP in (12c), by virtue of its locative preposition, matches the *wh*-pronoun *where*. When such a match triggers the operation of Discourse Inference, the independent constituent utterance then functions in the discourse role of the *wh*-pronoun in an elaborated structure of linguistic context:

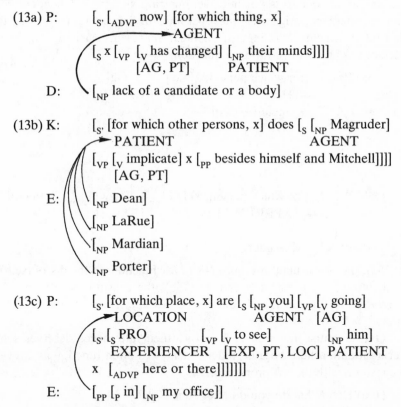

(13a) P: [$_{S'}$ [$_{ADVP}$ now] [for which thing, x]
            ────────►AGENT
            [$_S$ x [$_{VP}$ [$_V$ has changed] [$_{NP}$ their minds]]]]]
            [AG, PT]   PATIENT

       D: [$_{NP}$ lack of a candidate or a body]

(13b) K: [$_{S'}$ [for which other persons, x] does [$_S$ [$_{NP}$ Magruder]
            ──► PATIENT   AGENT
            [$_{VP}$ [$_V$ implicate] x [$_{PP}$ besides himself and Mitchell]]]]]
            [AG, PT]

       E: [$_{NP}$ Dean]
             [$_{NP}$ LaRue]
             [$_{NP}$ Mardian]
             [$_{NP}$ Porter]

(13c) P: [$_{S'}$ [for which place, x] are [$_S$ [$_{NP}$ you] [$_{VP}$ [$_V$ going]
            ──►LOCATION   AGENT   [AG]
            [$_{S'}$ [$_S$ PRO   [$_{VP}$ [$_V$ to see]   [$_{NP}$ him]
            EXPERIENCER   [EXP, PT, LOC] PATIENT
            x [$_{ADVP}$ here or there]]]]]]]]

       E: [$_{PP}$ [$_P$ in] [$_{NP}$ my office]]

In (13a), the constituent utterance NP functions in the discourse role of Agent for the predicate *has changed*; in (13b), a series of constituent utterance NPs function in the discourse role of Patient for the predicate *implicates*; and in (13c), the constituent utterance PP functions in the discourse role of Location.

Interpretation within the submodule of linguistic context also accounts for an interesting way in which discourse participants use question and answer sequences in conversation:

(14a) P: Who do you mean? Liddy?
(14b) P: Who knew better? Magruder?
       (*Transcripts* 1974: 256, 85)

A common occurrence in casual conversation is a speaker suggesting or guessing an answer to his or her own question with an independent constituent utterance, triggering the operation of Discourse Inference; the elaborated structure of linguistic context represents such a constituent utterance as an answer to the *wh*-question:

(15a) P: $[_{S'}$ [for which person, x] do $[_S$ $[_{NP}$ you]

→THEME   AGENT

$[_{VP}$ $[_V$ mean]   x]]]
  [AG, TH]

P: $[_{NP}$ Liddy]

(15b) P: $[_{S'}$ [for which person, x] $[_S$ x $[_{VP}$ $[_V$ knew] $[_{ADVP}$ better]]]]
→EXPERIENCER   [EXP, (PT)]

P: $[_{NP}$ Magruder]

In (15a), the constituent utterance NP *Liddy* functions in the discourse role of Theme for the predicate *mean*; in (15b), the constituent utterance NP *Magruder* functions in the discourse role of Experiencer for the predicate *know*.

One discourse function of VP constituent utterances deserves some special attention here because independent VPs often function as answers to questions with the *wh*-pronoun *what*:

(16a) H: What do you do after June 17th?
       P: Use the executive privilege on that.
(16b) P: What does Ziegler suggest as an alternative? Stonewall the Committee?
       (*Transcripts* 1974: 213, 258)

In each of these sequences, the *wh*-pronoun carries the θ-role of Patient. Within the submodule of linguistic context, the operation of Discourse

Inference assigns each VP constituent utterance to function in that discourse role within an elaborated structure of linguistic context:

(17a) H: [$_S$' [for which thing, x] do [$_S$ [$_{NP}$ you] [$_{VP}$ [$_V$ do]
           ➤PATIENT   AGENT   [AG,PT]
       ⎛ x   [$_{PP}$ after June 17th]]]]

   P: ⎝[$_{VP}$ [$_V$ use]   [$_{NP}$ the executive privilege] [$_{PP}$ on that]]
        [{AG}, PT]   PATIENT

(17b) P: [$_S$' [for which thing, x] does [$_S$ [$_{NP}$ Ziegler]
           ➤PATIENT   AGENT
       ⎛ [$_{VP}$ [$_V$ suggest]   x   [$_{PP}$ as an alternative]]]]
       ⎜ [AG, PT]

   P: ⎝[$_{VP}$ [$_V$ stonewall] [$_{NP}$ the Committee]]
        [{AG}, PT]   PATIENT

Within a discourse, the *wh*-pronoun *what* allows a match with both NP as well as VP constituent utterances as shown by examples (13a) and (17). The ability of VP constituent utterances to function in a discourse role points to a distinct difference between the representation of Logical Form in a competence model and the representation of linguistic context in a pragmatic model: within the highly constrained representation of Logical Form, a VP functions only as a predication; in contrast, within the less constrained submodule of linguistic context, a VP can function in a discourse role within an elaborated structure of linguistic context (cf. §4.2 for a discussion of other differences between the representation of Logical Form and the representation of linguistic context).

Participants in a discourse actively use their knowledge of the developing structure of linguistic context in order to construct questions and provide answers as contributions to a conversation. Consider the following sequence:

(18)   P: Then what the hell is in it for him?
       H: Immunity.
       P: Who grants immunity? The judges?
       (*Transcripts* 1974: 210)

Within the elaborated structure of linguistic context, the idiomatic question initiates a question and answer sequence in which the constituent utterance

NP *immunity* functions in the discourse role of Theme; the first speaker then asks another question and immediately uses an independent constituent utterance to suggest an answer functioning in the discourse role of Agent:

(19) P: [$_{S'}$ [$_{ADVP}$ then] [for which thing, x]
     ──────────►THEME
     [$_S$ x [$_{VP}$ [$_V$ is] [$_{PP}$ in it] [$_{PP}$ for him]]]]
                 [TH, GOAL]   GOAL

     H: [$_{NP}$ immunity]

     P: [$_{S'}$ [for which person, x] [$_S$ x [$_{VP}$ [$_V$ grants]
     ──►AGENT   [AG, PT]
     [$_{NP}$ immunity]]]]
     PATIENT

     P: [$_{NP}$ the judges]

The representations of the sequences in (11) - (19) demonstrate the ability of the submodule of linguistic context to describe the contribution of independent constituent utterances to a discourse consisting of question and answer sequences.

Another frequent discourse function of independent constituent utterances, especially PPs, is to elaborate discourse roles associated with a predicate within the structure of linguistic context. Example (10) in §4.1.1 illustrates an elaborated structure of linguistic context in which two constituent utterance PPs function in the discourse role of Goal; the following sequences include constituent utterance PPs that function in other discourse roles:

(20a) D: He was paid.
      P: By check?
(20b) P: He knew?
      D: Yes.
      P: About the Watergate?
      (*Transcripts* 1974: 66, 84)

Each constituent utterance matches an unrealized argument role associated with a predicate within the structure of linguistic context, triggering the operation of Discourse Inference:

(21a) D: [$_S$ [$_{NP}$ he]   [$_{VP}$ [$_V$ was paid]]]
           PATIENT   [(AG), PT, (INSTR), (LOC)]

     P: [$_{PP}$ [$_P$ by] [$_{NP}$ check]]

(21b) P: [$_S$ [$_{NP}$ he]   [$_{VP}$ [$_V$ knew]]]
           EXPERIENCER   [EXP, (PT)]

     D: [$_{ADVP}$ yes]

     P: [$_{PP}$ [$_P$ about] [$_{NP}$ the Watergate]]

The sequence in (21a) is an example of an interlocutor asking about a possible Instrument for the predicate *was paid* in the previous utterance; the match between the selection possibility of the passive predicate for an Instrument *by*-phrase and the constituent utterance PP with the same preposition provides the basis for the operation of Discourse Inference. The sequence in (21b) is an example of an interlocutor asking about a possible Patient for the predicate *know*; the match between the selection possibility of *know* for an *about*-phrase and the constituent utterance PP with the same preposition triggers the operation of Discourse Inference. Within these sequences, speakers use constituent utterances in order to suggest their understanding of a discourse role implicitly associated with a predicate in the structure of linguistic context.

Within a linguistic context, PP constituent utterances also function in discourse roles that already have been realized explicitly as in the following examples:

(22a) D: Hunt and Liddy were in his office.
     H: In Colson's office?
     D: In Colson's office.
(22b) P: Mitchell, apparently[,] had said something about clemency to people.
     H: To Liddy.
(22c) D: [T]hey had infiltrated it by a secretary.
     P: By a secretary?
     D: By a secretary and a chauffeur.
     (*Transcripts* 1974: 124, 269, 103)

In each of these sequences, a PP constituent utterance or a series of PP constituent utterances functions in a discourse role associated with a predicate:

(23a) D: [$_S$ [$_{NP}$ Hunt and Liddy] [$_{VP}$ [$_V$ were]   [$_{PP}$ in his office]]]
           THEME   [TH, LOC] LOCATION

    H: [$_{PP}$ [$_P$ in] [$_{NP}$ Colson's office]]

    D: [$_{PP}$ [$_P$ in] [$_{NP}$ Colson's office]]

(23b) P: [$_S$ [$_{NP}$ Mitchell] [$_{VP}$ [$_{ADVP}$ apparently] [$_V$ has said]
           AGENT   [AG, TH, GOAL]
           [$_{NP}$ something about clemency] [$_{PP}$ to people]]]
           THEME   GOAL

    H: [$_{PP}$ [$_P$ to] [$_{NP}$ Liddy]]

(23c) D: [$_S$ [$_{NP}$ they] [$_{VP}$ [$_V$ had infiltrated]   [$_{NP}$ it]
           AGENT   [AG, PT, INSTR] PATIENT
           [$_{PP}$ by a secretary]]]
           INSTRUMENT

    P: [$_{PP}$ [$_P$ by] [$_{NP}$ a secretary]]

    D: [$_{PP}$ [$_P$ by] [$_{NP}$ a secretary and a chauffeur]]

In (23a), the two PP constituent utterances function in the discourse role of
Location, and in (23b), the PP constituent utterance functions in the discourse role of Goal. In (23c), the predicate *infiltrate* selects (fairly unusu-
ally) a *by*-phrase for an Instrument, and the two PP constituent utterances
function in this discourse role. Within these sequences, speakers use independent constituent utterances in order to question or specify their understanding of a discourse role explicitly associated with a predicate in the
structure of linguistic context.

The representations of the sequences in (20) - (23) show that the submodule of linguistic context incorporates an important aspect of participants' knowledge about discourse: participants know not only what was
said, but also what was not said about any particular element in a discourse.
The basis for this knowledge of linguistic context is knowledge of the
expansion possibilities of lexical items, which is incorporated in the input
representation from Logical Form.

So far, the discussion has considered independent constituent utterances interpreted in discourse roles associated with a predicate within the structure of linguistic context. Another type of match triggering the operation of Discourse Inference within the submodule of linguistic context, however, is between an independent constituent utterance NP that follows a non-*wh*-pronoun within a discourse sequence. After the operation of Discourse Inference, the constituent utterance NP then specifies the pronoun and functions in its discourse role. In the discussion that follows I use the expression 'specification of pronouns' in order to emphasize the difference between this discourse phenomenon and the phenomenon of discourse or pragmatic anaphora. Generally speaking, discourse anaphora is an antecedent-anaphor relationship in which an antecedent precedes the pronoun; pragmatic anaphora is a relationship in which an anaphor receives its interpretation from an antecedent in the physical context of situation.[7] The specification of pronouns within discourse, in contrast, is a relationship in which the pronoun precedes its specification with an independent constituent utterance NP as in the following examples:

(24a) HP: He is apt to blast us all publicly.
     P: Sirica?
(24b) HP: [Y]ou need to get someone on the panel who knows politics.
     E: Former [g]overnor . . .
    (*Transcripts* 1974: 520, 194)

If a constituent utterance NP matches the features of a non-*wh*-pronoun, the operation of Discourse Inference can assign it to function in the discourse role of that pronoun within an elaborated structure of linguistic context. The basis for the match between a constituent utterance NP and a definite pronoun is a match based on the features of [animacy], [person], and [number]. In the sequence in (24a), the constituent utterance NP *Sirica* is [+animate], [3rd person], and [+singular], which matches the features of the pronoun *he*, so the NP functions in the discourse role of Theme:

(25)   HP: $[_S [_{NP}$ he] $[_{VP} [_V$ is] $[_{ADJP}$ apt]
      THEME   [TH]
      $[_{S'} [_S$ PRO $[_{VP} [_V$ to blast] $[_{NP}$ us all] $[_{ADVP}$ publicly]]]]]]
      AGENT   [AG,PT]   PATIENT

     P: $[_{NP}$ Sirica]

The single feature of [animacy] is the basis for the match between a constituent utterance and an indefinite pronoun. In the example in (24b), the constituent utterance NP *former governor* matches the [+animate] feature of the indefinite pronoun *someone* and functions in the discourse role of Patient; the third person NP does not match the features of the second person pronoun *you*, so the constituent utterance is not interpreted as a match to that pronoun:

(26) HP: [$_S$ [$_{NP}$ you]   [$_{VP}$ [$_V$ need]
          EXPERIENCER   [EXP]
          [$_{S'}$ [$_S$ PRO   [$_{VP}$ [$_V$ to get]
             AGENT   [AG,PT]
          [$_{NP}$ someone on the panel who knows politics]]]]]]
          PATIENT

    E: [$_{NP}$ former governor]

In both of these sequences, the NP constituent utterance specifies a pronoun by functioning in its discourse role.

The operation of Discourse Inference correctly predicts ambiguity in the specification of pronouns within discourse sequences. Consider the example of (24a) with one slight change:

(27) A: He is apt to blast him publicly.
      B: Sirica?

In this sequence, the NP constituent utterance *Sirica* matches both third person singular pronouns in the previous utterance, and the representation of linguistic context shows the connections between the NP and both pronouns:

(28) A: [$_S$ [$_{NP}$ he] [$_{VP}$ [$_V$ is] [$_{ADJP}$ apt]
          THEME   [TH]
          [$_{S'}$ [$_S$ PRO   [$_{VP}$ [$_V$ to blast] [$_{NP}$ him] [$_{ADVP}$ publicly]]]]]]
             AGENT   [AG,PT]   PATIENT

      B: [$_{NP}$ Sirica]

The elaborated structure of linguistic context accurately represents both of the possible matches for the NP constituent utterance.

Participants in a discourse often use constituent utterance NPs to ask questions about and with pronouns as in the following sequences:

(29a) P: They aren't involved in the damn thing are they? O'Brien and Parkinson?

(29b) E: The two of them put on a little charade for me in the office.
  P: Shapiro and Colson?
  E: Yes.
  (*Transcripts* 1974: 186, 240)

Example (29a) is similar to previous examples in which the speaker uses an independent constituent utterance to suggest an answer to his or her own question; here, the speaker immediately uses a constituent utterance NP to specify a pronoun in his previous utterance. The conjoined constituent utterance NP matches the features of the plural pronoun *they*, triggering the operation of Discourse Inference and resulting in an elaborated structure of linguistic context:

(30) P: $[_S [_{NP}$ they] $[_{VP} [_V$ aren't] $[_{ADJP}$ involved] $[_{PP}$ in the damn thing]]
  ↗THEME [TH, LOC]   LOCATION
  $[_{S'}$ are they]]

  P: $[_{NP}$ O'Brien and Parkinson]

In example (29b), the second speaker, President Nixon, uses a constituent utterance NP to suggest a specification for a pronoun in the utterance of the first speaker, John Ehrlichman. The conjoined constituent utterance NP matches the features of the plural pronoun *them* and functions in the discourse role of Agent:

(31) E: $[_S [_{NP}$ the two of them] $[_{VP} [_V$ put on]
  ↗AGENT   [AG, PT, GOAL, LOC]
  $[_{NP}$ a little charade] $[_{PP}$ for me] $[_{PP}$ in the office]]]
  PATIENT   GOAL   LOCATION

  P: $[_{NP}$ Shapiro and Colson]

In the discourse sequence in (29b), Ehrlichman, the original speaker, indicates his agreement with the President's specification of the pronoun by saying *yes*.

Participants in a discourse sometimes use a series of constituent utterances to specify a pronoun as in the following sequence:

(32) E: Everybody knew about it?
  H: Mitchell, Haldeman, Colson, Dean, the President.
  (*Transcripts* 1974: 234)

Each constituent utterance NP matches the [+animate] feature of the indefinite pronoun *everybody* in an elaborated structure of linguistic context:

(33) E: [$_S$ [$_{NP}$ everybody]   [$_{VP}$ [$_V$ knew]   [$_{PP}$ about it]]]
            EXPERIENCER   [EXP, PT]   PATIENT

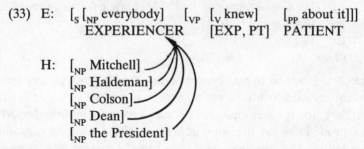

        H: [$_{NP}$ Mitchell]
             [$_{NP}$ Haldeman]
             [$_{NP}$ Colson]
             [$_{NP}$ Dean]
             [$_{NP}$ the President]

Each NP in the series functions in the discourse role of Experiencer.

The representations of the sequences in (24) - (33) illustrate the ability
of the submodule of linguistic context to account for the specification of
pronouns with independent constituent utterance NPs. The specification of
pronouns is one of the most interesting uses of independent constituent
utterances within discourse sequences, allowing discourse participants to
question, contradict, and clarify their use and understanding of pronouns.[8]

The discussion above has concentrated exclusively upon independent
constituent utterances functioning in discourse roles such as Agent, Patient,
Goal, and so on. Some PP constituent utterances and all ADJP and ADVP
constituent utterances, however, function as modifiers that expand previous elements in a discourse, and the submodule of linguistic context
describes this type of interaction among utterances as well. Expansion possibilities for modifiers, generally speaking, include matches between
ADJPs and PPs for NPs as well as matches between ADVPs and PPs for
VPs as in the following sequences:

(34a) L: Are we clear?
      C: Crystal.
      (*Cagney and Lacey*, January 19, 1988)
(34b) P: Yeah, in other words, you stay in the job.
      K: Until the trial.
      (*Transcripts* 1974: 397)

When a constituent utterance matches an expansion possibility for a modifier of an element in the previous structure of linguistic context, the operation of Discourse Inference can assign the constituent utterance to function
as that modifier in an elaborated structure of linguistic context; the arrows

that connect the constituent utterances to their discourse functions as modifiers attach to the specific lexical item:

(35a) L: $[_{S'}$ are $[_S$ $[_{NP}$ we] $[_{VP}$ $[_{ADJP}$ clear]]]]

C: $[_{ADJP}$ crystal]

(35b) P: $[_{S'}$ $[_{ADVP}$ yeah] $[_{PP}$ in other words] $[_S$ $[_{NP}$ you]
THEME
$[_{VP}$ $[_V$ stay] $[_{PP}$ in the job]]]]

[TH, LOC] LOCATION
K: $[_{PP}$ $[_P$ until] $[_{NP}$ the trial]]

In (35a), the constituent utterance ADJP matches the idiomatic possibility of an ADJP modifier for *clear*; in (35b), the constituent utterance PP matches the possibility of a modifier of time for the predicate *stay*. These sequences illustrate constituent utterances functioning as modifiers, thereby expanding previous elements in a structure of linguistic context.[9]

The operation of Discourse Inference also accounts for independent constituent utterances functioning as modifiers that answer *wh*-questions in which the *wh*-pronoun does not carry a specific θ-role. The *wh*-pronouns *when* and *how*, for example, do not carry a θ-role in Logical Form representation, but they introduce questions of time and manner, and independent constituent utterances frequently function as answers to these types of question:

(36a) P: How long will it take?
D: About fifteen minutes.
(36b) E: How was the golf?
K: Half good and half bad.
(*Transcripts* 1974: 154-155, 340)

After the operation of Discourse Inference, the elaborated structure of linguistic context represents the discourse function of the constituent utterances:

(37a) P: $[_{S'}$ [how long, x] will $[_S$ $[_{NP}$ it] $[_{VP}$ $[_V$ take] x]]]

D: $[_{PP}$ $[_P$ about] $[_{NP}$ fifteen minutes]]

(37b) E: $[_{S'}$ [how, x] was $[_S [_{NP}$ the golf] $[_{VP}$ x]]]

K: $[_{ADJP}$ half good and half bad]

In (37a), the constituent utterance PP matches the *wh*-pronoun *how long* and functions as a modifier of time; in (37b), the constituent utterance ADJP matches the *wh*-pronoun *how* and functions as a modifier of manner.

As it did for the specification of pronouns, the operation of Discourse Inference predicts discourse-level ambiguity in possible matches between constituent utterances and their discourse functions as modifiers. Consider the following sequence which contains a constituent utterance ADVP:

(38)   H: We stand ready to meet this offer whenever the enemy is willing to talk.

E: Seriously.

(*Transcripts* 1974: 305)

The operation of Discourse Inference can assign the ADVP to function as an expansion of a number of verbal elements within the previous utterance:

(39)   H: $[_S [_{NP}$ we] $[_{VP} [_V$ stand] $[_{ADJP}$ ready] $[_{S'} [_S$ PRO $[_{VP} [_V$ to meet]

$[_{NP}$ this offer] $[_{S'}$ whenever $[_S [_{NP}$ the enemy] $[_{VP} [_V$ is willing]

$[_{S'} [_S$ PRO $[_{VP} [_V$ to talk]]]]]]]]]]]]

E: $[_{ADVP}$ seriously]

Deciding exactly which verbal element(s) the ADVP refers to is a type of pragmatic interpretation that has to take place beyond the submodule of linguistic context since this submodule is restricted to discourse-based interpretation. In this case, background information about the particular parties being discussed or the topic of this sequence might function to establish an association between the ADVP and one verbal element (possibly the last one, *to talk*); such information-based interpretation, however, has to take place within the second submodule of the pragmatic model since that submodule incorporates knowledge from beyond the linguistic context (cf. §1.2 and Ch. 5, where the interpretation based on knowledge from beyond the linguistic context is discussed in more detail).

The final type of discourse-based interpretation I discuss in this subsection concerns some aspects of the interpretation of discourse-based anaphora. Some independent pronouns in or as constituent utterances receive part of their interpretation through the operation of Discourse Inference within the submodule of linguistic context; in certain cases, the operation of Discourse Inference sets up the possibility of discourse anaphora. Consider the following sequences in which each pronoun receives a free index i according to the principles of Binding theory (cf. §3.2 and §3.3):[10]

(40a) A: Someone gave a book to John.
      B: Me.
(40b) A: John gave a book to someone.
      B: Me.
(40c) A: That book is someone's.
      B: Mine.
(40d) A: John hurt someone by releasing information.
      B: Himself.
(40e) A: The Senators voted down a pay cut.
      B: For themselves?
(40f) A: Who are John and Mary exchanging information with?
     B: Each other.

Within an elaborated structure of linguistic context, the constituent utterances function as specifications of indefinite pronouns or as answers to questions: in (40a) - (40d), the constituent utterance pronouns match the [+animate] feature of the indefinite pronoun *someone* and function in the role of Source in (40a), Goal in (40b), Location in (40c) (Jackendoff (1972) analyzes possessives as Locations), and Patient in (40d). In (40e), the PP *for themselves* functions as a Goal for the predicate *vote*; and in (40f), the NP *each other* answers the question and functions in the Goal role of the *wh*-pronoun *who*:

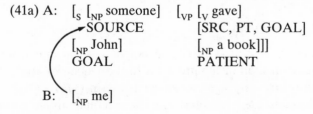

(41a) A: $[_S$ $[_{NP}$ someone] $[_{VP}$ $[_V$ gave]
        SOURCE   [SRC, PT, GOAL]
        $[_{NP}$ John] $[_{NP}$ a book]]]
        GOAL   PATIENT

    B: $[_{NP}$ me]

(41b) A: [$_S$ [$_{NP}$ John]   [$_{VP}$ [$_V$ gave]
           SOURCE   [SRC, PT, GOAL]
           [$_{NP}$ a book]   [$_{PP}$ [$_P$ to] [$_{NP}$ someone]]]]]
           PATIENT   GOAL

      B: [$_{NP}$ me]

(41c) A: [$_S$ [$_{NP}$ that book] [$_{VP}$ [$_V$ is]   [$_{NP}$ someone's]]]
           THEME   [TH, LOC]   LOCATION

      B: [$_{NP}$ mine]

(41d) A: [$_S$ [$_{NP}$ John] [$_{VP}$ [$_V$ hurt]   [$_{NP}$ someone]
           AGENT   [AG, PT]   PATIENT
           [$_{PP}$ by releasing information]]]

      B: [$_{NP}$ himself]

(41e) A: [$_S$ [$_{NP}$ the Senators] [$_{VP}$ [$_V$ voted down]
           AGENT   [AG, PT, (GOAL)]
           [$_{NP}$ a pay cut]]]
           PATIENT

      B: [$_{PP}$ [$_P$ for [$_{NP}$ themselves]]

(41f) A: [$_{S'}$ [for which person, x] [$_S$ [$_{NP}$ John and Mary]
            GOAL   SOURCE
           [$_{VP}$ [$_V$ are exchanging] [$_{NP}$ information] [$_{PP}$ [$_P$ with] x]]]]
           [SRC, PT, GOAL] PATIENT

      B: [$_{NP}$ each other]

After the operation of Discourse Inference assigns the constituent utterances discourse functions, all of the pronouns in the sequences above can
find acceptable discourse or pragmatic antecedents. In (41a) - (41c), the
match between the constituent utterance and the indefinite pronoun *someone* identifies the discourse function of the constituent utterances; the
speaker in the context of situation functions as the pragmatic antecedent for
the first person pronouns. In (41d), the singular third person NP *John* can

function as a discourse antecedent for the singular third person reflexive *himself* when the reflexive is functioning in the discourse role of Patient. In (41e), the plural NP *Senators* can function as the antecedent for the plural reflexive *themselves* when the PP is functioning in the discourse role of Goal. In (41f), the conjoined third person NP *John and Mary* can function as the antecedent for the plural reciprocal *each other* when the reciprocal is functioning in the discourse role of Goal.

There seems to be a general constraint that pronouns in or as independent constituent utterances somehow receive an interpretation through discourse and/or pragmatic anaphora.[11] When a pronoun has no antecedent, it is unacceptable, even if the operation of Discourse Inference assigns it a discourse function. Consider the following examples:

(42a) A: John hurt someone by releasing information.
      B: #Themselves
(42b) A: Who is John exchanging information with?
      B: #Each other
(42c) A: The Senators voted down a pay cut.
      B: #For himself?

In (42a), assuming that there is no set of entities in the context of situation providing a pragmatic antecedent for the pronoun, the third person plural pronoun *themselves* does not have a discourse antecedent in *John*, so even though the operation of Discourse Inference can assign the pronoun to function in the discourse role of Patient because it matches the [+animate] feature of the indefinite pronoun *someone*, the reflexive is unacceptable because it has no antecedent in discourse or in the context of situation. In (42b), again assuming that there is no physical context of situation providing a pragmatic antecedent for the reciprocal pronoun, the plural form of *each other* does not have an antecedent in the singular NP *John*, so even though the operation of Discourse Inference assigns the pronoun to function in the discourse role of Goal, it is unacceptable because it has no antecedent. In (42c), too, assuming that there is neither a 'larger than life' figure (cf. note 36 in Chapter Three) nor an individual in the context of situation to serve as the pragmatic antecedent, the singular reflexive *himself* fails to find a discourse antecedent and is therefore unacceptable. In these examples, the combination of the operation of Discourse Inference and discourse or pragmatic anaphora fails to arrive at an acceptable interpretation of the pronouns in or as constituent utterances.

The examples of discourse-based interpretation in this subsection have included answers to questions, specifications of pronouns, and other expansions of previous elements within the linguistic context. To describe the interpretation of these examples, the Principle of Linguistic Context creates a structure that allows interaction among the utterances in a discourse sequence. The operation of Discourse Inference elaborates that structure of linguistic context by assigning a constituent utterance to a discourse function. This elaborated structure is the representation of linguistic context within the first submodule of the pragmatic model of the interpretation of independent constituent utterances.

4.1.3 *The condition of acceptability within the submodule of linguistic context*

Within the submodule of linguistic context in the pragmatic model, the operation of Discourse Inference describes one hypothesis in the interpretation of an independent constituent utterance: participants attempt to fit a constituent utterance into the previous linguistic context in order to determine its discourse function. The operation of Discourse Inference, however, does not provide a procedure that interprets all constituent utterances satisfactorily, including some that appear to fit into the ongoing structure of linguistic context. Consider the following sequences (the notation (#) indicates that the pragmatic unacceptability is particular to the case explained in parentheses):[12]

(43a) A: John's dissertation in political science was approved.
       B: By the whole committee?
(43b) A: John's dissertation in political science was approved.
       B: (#)By the deadline? (with reading as an Agent)
(43c) B: By the deadline? (with reading as modifier of time)

While the operation of Discourse Inference seems to work smoothly in interpreting the function of the PP constituent utterance in (43a) in the discourse role of Agent for the passive predicate *was approved*, the interpretation of the *by*-phrase in (43b) as an Agent seems unacceptable. Instead, the PP constituent utterance is best interpreted as a modifier of time as in (43c). The operation of Discourse Inference describes implicated meaning based on a match within the structure of linguistic context; in and of itself, however, it does not establish any criteria for determining the acceptability or unacceptability of independent constituent utterances in discourse functions.

The concept of what is acceptable and what is unacceptable has received only sporadic attention in research on pragmatics. Researchers often claim, presumably based on their intuitions, that a particular utterance is pragmatically unacceptable without offering any explanation for its status (cf., for example, Hankamer and Sag 1976). A few researchers have described the concepts of pragmatic acceptability and unacceptability in nonformal terms; Grice, for example, says: "But at each stage SOME possible conversational moves would be excluded as conversationally unsuitable" (1975: 45; author's emphasis), but he does not suggest any specific ways in which discourse participants decide what type of utterance would constitute an unsuitable conversational move. For the purposes of developing the pragmatic model, however, the concepts of acceptability and unacceptability require a more explicit characterization.

It is possible to construct many discourse sequences that contrast in terms of intuitions regarding the pragmatic acceptability and unacceptability of discourse-based interpretation:

(44a) A: Who will give John a job?
      B: Nobody.
(44b) B: Congress.
(44c) B: #The tree in front of his house
(44d) B: #Grape Nuts cereal

The operation of Discourse Inference predicts that each of the constituent utterance NPs can function as a Source within the elaborated structure of linguistic context of the question and answer sequence; examples (44a) and (44b) seem acceptable, but examples (44c) and (44d) seem unacceptable. It is important to note here that the constituent utterances are pragmatically acceptable or unacceptable within specific discourse sequences; the acceptable and unacceptable utterances in (44a) - (44b) and (44c) - (44d) could be unacceptable and acceptable, respectively, in different sequences:

(45a) A: Something blocks John's view of the Washington monument.
      B: #Nobody
(45b) A: John eats the same thing for breakfast every day.
      B: #Congress

(45c) A: Something blocks John's view of the Washington monument.
      B: The tree in front of his house.
(45d) A: John eats the same thing for breakfast every day.
      B: Grape Nuts cereal.

A specific discourse sequence is crucial to intuitions of the pragmatic acceptability or unacceptability of independent constituent utterances, which suggests that the boundaries for any specific condition describing acceptability and unacceptability consist of the structure created by the Principle of Linguistic Context.

A nonformal explanation of the pragmatic intuitions about constituent utterances within different discourse sequences reveals the properties of acceptability and unacceptability that each of the examples has in common. With respect to the sequences in (44), people and institutions give or do not give jobs; individuals like *nobody* and organizations such as *Congress* typically function in this capacity. A *tree* and a *cereal*, on the other hand, typically do not function as Sources in giving a job. The same kind of explanation holds for the sequences in (43): a committee typically has the authority to approve a dissertation; in contrast, a deadline typically does not function as an Agent although it can function as a modifier of time.

In each of the explanations above, knowledge of the typicality of a situation in the real world governs the acceptability or unacceptability of the discourse function of an independent constituent utterance. This concept of knowledge about typical situations in the world has been described as "practical knowledge" in the work of Miller, who explains how it operates in disambiguation:

> *The Smiths saw the Rocky Mountains while they were flying to California.*
> Most people fail at first to notice the ambiguity, because the interpretation in which the Smiths are flying is far more salient than interpretations in which the Rocky Mountains are. The reason is obvious. Anyone who knows what mountains are knows that they do not fly. This fact — that mountains do not fly — is practical knowledge. It is not a fact that can be discovered by consulting dictionaries and would not be included in any reasonable account of a person's lexical knowledge. Yet it affects the interpretation of the ambiguous sentence almost as directly and immediately as does any [lexical] knowledge. (1977: 400-401)

Miller argues that judgments often rely on systems of practical knowledge. He acknowledges that a fully developed theory of practical knowledge would be a systematic account of human knowledge and thinking and that such a theory does not presently exist, but he claims that using the concept of practical knowledge is superior to attempting to account for such knowledge within semantics:

> Some linguists would say that *Mountains fly* violates the selectional restrictions of *fly*, and that is true enough. But why does it violate the selectional restrictions? Do we assume some special semantic category of flyable objects from which mountains are excluded? Or do we assume some inferential process that finds a contradiction between flying and being part of the earth's surface? The inferential process seems more plausible than an *ad hoc* list of flyable objects. . . [I]nferences based on practical knowledge and prevailing circumstances are the ultimate court of appeal. (1977: 409-410)

Miller's arguments hold as reasons not to attempt any integration of knowledge about the real world into the submodule of linguistic context in a pragmatic model.

The submodule of linguistic context in the pragmatic model describes discourse-based interpretation, but the operation of Discourse Inference operates blindly, creating a representation of linguistic context that needs to be governed by Miller's "court of appeals." The representation of linguistic context needs a point of contact with practical knowledge about the real world. The concept of practical knowledge is abstract; such abstraction, however, is necessary for it to have predictive power with respect to the acceptability or unacceptability of constituent utterances. The concept, or at least the term, represents the interface between the representation of linguistic context in the pragmatic model and general knowledge about the world as it is represented (somehow) in the mind of a native speaker or in the models proposed in cognitive science.

In this work, I do not even attempt to discuss the many complex issues connected with the representation of knowledge about the world in cognitive models. The work of Clark and Clark (1977) describes early attempts to explore the representation of encyclopedic knowledge; in recent years, there has been an explosion in cognitive science research on the representation of knowledge and the operations of thinking that utilize such general knowledge (cf., for example, Chs. 2-3 of Stillings et al. 1987, and references therein; Pylshyn 1984; Johnson-Laird 1983; Joshi, Webber and Sag 1981; Fauconnier 1985; Johnson 1987; Newmeyer 1988c). In addition to work in cognitive science, work in artificial intelligence also examines the problem of the representation and the use of knowledge about the world (cf. Chs. 4-

5 of Stillings et al. 1987, and references therein). (It should be noted here that the references cited above are not all compatible with the theory of nonsentential constituents being developed in this work; in particular, as Levinson (1985) notes, many of the models being developed in cognitive science and artificial intelligence specifically reject the notion of autonomous grammar and/or pragmatic inference as an operation specialized to the interpretation of language.)

The pragmatic model of the interpretation of independent constituent utterances requires a condition governing the acceptability of a representation of linguistic context, and this condition requires contact with some model of practical knowledge about the world; the structure of that model, however, is an open issue in cognitive science and therefore in linguistics. Consequently, I beg the question of exactly what nature of cognitive model has contact with the pragmatic model. The pragmatic model, however, requires a separation between its domain and the domain of a cognitive model because such a separation restricts a pragmatic model to the limited domain of utterance interpretation, which does not encompass all aspects of knowledge and thinking.

Knowledge about the world does not affect making an inference according to the operation of Discourse Inference; it merely confirms the arrived-at interpretation as acceptable or overrules it as unacceptable. The interaction proposed here is the common sense check on the results of discourse-based pragmatic inference: the concept of practical knowledge governs the elaborated representation of linguistic context by confirming or overruling the result of the operation of Discourse Inference for the interpretation of the discourse function of constituent utterances. It is, in short, a limited interaction between the pragmatic model and a model of the world. It is the specific interface point at which the submodule of linguistic context is partially autonomous with respect to systems of knowledge beyond itself.

The following Condition of Acceptability describes this interaction between the representation of an interpretation within the submodule of linguistic context and knowledge of typicality in the world:

(46) *Condition of Acceptability within the Submodule of Linguistic Context*
      Within a representation of linguistic context, an independent constituent utterance is pragmatically acceptable if it can perform its implicated discourse function according to the operation

of Discourse Inference; otherwise, it is deemed unacceptable (and marked #). The basis for a judgment of acceptability or unacceptability is practical knowledge of typical situations in the world.

This Condition governs the results of the operation of Discourse Inference within the submodule of linguistic context in the pragmatic model.

Claiming that the Condition overrules the results of the operation of Discourse Inference describes two situations of discourse-based interpretation. In the first situation, based on knowledge of typicality in the real world, a constituent utterance cannot function in its implicated discourse role, and, as such, is judged unacceptable. This situation encompasses examples in which the operation of Discourse Inference predicts an anomalous result as in the examples of (44) repeated here:

(47a) A: Someone will give John a job.
       B: #The tree in front of his house
(47b) B: #Grape Nuts cereal

In the second situation of interpretation that the Condition governs, an unacceptable constituent utterance cannot function in a discourse role even though there is a potential match as in the examples of (43) repeated here as part of (48):

(48a) A: John's dissertation in political science was approved.
       B: (#)By the deadline? (w/ reading as Agent)
       B: By the deadline? (w/ reading as modifier)
(48b) A: John gave expert testimony.
       B: (#)To no avail (w/ reading as Goal)
       B: To no avail. (w/ reading as modifier)
(48c) A: John refused to hurt himself by testifying publicly.
       B: (#)With any success? (w/ reading as Instrument)
       B: With any success? (w/ reading as modifier)
(48d) A: John left angrily.
       B: (#)From pique? (w/ reading as Location)
       B: From pique? (w/ reading as modifier)

In each of these examples, the Condition predicts that the PP constituent utterances are unacceptable in the functions of the discourse roles implicated by the operation of the operation of Discourse Inference: the PP constituent utterances cannot function in the discourse roles of Agent in (48a),

Goal in (48b), Instrument in (48c), and Location in (48d), so the Condition of Acceptability marks them as pragmatically unacceptable with that reading. The Condition, however, predicts that the PP constituent utterances are acceptable in the discourse function of modifier, which also is predicted by the operation of Discourse Inference: in (48a), for example, the PP constituent utterance can function as a modifier of time; in (48b) and (48c), the PP constituent utterances can function as modifiers of result, and in (48d), the PP can function as a modifier of manner. These examples are similar to Miller's example of the disambiguation of a pronoun; in these cases, practical knowledge of the real world dictates the modifier interpretation rather than the discourse role interpretation, and the process is so rapid that alternate interpretations most often are not even noticed by participants in an ongoing conversation. The pragmatic model, though, has to describe how these determinations are made, and the Condition of Acceptability does that.

The explication above establishes a theoretical separation between the application of the Principle of Linguistic Context, the operation of Discourse Inference, and the judgment of the Condition of Acceptability. In the actual process of interpretation, however, all of these constructs may function together, perhaps even simultaneously, in order to arrive at a discourse-based interpretation of a constituent utterance. One particular combination seems especially powerful: if the operation of Discourse Inference and the Condition of Acceptability describe and verify one particular interpretation of a discourse function for a constituent utterance, other possibilities may not even be noticed or calculated. But even though the actual process of interpretation may mix or cut short the different operations, the submodule presented here does not make any claims about the real-time or psychological processing of utterances in a discourse. The description of interpretation within the submodule of linguistic context is theoretical; it has to describe all of these operations separately because each one makes a different contribution to the discourse-based interpretation of a constituent utterance: the Principle of Linguistic Context creates the structure of linguistic context in which interpretation takes place; the operation of Discourse Inference describes the interaction among utterances in which a constituent utterance receives a discourse function within an elaborated structure of linguistic context; and the Condition of Acceptability governs the resulting representation of linguistic context.

4.2   Arguments supporting the submodule of linguistic context

In this section, I present arguments in support of the claim that the submodule of linguistic context offers a theoretically principled way of describing the discourse-based interpretation of constituent utterances. In §4.2.1, I compare the pragmatic account of interpretation presented here with competing accounts of interpretation based on an ellipsis theory of independent major lexical category utterances; I also discuss differences between the component of Logical Form in the competence model and the submodule of linguistic context in the pragmatic model, arguing that one theoretical advantage of the submodule of linguistic context is its ability to distinguish between its representation of indeterminate implicated meaning and its input representation of determinate semantic meaning. In §4.2.2, I consider the submodule of linguistic context within a wider theoretical framework, explaining how it complements aspects of other theories of pragmatic interpretation.

4.2.1   *Competing accounts of interpretation*

The most significant claim made in this work is that a theory of the structure and interpretation of nonsentential constituents requires two interacting models: a competence model accounting for the grammar of nonsentential constituent structures and a pragmatic model accounting for the interpretation of independent constituent utterances in context. Within the broad framework of Chomskyan linguistics, the interaction between models is necessary in order to provide a modular account of the meaning of independent constituents: the output of a competence model is a representation of meaning narrowly defined as Logical Form representation, which becomes the input to a pragmatic model; the output of a pragmatic model is a representation of meaning broadly defined as interpretation in context.

Another claim made in this work is that a pragmatic model describing interpretation in context consists of two submodules, the submodule of linguistic context and the submodule of conversational context. The previous section of this chapter described the first submodule within the pragmatic model, in which the input of a Logical Form representation for a structure becomes a representation of an utterance within a structure of linguistic context as described by the Principle of Linguistic Context. A structure of linguistic context creates the opportunity for independent constituent utterances to interact with other utterances by functioning as discourse roles or modifiers as described by the operation of Discourse Inference. Within an elaborated structure of linguistic context, the interpretation of a constituent utterance is judged for appropriateness as described by the Condition of Acceptability. I claim that this description of interpretation within the sub-module of linguistic context provides a theoretically satisfying account of the discourse-based interpretation of independent constituent utterances, especially in comparison to accounts of interpretation based on an ellipsis theory of independent major lexical categories.

An ellipsis theory traditionally claims that the interpretation of an independent major lexical category depends upon the semantic representation of its full sentence source: a full sentence semantic representation is required in Sag's (1976) theory, and Morgan explicitly claims that "[P]roperties of full sentences will bear directly on the . . . interpretation of fragments" (1973: 724). Another competing account of the interpretation of independent major lexical categories is based on the work of Sperber and Wilson (Wilson and Sperber 1981, 1986; Sperber and Wilson 1986). This theory assumes that independent major lexical categories are generated by grammatical ellipsis, and it claims that nonsentential utterances are interpreted through pragmatic inference, although the inference is of a radically different sort than the operation of Discourse Inference proposed in this work.

Wilson and Sperber claim that a single principle of relevance is sufficient and powerful enough to constitute a full theory of pragmatic interpretation, explicating the Principle of Relevance as follows:

> [(i)] Other things being equal, the greater the contextual effects, the greater the relevance.
>
> [(ii)] Other things being equal, the smaller the processing effort, the greater the relevance.
>
> Let us say that an utterance (or more generally an act of inferential communication) which, on the one hand, achieves an adequate range of contextual effects, and on the other hand, achieves it for the minimum justifiable processing effort, is *optimally relevant*.
>
> Principle of Relevance
> Every act of inferential communication carries a guarantee of optimal relevance. (1986: 74-75; authors' emphasis)

One of the most controversial features of Sperber and Wilson's work is that they specifically claim that pragmatic inference based on relevance is necessary to arrive at an interpretation of both the explicit (propositional) content as well as the implicit (implicated) content of an utterance. They cite the following example as an utterance which requires interpretation of its explicit propositional content:

> [(i)]   His food is not hot enough.
> The hearer of [(i)] must not only recover the semantic representation of the sentence uttered, but decide who the referential expression 'he' [sic] refers to, whether the ambiguous word 'hot' means *very warm* or *spicy*, whether the vague expression 'his food' refers to the food he cooked, the food he brought, the food he served, the food he is eating, etc., and what this food is claimed to be not hot enough *for*. (1986: 67; authors' emphasis)

Although not all researchers would agree that Wilson and Sperber's list above necessarily represents propositional content, the example illustrates their general claim that grammar often underdetermines content and that pragmatic inference is required to recover the assertion or proposition associated with an utterance.

Wilson and Sperber's theory of relevance incorporates two strong claims: first, that the operation of pragmatic inference functions to recover part of the propositional content of utterances; and second, that the Principle of Relevance is sufficient and powerful enough to establish the exact explicatures and implicatures that make up a single, determinate interpretation for an utterance, defining determinacy as "the interpretation intended by the speaker; this is the only interpretation it is worth the hearer's effort to recover. . . .[E]very utterance has at most one interpretation which is consistent with the principle of relevance" (1986: 67, 76). The following discussion concentrates upon Sperber and Wilson's claim that pragmatic inference based on Relevance recovers propositional content because this is the part of their theory that interacts with ellipsis.[13]

Sperber and Wilson call a proposition specified by the operation of pragmatic inference an 'explicature', defining it as an enriched proposition which contains the content of the utterance as a subpart (1986: 181-182). Following Sperber and Wilson, Carston (1985a,b) cites ellipsis as an example of a conversational phenomenon that requires the recovery of propositional content by means of pragmatic inference:

> Supplying ellipsed material is an obvious case of underspecification by linguistic meaning, so phrasal or lexical utterances such as "On the table," "Telephone," are standardly instantly understood as conveying complete propositions — a large portion of such propositions retrieved has clearly been pragmatically derived. Now ellipsis is a case where a proposition would be hopelessly incomplete without such pragmatic additions; presum-

ably the logical form output by the grammar constrains the shape of the
required completion. (1985a: 5)

Carston explicates the following example (without specifying how the grammar constrains the form of an explicature):

> [F]or example, if B comes into the kitchen carrying a box of groceries and
> A says:
>> On the table, please.
> B will instantly understand A as having *said* something like, "I want you to
> put the groceries on the table", i.e., a large portion of the proposition
> expressed here has been derived pragmatically. (1985b: 5; author's
> emphasis)

Carston's assumption that a nonsentential utterance is associated with a
sentence-like proposition is similar to Morgan's statement about the semantic interpretation of sentence fragments: "I will not argue here for the obvious fact that [fragments] have the *semantic* import of full sentences" (1973:
721; author's emphasis).

The ellipsis theories of Morgan and Carston assume that interpretation
of an independent major lexical category consists of a determinate semantic
representation or a determinate set of explicatures specifying propositional
content. But the interpretation of nonsentential utterances may not be as
straightforward as Morgan and Carston suggest because issues of indeterminacy quickly complicate the picture. The major problem with both these
views of the interpretation of nonsentential utterances is that a single, well-
formed semantic or propositional representation is not available for all
independent major lexical category utterances (cf. §1.2). But within their
respective theoretical frameworks of ellipsis, Morgan and Carston are
forced to conclude that a determinate interpretation does exist for any particular nonsentential utterance; thus, their theoretical frameworks are
incapable of accounting for the indeterminacy that actually characterizes
most pragmatic interpretation.

Following the work of Grice, however, as I do here in the development
of the pragmatic model, allows an account of the interpretation of independent constituent utterances to encompass and explain indeterminacy, where
indeterminacy is defined as the possibility of different interpretations for an
utterance. Within the submodule of linguistic context, the operation of Discourse Inference creates implicatures which connect an independent constituent utterance to a discourse function; these implicatures represent
indeterminate meaning. Carston, though, argues against such an implica-

ture-based account of nonsentential utterances. Following Sperber and Wilson, she claims that recovery of determinate propositional content, while a pragmatic process, does not result in the formation of implicatures: "[M]ost pragmatists employing Gricean maxims have adopted as a basic working principle the view that anything which is not part of the linguistic meaning of expressions used in the utterance must be a[n] . . . implicature, i.e., anything pragmatic is an implicature" (1985a: 4-5). In the following argument, however, I show that an implicature-based description provides a theoretically satisfying account of the indeterminate interpretation of independent constituent utterances.

Consider once more the representation of linguistic context for the first speaker's utterances in this discourse sequence:

(49)   P: Who grants immunity? The judges?
       E: Sirica grants immunity in the Grand Jury proceedings; Ervin grants it in Congressional proceedings; the Attorney General can grant it in anything.
       (*Transcripts* 1974: 210)

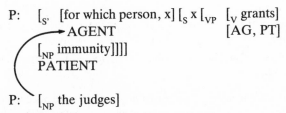

P: $[_{S'}$ [for which person, x] $[_S$ x $[_{VP}$ $[_V$ grants]
     →AGENT   [AG, PT]
     $[_{NP}$ immunity]]]]
     PATIENT

P: $[_{NP}$ the judges]

Within the elaborated structure of linguistic context, the NP constituent utterance matches the *wh*-pronoun, and on this basis the operation of Discourse Inference assigns the constituent utterance to function in the discourse role of Agent. Within the submodule of linguistic context, this discourse-based interpretation proceeds in the manner of inferential communication of meaning$_{nn}$ (non-natural meaning, or intentional meaning) as originally described by Grice (1957) and explicated here by Levinson:

S meant$_{nn}$ [intentionally communicated/implicated] z
by uttering U [an utterance] if and only if:
(i)   S intended U to cause some effect z in recipient H
(ii)   S intended (i) to be achieved simply by H recognizing that intention (i)
Here, S stands for speaker, . . . H for hearer, or more accurately, the intended recipient; 'uttering U' for utterance of a linguistic token; . . . and

z for (roughly) some belief or volition invoked in H. . . .[C]ommunication consists of the 'sender' intending to cause the 'receiver' to think or do something, just by getting the 'receiver' to recognize that the 'sender' is trying to cause that thought or action. So communication is a complex kind of intention that is achieved or satisfied just by being recognized. In the process of communication, the sender's 'communicative intention' becomes **mutual knowledge**. . . .Attaining this state of mutual knowledge of a communicative intention is to have successfully communicated. (1983: 16; author's emphasis)

In the case of the discourse-based interpretation of the sequence in (49), the speaker, President Nixon, intends the NP constituent utterance to function as an Agent of the predicate *grant* within the structure of linguistic context. The hearer, John Ehrlichman, seems to recognize this intention and correctly interpret the function of the NP as an Agent, judging from his answer in which he specifies several possible agents for granting immunity. What both speaker and hearer have in common for the interpretation of the constituent utterance NP is the structure of linguistic context as the basis for the operation of Discourse Inference. The elaborated structure of linguistic context then represents the mutual knowledge of the interpretation of the independent constituent utterance.

Levinson offers the generally accepted characterization of inference as the process used to bridge "the gap between what is literally *said* and what is conveyed" (1983: 98; author's emphasis). Grice adds an important qualification to this framework:

[F]or x to have meaning$_{nn}$ [implicated meaning], the intended effect must be something which in some sense is within the control of the audience. (1957: 58)

With respect to the submodule of linguistic context, what is under the control of the discourse participants is knowledge of the structure of linguistic context; what hearers do is draw inferences about the intentions of a speaker with respect to fitting an independent constituent utterance into this structure of linguistic context. This process of discourse-based interpretation is described by the operation of Discourse Inference, which is one specific type of inference within the general description proposed by Grice; using Levinson's terminology, it is one specific process by which discourse participants bridge the gap between what is said and what is interpreted, in this case, within the linguistic context.[14]

The operation that assigns an independent constituent utterance to function in a specific discourse role within a structure of linguistic context must be an inferential operation within a pragmatic model; in contrast to the assumptions of an ellipsis theory, it cannot be some kind of extension of the rules of syntactic or semantic derivation in a grammar, nor can it be some kind of deductive rule recovering determinate propositional content. Consider, for instance, the contrast in the assignment of the θ-role of Agent as an aspect of a grammatical derivation compared to the assignment of an independent constituent utterance functioning in the discourse role of Agent as an aspect of a pragmatic interpretation. Within the grammar, a predicate in a sentence structure may select Agent as a θ-role, and a subject NP canonically functions as this argument as the following LF representation shows:

(50) $[_S [_{NP}$ the judges] $[_{VP} [_V$ grant] $[_{NP}$ immunity]]]
      AGENT   [AG, PT]   PATIENT

The assignment is an automatic one specified by a combination of the lexical entry for the verb as well as the presence of a NP in subject position. In contrast, consider the following discourse sequences:[15]

(51a) P: Who grants immunity? The judges?
       (*Transcripts* 1974: 210)
(51b) A: Who grants immunity?
       B: (#)Red lights! (with reading as Agent)

In (51a), the constituent utterance NP *the judges* functions acceptably in the discourse role of Agent within an elaborated structure of linguistic context. In (51b), however, the interpretation of the NP *red lights* as an agent granting immunity seems atypical, so the constituent utterance is marked unacceptable by the Condition of Acceptability within the submodule of linguistic context (although the NP might receive an interpretation within the submodule of conversational context where interpretation can be based on the physical context of situation). The point here is that the operation of Discourse Inference which arrives at an interpretation of discourse function is not automatic and determinate as is the operation of rules which arrive at a semantic representation of θ-assignment within a grammatical derivation. A discourse-based inference can be overruled by the Condition of Acceptability, as the example in (51b) illustrates. The pragmatic model of the interpretation of constituent utterances has to be flexible enough to create different interpretations of independent constituent utterances; it is able to do so because its mechanism, the operation of Discourse Inference, is a type of pragmatic inference, which arrives at an indeterminate interpretation of meaning.

Grice (1975) lists five defining features of implicatures, which I consider here in relation to the discourse-based interpretation of independent constituent utterances. One of these features is indeterminacy, which Grice characterizes as the possibility of "various" inferential interpretations of an utterance (1975: 58). Indeterminacy is characteristic of the interpretation of many independent constituent utterances within the pragmatic model, as shown in the examples of (51) and again in the following sequences:

(52a) A: What did John say about the drive around Washington?
      B: Red lights.
(52b) A: What did John say about the drive around Washington?
      B: Red lights!

In (52a), the constituent utterance NP could function in the discourse role of Theme in an elaborated structure of linguistic context:

(53) A: $[_{S'}$ [for which thing, x] did $[_S [_{NP}$ John] $[_{VP} [_V$ say]   x
           ⟶THEME   AGENT   [AG, TH]
           $[_{PP}$ about the drive around Washington]]]]

      B: $[_{NP}$ red lights]

In this interpretation, the independent constituent utterance functions as an answer to the question: what John said about the drive around Washington, perhaps in a conversation about the frustrating nature of a drive in a congested city, was *red lights* (possibly implying that the large number of red lights was the reason for the frustrating nature of the drive, although this additional interpretation would have to take place within the submodule of conversational context where interpretation can be based on information about the topic of conversation; cf. §5.1). The discourse role of Theme, however, is not the only interpretation possible for the NP. In (52b), perhaps aided by clues from events in the physical context of situation, especially if that context of situation is in an automobile, the constituent utterance NP could function as a warning or reminder about upcoming red lights (again, this specific interpretation, too, would take place within the submodule of conversational context where interpretation can be based on information about the physical context of situation). It is possible to overrule a discourse-based interpretation based on the physical context as in (52b); it is also possible to ignore a possible interpretation based on a physical context of situation in favor of a discourse-based interpretation as in (52a). In short, the interpretation of the NP is indeterminate because at least two different interpretations are available, and the pragmatic model reflects this indeterminacy by describing different ways in which an utterance can be interpreted (cf. Chapter Five for additional discussion of indeterminacy in pragmatic interpretation *contra* Sperber and Wilson).

In work considering Grice's defining features of implicatures, Sadock (1978, 1981) and Hirschberg (1985) argue that the most distinctive feature of an implicature is that it is defeasible — it can be canceled based on contextual information, as in examples (51b) and (52b) above, or it can be canceled based on an explicit statement that denies the implicature. Consider the assignment of the θ-role Patient as an aspect of derivation in grammar versus the assignment of the discourse role of Patient as the result of an operation of Discourse Inference in a pragmatic model of interpretation. Within the grammar, the assignment of a θ-role cannot be canceled; any attempt to do so with the addition of a cancellation clause results in semantic anomaly:

(54) A: What did John say about the drive around Washington?
     B: *John said *red lights* about the drive around Washington, but he didn't say *red lights* about the drive around Washington, he was warning Mary about upcoming red lights at the next corner.

In contrast, the addition of a cancellation clause to a NP constituent utterance simply cancels the implicature and doesn't result in anomaly:

(55) A: What did John say about the drive around Washington?
     B: Red lights, but he didn't say *red lights* about the drive around Washington, he was warning Mary about upcoming red lights at the next corner.

Because the association between the NP *red light* and the discourse role of Patient is an implicature, it can be qualified and/or canceled with additional information.

Not all speakers agree that (54) and (55) are, respectively, semantically anomalous and pragmatically acceptable. Although there is general agreement that (54) is semantically anomalous because it is contradictory, some see (55) as equally contradictory (Horn, Ward, Lapointe, personal communication). Sadock (1978, 1981), though, notes that it is not always possible to apply cancellation as a criterion for distinguishing implicatures, especially if those implicatures are the result of generalized inference. The operation of Discourse Inference is a type of generalized inference (cf. §4.2.2), and, as Sadock predicts, its implicatures are difficult to cancel. There is, though, I believe, a noticeable distinction in acceptability between (54) and (55): (54) is clearly unacceptable on semantic grounds because it is a fully specified contradiction; (55), however, seems more acceptable on pragmatic grounds because it does not contradict an aspect of grammatical derivation; it merely cancels an implicature.

Although the cancellation test does not provide a straightforward way to make a distinction between semantic meaning and implicated meaning with respect to the interpretation of nonsentential constituents, independent constituent utterances do interact with a notion of cancelability in an interesting way. In an explication of Grice's feature of defeasibility, Levinson uses the following set of examples:

(56a) John has three cows.
(56b) John has two cows.
(56c) John has only three cows and no more.
(56d) *John has three cows, if not two
(56e) *John has three cows and maybe none
(56f) John has three cows, in fact, ten.
(56g) John has three cows and maybe more.
(1983: 115-116)

He explains that the sentence in (56a) has both semantic entailments and pragmatic implicatures: John's owning three cows entails that he owns two cows as specified in (56b); his owning three cows implicates that he owns no more than three cows as described in (56c). In (56d) and (56e), an attempt to cancel the entailments results in semantic anomaly. Additional material, though, easily cancels the implicature that John owns only three cows, as seen in the felicitous sentences (56f) and (56g).

The non-defeasibility of semantic meaning and the defeasibility of pragmatic meaning reflect the basic difference between the representation of determinate meaning at the level of Logical Form and the representation of implicated meaning within the submodule of linguistic context. As examples (56d) and (56e) show, the semantic entailments of sentential structures are non-defeasible at the highly constrained level of Logical Form representation. Consider, however, the following examples of discourse sequences with independent constituent utterances:

(57a) A: John has three cows.
      B: Ten.
(57b) B: Ten, if not more.
(57c) B: Two.
(57d) B: One, if any.

The operation of Discourse Inference assigns each of the independent constituent utterances to function in the role of modifier for the NP *cows*. Consider, first, the sequences in (57a) and (57b) in comparison to the sentences in (56f) and (56g):

(58a) A: $[_S [_{NP} \text{John}] [_{VP} [_V \text{has}] \quad [_{NP} [_{ADJP} \text{three}] [_N \text{cows}]]]]$
            AGENT   [AG, TH]   THEME

      B: $[_{ADJP} \text{ten}]$

(58b) A: $[_S [_{NP} \text{John}] [_{VP} [_V \text{has}] \quad [_{NP} [_{ADJP} \text{three}] [_N \text{cows}]]]]$
            AGENT   [AG, TH]   THEME

      B: $[_{ADJP} \text{ten, if not more}]$

As in sentences (56f) and (56g), the addition of information from the constituent utterances cancels the implicature associated with the previous utterance within the structure of linguistic context, namely, the implicature that John has three and only three cows.

Now consider the contrast between the independent constituent utterances in (57c) and (57d) in comparison to the sentences in (56d) and (56e). The sentences in (56d) and (56e) cannot include material that contradicts their semantic entailments. The elaborated structure of linguistic context for (57c) and (57d), however, shows that constituent utterances can function to contradict the semantic entailments of the previous utterance in the linguistic context:

(59a) A: $[_S [_{NP} \text{John}] [_{VP} [_V \text{has}] \quad [_{NP} [_{ADJP} \text{three}] [_N \text{cows}]]]]$
            AGENT   [AG, TH]   THEME

      B: $[_{ADJP} \text{two}]$

(59b) A: [$_S$ [$_{NP}$ John]   [$_{VP}$ [$_V$ has]   [$_{NP}$ [$_{ADJP}$ three] [$_N$ cows]]]]
            AGENT   [AG, TH]   THEME

     B: [$_{ADJP}$ one, if any]

Because the discourse function for each constituent utterance is the result of an inference, it is possible to use a constituent utterance to cancel implicatures as well as entailments associated with previous utterances in the linguistic context. Since the submodule of linguistic context does not represent determinate semantic meaning, it is able to describe independent constituent utterances performing one of their most frequent discourse functions, that of contradicting the meaning of a previous utterance by canceling its entailments.

Sadock (1978) proposes the notion of reinforceability, an additional test for distinguishing an implicature. Reinforceability is similar to defeasibility because it states an implicature explicitly; defeasibility, though, cancels the implicature, while reinforceability affirms or repeats it. Sadock offers the following example:

(60)   Maggie ate some, but not all, of the cheddar.
       (1978: 294)

In this case, *not all* explicitly states the generalized implicature associated with *some*. The test of reinforceability also illustrates the differences between the Logical Form representation of sentences and the representation of linguistic context for independent constituent utterances. At Logical Form, explicitly stating, by actually repeating, the semantic meaning of a sentence results in anomaly from redundancy:

(61)   *John left; John left.

The implicated discourse function of a constituent utterance, however, can be explicitly stated without anomaly:[16]

(62)   A: Who left?
       B: John; John left.

The implicature connecting an independent constituent utterance to its discourse function passes Sadock's test of reinforceability.

Other features that Grice (1975) associates with implicatures are non-detachability, non-conventionality, and calculability, and all of these, too, are associated with the implicatures resulting from the operation of Discourse Inference within the submodule of linguistic context. Except for implicatures arising from Grice's maxim of Manner, non-detachability means that an implicature is attached to the meaning of an expression rather than its linguistic form; in other words, as Levinson points out, changing an expression into synonyms will not cancel the implicature (1983: 116). The discourse-based interpretation of independent constituent utterances is non-detachable as the following examples demonstrate:

(63a) Who grants immunity? Federal judges?
(63b) Who grants immunity? Federal justices?
(63c) Who grants immunity? The honorable members of the Federal bench?

In all three cases, the elaborated structure of linguistic context indicates that the NPs are interpreted with the discourse function of Agent:

(64a) A: $[_{S'}$ [for which person, x] $[_S$ x $[_{VP} [_V$ grants]
          ⟶AGENT   [AG, PT]
          $[_{NP}$ immunity]]]]
          PATIENT

    A: $[_{NP}$ Federal judges]

(64b) A: $[_{S'}$ [for which person, x] $[_S$ x $[_{VP} [_V$ grants]
          ⟶AGENT   [AG, PT]
          $[_{NP}$ immunity]]]]
          PATIENT

    A: $[_{NP}$ Federal justices]

(64c) A: $[_{S'}$ [for which person, x] $[_S$ x $[_{VP} [_V$ grants]
          ⟶AGENT   [AG, PT]
          $[_{NP}$ immunity]]]]
          PATIENT

    A: $[_{NP}$ the honorable members of the Federal bench]

The synonymous NPs in (64a) and (64b) as well as the paraphrase NP in (64c) all receive the same interpretation in the representation of linguistic context by virtue of the ability of an independent constituent utterance NP to match the *wh*-pronoun, not by virtue of the internal form of any particular NP. The implicature representing the discourse function of Agent is non-detachable because it is associated with the meaning of the constituent utterances, not their form.

Grice's feature of non-conventionality means that the implicature associated with an expression cannot be the result solely of the literal meaning of the words; an implicature has to be the result of using, or as Grice puts it, "employing" words in a certain way (1975: 58). Non-conventionality also is characteristic of the interpretation of the examples in (63) - (64): the implicature associating either NP, *Federal judges/justices* or *the honorable members of the Federal bench*, to the discourse role of an Agent granting immunity does not follow from the referential meaning of the NPs alone; rather, it follows from the use of the NPs within a structure of linguistic context, which triggers the operation of Discourse Inference to assign the discourse function of Agent to the NPs.

Finally, according to Levinson, Grice's feature of calculability means that an argument should be able to show how "it follows that an addressee would make the inference in question" (1983: 117). The whole purpose of developing the theoretical apparatus within the submodule of linguistic context is to make explicit the calculation of inferences that assign independent constituent utterances to their discourse functions. The Principle of Linguistic Context creates a structure of linguistic context for each utterance in a discourse sequence; this structure is the area, so to speak, for the calculation of an inference within its boundaries. Based on a match between an independent constituent utterance and an expansion possibility of a previous element within the structure of linguistic context, each and every operation of Discourse Inference is a calculation arriving at an interpretation of the function of a constituent utterance. The result of the calculation, the specific implicature, is checked for appropriateness by the Condition of Acceptability. All of the constructs within the submodule of linguistic context function together to calculate a discourse-based interpretation for a constituent utterance.

An implicature, according to Grice, is "distinct" from what is said (1975: 43). This is precisely why a pragmatic model with a submodule of linguistic context is a necessary part of a theory of the structure and interpretation of nonsentential constituents. Logical Form represents determinate semantic meaning, but the pragmatic model builds upon semantic meaning to represent implicated meaning; the submodule of linguistic context accounts for the portion of implicated meaning that is discourse-based. A consideration of contrasting question and answer sequences illustrates the difference between determinate meaning described by Logical Form representation and implicated meaning described within the submodule of linguistic context in the pragmatic model. Consider the following sequences once more:

(65a) P: Who grants immunity? The judges?
           (*Transcripts* 1974: 210)
(65b) A: Who grants immunity?
      B: The judges grant immunity.

Their representations within the submodule of linguistic context indicate a significant difference between the two sequences:

(66a) P: [$_{S'}$ [for which person, x] [$_S$ x   [$_{VP}$ [$_V$ grants]
           AGENT   [AG, PT]
           [$_{NP}$ immunity]]]]
           PATIENT

      P: [$_{NP}$ the judges]

(66b) [$_S$ [$_{NP}$ the judges] [$_{VP}$ [$_V$ grant]   [$_{NP}$ immunity]]]
      AGENT   [AG, PT]   PATIENT

The speaker in (66a) has implied that the constituent utterance NP functions as an answer to the question, and the arrow formally describes the implicature within an elaborated structure of linguistic context. The answer is not a full sentence as in the contrasting example of (66b). Although speakers in both (66a) and (66b) answer the question, the representation of linguistic context formalizes the difference between answering with a full sentence and implicating an answer by elaborating the structure of linguistic context. The submodule of linguistic context within the pragmatic model thus represents the subtle, but real, difference between implicating an answer and stating a full sentence as an answer to a *wh*-question in the performance of a discourse, a difference in representation that allows the pragmatic model to maintain a principled distinction between the representation of determinate literal meaning at Logical Form and the representation of indeterminate implicated meaning within the submodule of linguistic context.

    In contrast to Morgan's (1973) view of semantic interpretation and Carston's (1985a,b) view of propositional interpretation of nonsentential utterances, I claim that the use of an independent major lexical category in a discourse is not the assertion of a unique proposition; it cannot be since the speaker has not actually uttered one. The use of an independent constituent utterance is, instead, the elaboration of a proposition already extant within the discourse, an elaboration by means of an implicature. Neither Morgan nor Carston has any way of distinguishing between a sentential versus a nonsentential answer to a question as in example (66) above. Nor do they have any way of explaining why the interpretation of nonsentential utterances is theoretically characterized by indeterminacy, as well as all of the other criteria for implicatures, including reinforceability, (arguably) cancelability, non-detachability, non-conventionality, and calculability. The implicatures that result from the operation of Discourse Inference pass all the tests for implicatures; it is reasonable to conclude, therefore, that the discourse-based interpretation of these constituent utterances takes place by means of implicatures, not propositions.

In sum, the submodule of linguistic context in the pragmatic model builds upon the input of Logical Form to describe the discourse-based interpretation of independent constituent utterances that fit into a structure of linguistic context. The submodule of linguistic context in the pragmatic model is distinct from its input component of Logical Form in two main ways: first, it describes a process of inference rather than a process of derivation, which means that it describes indeterminate implicated meaning rather than determinate semantic meaning; and second, it represents context-based interpretation based on information from discourse rather than semantic meaning based on information from language structure. The arguments above are necessary in order to motivate the component of Logical Form and the submodule of linguistic context as separate but interacting parts of the theory of the structure and interpretation of nonsentential constituents.

4.2.2 *The wider framework*

The submodule of linguistic context consists of three internal constructs: the Principle of Linguistic Context, the operation of Discourse Inference, and the Condition of Acceptability, and each of these constructs contributes to a partially autonomous and partially modular account of the discourse-based interpretation within the pragmatic model of the interpretation of independent constituent utterances. In this subsection, I consider these constructs, showing how each one incorporates constraints which characterize the nature of the autonomy and modularity that define the submodule of linguistic context and the pragmatic model. I then discuss the ways in which the work presented here complements other recent work in pragmatics.

In §1.2, I argued that the interaction between the competence model of nonsentential constituent structures and the pragmatic model of independent constituent utterances is a modular interaction because the two models contribute explanations of different aspects of the meaning of independent constituents: the competence model accounts for the limited amount of context-free meaning provided by the semantic representation of a nonsentential constituent structure; the pragmatic model accounts for the large amount of context-dependent meaning provided by the pragmatic interpretation of an independent constituent utterance, with the submodule of linguistic context describing discourse-based interpretation and the submodule of conversational context describing information-based interpretation. In §1.2, I also claimed that the nature of the pragmatic model of the interpretation of constituent utterances is both partially autonomous and partially modular: the model is only partially autonomous because it interacts with systems beyond itself, including models of knowledge about the world; the model is only partially modular because its two submodules share crucial properties, notably the operation of pragmatic inference.

The statement of the Principle of Linguistic Context (cf. (7) in §4.1.1) establishes the modularity of the pragmatic model by explicitly describing the interaction of the competence model and the pragmatic model: the semantic representation of a structure becomes the pragmatic representation of an utterance. In Zwicky's (1984) terms, this weakly autonomous interaction takes place through an interface representation; the interaction also is fuzzily autonomous because the component of Logical Form and the submodule of linguistic context share properties, in particular the expansion possibilities of lexical items, which are crucially important for discourse-based interpretation. The Principle also contributes to a distinct characterization of the submodule of linguistic context in comparison to the submodule of conversational context by defining the linguistic context as a series of utterances. The linguistic context as created by the Principle is dynamic, capable of growing and changing as participants add, elaborate, and modify utterances and make inferences about their interaction. In this way, the submodule reflects not a static concept of meaning limited to a single structure but an interactive concept of meaning as a discourse-based interpretation that develops through the interaction of utterances within a linguistic context.

The partially modular nature of the pragmatic model of the interpretation of independent constituent utterances is based upon the structure-building principles, the operation of pragmatic inference, and the conditions governing acceptability, which are common to its two submodules, but interpretation within each submodule is based on a different kind of contextual information and a different type of pragmatic inference. The operation of Discourse Inference is the specific mechanism for interpretation based on the linguistic context; its statement (cf. (9) in §4.1) incorporates the major constraint upon the type of context-based interpretation described within the submodule. This constraint limits the submodule of linguistic context to describing discourse-based interpretation because the operation of Discourse Inference is triggered only when there is a match between a constituent utterance and an expansion possibility of a previous element in the structure of linguistic context. This discourse-based constraint explicitly ties the operation of Discourse Inference solely to the linguistic context and functions to define interpretation based on linguistic context as a distinct submodule within the pragmatic model of the interpretation of constituent utterances.

Within the submodule of linguistic context, the Condition of Acceptability is the theoretical construct that bears the burden of constraining the partially autonomous nature of the submodule of linguistic context. Within the submodule, the Principle of Linguistic Context and the operation of Discourse Inference operate autonomously; only the result of the inference, the representation of linguistic context, is checked by the Condition of Acceptability, which is connected to knowledge about the world. The Condition of Acceptability, in essence, allows knowledge about the world to confirm or overrule a discourse-based interpretation. Within the submodule of linguistic context, this is an extremely restricted interaction with a model of knowledge about the world since it takes place only through this one construct; the partial autonomy of the submodule is, therefore, highly constrained.

An interesting implication arising from the acknowledgment that the pragmatic model is only partially autonomous is the fact that discourse-based interpretation cannot be assumed to belong within a grammar or an extension of a grammar (as, e.g., in van Dijk 1977). Fodor's (1983) definition of the language faculty as an autonomous module specifies that it must be informationally encapsulated; in other words, a grammar has access to grammatical information only. The fact that the submodule of linguistic context in the pragmatic model requires interaction with some model of knowledge about the world through the Condition of Acceptability shows that discourse-based interpretation cannot be part of a module of grammar.

The development of the pragmatic model of the interpretation of constituent utterances is based in part on the work of Grice and in part on recent research growing out of radical pragmatics, in particular, work by Horn (1984) and Levinson (1983, 1985, 1987a,b,c; Atlas and Levinson 1981). The general orientation of radical pragmatics, according to Cole, investigates the hypothesis that "many linguistic phenomena, which had previously been viewed as belonging to the semantic subsystem, in fact belong to the pragmatic subsystem" (1981: xi). The object of investigation in radical pragmatics, Sadock suggests, is "the intricate symbiosis that characterizes the association between structure and function in natural language" (1984: 147). The general orientation of the theory of nonsentential constituents presented here is that of radical pragmatics because it explicitly shifts the burden of accounting for the majority of the meaning of independent constituents from semantics to pragmatics. The interaction between the competence model and the pragmatic model is a formal reflection of the symbiotic relationship between the two components of the theory, the structural component of the model of grammar and the functional component of the pragmatic model. The development of the pragmatic model is an attempt to describe how the pragmatic interpretation of nonsentential constituents takes place within this framework.

One direction of recent work in radical pragmatics has been a re-examination of Grice's (1975) Cooperative Principle and maxims. Surveying this work, Levinson (Horn and Levinson 1987) compares neo-Gricean work, which remains close to Grice's original idea of the Cooperative Principle with a small number of maxims, with post-Gricean work, which suggests a more reductionist program to one or two general maxims. Levinson identifies work by himself and Horn as neo-Gricean; he classifies work by Sperber and Wilson as post-Gricean. The previous subsection offered arguments against the post-Gricean view of ellipsis; the following discussion shows how the submodule of linguistic context, and especially the operation of Discourse Inference, fits in with recent work in neo-Gricean pragmatics.

Horn (1984) suggests that Grice's (1975) maxims describing interpretation are derived from two competing principles: a principle of least effort, which describes the speaker's perspective on communication, and a principle of sufficient effort, which describes the hearer's perspective.[17] Setting aside the maxim of Quality, which both Grice and Horn describe as a basic feature of any cooperative conversation, Horn divides Grice's maxims into two groups according to their contribution to the principles of least effort and sufficient effort.[18] Grice's first maxim of Quantity ("Make your contribution as informative as is required (for the current purposes of the exchange)") and the first two maxims of Manner ("Avoid obscurity of expression" and "Avoid ambiguity") are collapsed into what Horn calls the Q-Principle, which represents the hearer's perspective on what the speaker should do in communication:

Q-Principle
Make your contribution SUFFICIENT;
Say as much as you can (given Quality and R).

Grice's second maxim of Quantity ("Do not make your contribution more informative than is required"), the maxim of Relation ("Be relevant"), and the last two maxims of Manner ("Be brief (avoid unnecessary prolixity)" and "Be orderly") are collapsed into what Horn calls the R-Principle, which represents the speaker's perspective on communication:

R-Principle
Make your contribution NECESSARY;
Say no more than you must (given Q).

These two principles are the basis for inferences that license different types of implicatures. The Q-Principle accounts for generalized scalar and clausal implicatures: for example, in the sentence *Some of the boys went to the party*, the Q-Principle licenses the scalar implicature *Not all of the boys went to the party*.[19] The R-Principle accounts for indirect speech acts: for the question *Can you pass the salt?* the R-Principle licenses the implicature *Pass the salt*; it also accounts for some of the properties of negation. Both the Q-Principle and the R-Principle license implicatures that go beyond what was said: the Q-Principle most often licenses negative implicatures (*some* +⟩ *not all*), while the R-Principle most often licenses positive implicatures (*Can you pass the salt?* +⟩ *Pass the salt*).

Levinson further suggests that the R-Principle (his I-Principle), which is a type of inference creating positive and specific implicatures that go beyond what was said, extends to a number of interesting cases. In addition to Horn's examples of indirect speech acts and negation, Levinson lists the following types of I-based implicatures:[20]

(67a) Conjunction Buttressing

John turned the key and the engine started.

+⟩He turned the key *and then* the engine started. (temporality)

+⟩He turned the key *and thereby* caused the engine to start. (causality)

+⟩He turned the key *in order to make* the engine start. (teleology)

(67b) Conditional Perfection

If you mow the lawn, I'll give you $5.

+⟩If and only if you mow the lawn will I give you $5.

(67c) Bridging

John unpacked the picnic. The beer was warm.

+⟩The beer was part of the picnic.

John was put in the cell. The window was barred.

+⟩The cell has a window.

(67d) Membership Categorization Devices

The baby cried. The mummy picked it up.

+⟩'The mummy' was the mother of the crying baby.

(67e) Inference to Stereotype

John said 'Hello' to the secretary, and then he smiled.

+⟩John said 'Hello' to the female secretary, and then he (John) smiled.

(67f) Mirror Maxim

Harry and Sue bought a piano.

+⟩They bought it together, not one each.

(67g) Frames

John pushed the cart to the checkout.

+⟩John pushed the cart full of groceries to the supermarket checkout in order to pay for them, etc.

(67h) Preferred Coreference

John came in and he sat down.

+⟩John came in and he, John, sat down.

(1987a: 65)

In each of these cases, the implicature is a more specific interpretation of what was said in the sentence.

Levinson expands Horn's R-Principle by suggesting that the following maxims govern R (or I)-inferences to a specific interpretation:

Speaker's Maxim: The Maxim of Minimization
"Say as little as necessary" i.e. produce the minimal linguistic clues sufficient to achieve your communicational ends, bearing Q in mind
Recipient's corollary: Enrichment Rule
"Amplify the informational content of the speaker's utterance, by finding a *more specific* interpretation, up to what you judge to be the speaker's intended point" (1987a: 68; author's emphasis)

He sums up his maxims with the slogan "the less you say the more you mean" (1987a: 62).

The pragmatic theory of the interpretation of constituent utterances presented here complements Horn and Levinson's work in neo-Gricean pragmatics in a number of ways, especially their work on R/I-inferences to a specific interpretation. The use of a constituent utterance is an example *par excellence* of Levinson's slogan "the less you say the more you mean" because its interpretation through the operation of Discourse Inference is an example of generalized I/R-inference to a specific, informationally enriching implicature. Consider a familiar example of the discourse-based interpretation of a constituent utterance as described by the submodule of linguistic context in the pragmatic model:

(68) P: Who grants immunity? The judges?
      (*Transcripts* 1974: 210)

The representation of the elaborated structure of linguistic context describes the implicature that results from the operation of Discourse Inference:

(69) P: [$_{S'}$ [for which person, x] [$_S$ x   [$_{VP}$ [$_V$ grants]
            ➤AGENT   [AG, PT]
        ⎛   [$_{NP}$ immunity]]]]]
        ⎜   PATIENT
        ⎝
      P: [$_{NP}$ the judges]

With the utterance of an independent constituent, the speaker accomplishes the informationally richer communication that the NP functions in the discourse role of Agent for the predicate *grants immunity*. Furthermore, the operation of Discourse Inference that creates the implicature associating the NP with the discourse function of Agent is one that is generalized: unless canceled by specific clauses or by other contextual information, the operation of Discourse Inference goes through (cf. the discussion of examples (51) and (52) above). The use of a constituent utterance is a minimal utterance, and the interpretation of a constituent utterance is a maximal enrichment; thus, the discourse-based interpretation described within the submodule of linguistic context complements Levinson's description of R/I-Principle informativeness. The operation of Discourse Inference could be added to the list in (67) as a specific example of generalized R/I-inference.

The account of interpretation presented here, however, has an interesting difference from Levinson's description of R/I-inference. Within the submodule of linguistic context, the Condition of Acceptability functions to separate knowledge about the world from the operation of Discourse Inference; in this way, the pragmatic model is constrained to describing interpretation rather than general knowledge. Since generalized implicatures are supposed to be calculated in any context except where specifically canceled, it seems to make sense to limit the place of context as strictly as possible when dealing with generalized inference, and a separate Condition of Acceptability does that. This separation of interpretation from any systems of information that interact with it allows the partially autonomous pragmatic model to describe interpretation as an ability to make inferences apart from, yet connected to, general knowledge about the world.

4.3 Conclusion

To account for discourse-based interpretation of independent constituent utterances, this chapter described interpretation within the submodule of linguistic context. Within the submodule, the Principle of Linguistic Context first creates a structure of linguistic context for each utterance within a discourse sequence; the operation of Discourse Inference then elaborates that structure of linguistic context by assigning a discourse function to the constituent utterance; and the Condition of Acceptability governs the results of the operation of Discourse Inference by confirming or overruling the interpretation of a constituent utterance within a representation of linguistic context. Independent constituent utterances interpreted within this submodule are ones which fit into the linguistic context by functioning as discourse roles or modifiers in discourse sequences. Typical discourse sequences interpreted within the submodule of linguistic context include independent constituent utterances functioning as answers to questions, specifications of pronouns, and other expansions of previous elements in a structure of linguistic context.

Arguments supporting the claim that the submodule of linguistic context offers a theoretically satisfying account of discourse-based interpretation came from a variety of sources. First, arguments showed that derivation within the grammatical component of Logical Form and inference within the submodule of linguistic context are theoretically distinct: a grammatical derivation is a determinate assignment of meaning; in contrast, a pragmatic inference creates implicatures that describe indeterminate implicated meaning. These implicatures satisfy all of the criteria for implicatures; they are indeterminate, (somewhat) cancelable, reinforceable, non-detachable, non-conventional, and calculable. Second, arguments compared this account of interpretation with accounts of interpretation from an ellipsis theory of sentence fragments (Morgan 1973; Carston 1985a,b), showing that the pragmatic account presented here provides a principled distinction between uttering a proposition by using a full sentence and elaborating a proposition by using an independent constituent utterance. Finally, the submodule of linguistic context was shown to be compatible with recent work in radical pragmatics; in particular, the operation of Discourse Inference was shown to be a type of generalized inference because the calculation of a discourse function for a constituent utterance goes through in all contexts unless specifically canceled. The implicatures that result from the operation of Discourse Inference are specific and informationally-enriching interpretations of independent constituent utterances within their linguistic contexts.

5. The Representation of Conversational Context in the Pragmatic Model

5.0 Introduction

The previous chapter described the submodule of linguistic context within a pragmatic model of the interpretation of independent constituent utterances, constraining it to the domain of discourse-based interpretation. Not all constituent utterances, however, can be interpreted based solely on information from the linguistic context, and this chapter describes the submodule of conversational context, defining its domain as the information-based interpretation of constituent utterances, where information is a general notion incorporating multiple sources of knowledge.

The input to the submodule of conversational context is the representation of linguistic context. Within the submodule, a Principle of Conversational Context, an associated operation of Cooperative Inference, and a Condition of Acceptability combine to describe interpretation based on information from the conversational context:

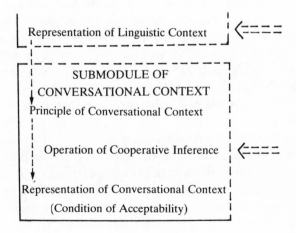

The concept of conversational context here is defined broadly enough to incorporate the Cooperative Principle (Grice 1975) and to encompass a number of domains of knowledge and information, including (at least) the physical context of situation, the topic of the conversation, the background knowledge of the discourse participants, and their general knowledge about the world. Such a broad concept of conversational context at first may seem unconstrained, but it reflects the interpretive abilities of discourse participants, who assume cooperation and then use information from a wide variety of sources in order to arrive at an interpretation of an independent constituent utterance. A broad definition of conversational context also provides a way of accounting for the indeterminacy that characterizes pragmatic interpretation (cf. §1.2): an utterance may receive an interpretation within more than one domain, and when a different domain within the conversational context is privileged in the interpretation of an utterance, the result is a different interpretation.

A typical case of interpretation within the submodule of conversational context describes the relevance of an independent constituent utterance within some aspect of the shared conversational context of discourse participants. Consider the following sequence:

(1)   A: I wonder how we can get immunity for the Executive staff.
             (DOOR SLAMS)
       B: John Mitchell.

Different domains of the conversational context generate different interpretations for the constituent utterance. If the privileged domain is the physical context of situation, then the NP *John Mitchell* might be interpreted as a suggestion about the person who slammed the door. On the other hand, if the privileged domain is not the context of situation and is instead the topic of conversation, which is immunity, then the NP might be interpreted as a suggestion about John Mitchell's ability to provide immunity for the Executive staff. In this chapter, I argue that this kind of indeterminacy arising from the possibility of different interpretations for an independent constituent utterance can be accounted for by privileging different domains within the conversational context.

In the following sections of this chapter, I first describe interpretation within the submodule of conversational context in §5.1; in §5.2, I then present arguments supporting the claim that the submodule of conversational context offers a theoretically satisfying description of the information-based interpretation of independent constituent utterances.

5.1 The submodule of conversational context

This section describes interpretation within conversational context as the second submodule within the pragmatic model of the interpretation of independent constituent utterances. In the following subsections, I describe the Principle of Conversational Context and its associated operation of Cooperative Inference in §5.1.1 and present examples of interpretation within the submodule of conversational context in §5.1.2; I then discuss the Condition of Acceptability governing the representation of conversational context in §5.1.3.

5.1.1 *The principle of conversational context and the operation of cooperative inference*

In order to fill the gap between what discourse participants say and what they mean in a total sense, both submodules of the pragmatic model have Gricean inference as their central mechanism; the operation of inference generates hypotheses about the implicated meaning of an independent constituent utterance. Within the submodule of linguistic context, the operation of Discourse Inference is generalized because it calculates the discourse function of a constituent utterance regardless of context; within the submodule of conversational context, however, the operation of inference is particularized, that is, implicatures are calculated within the specific conversational context of the constituent utterance under interpretation.

Particularized inferences are based on knowledge of Grice's Cooperative Principle as the quintessential feature of conversational exchanges: the Cooperative Principle licenses a discourse participant to assume that an utterance represents a cooperative contribution within the conversational context. Grice describes the Cooperative Principle as follows:

> We might then formulate a rough general principle which participants will be expected (*ceteris paribus*) to observe, namely: Make your conversational contribution such as is required, at the stage at which it occurs, by the accepted purpose or direction of the talk exchange in which you are engaged. One might label this the COOPERATIVE PRINCIPLE. (1975: 45; author's emphasis)

He goes on to explain that the Cooperative Principle is the basis for the inferences that discourse participants make in order to interpret an utterance:

> [T]he CP . . . [is] the basis for the assumption which we seem to make, and on which (I hope) it will appear that a great range of implicatures depend, that talkers will in general (*ceteris paribus* and in the absence of indications to the contrary) proceed in the manner that these principles describe. (1975: 47-48)

Levinson emphasizes the centrality of the Cooperative Principle in any theory of pragmatic interpretation by pointing out that "inferences arise to preserve the assumption of cooperation" (1983: 102). He also describes the strength of the Cooperative Principle, characterizing the "remarkable robustness of the assumption of cooperation" as evidenced by the fact that "utterances are still read as underlyingly cooperative if this is at all possible" (1983: 109).[1]

Grice's maxim of Relation has been seen as a powerful source of particularized inferences within specific conversational contexts. Grice himself leaves the maxim "Be relevant" mostly unexplained, remarking, though, that violations of the maxim of Relation are "rare" (1975: 54). Recognizing the importance of the notion of relevance, Sperber and Wilson (1986) go so far as to conclude that nothing else has any theoretical significance in pragmatic interpretation.[2] Levinson, though, offers a less reductionist position with enough power and flexibility to serve as the starting point for a specification of the concept of relevance within the pragmatic model under development here; explicating Grice's notion of Relation, he points out its importance:

> The inference seems to work roughly like this: assume [an] utterance is relevant. . . . [I]t is clear that such inferences are fundamental to our sense of coherence in discourse: if the implicatures were not constructed on the basis of the assumption of relevance, many adjacent utterances in conversation would appear quite unconnected. (1983: 107)

He also notes that relevance seems to have special importance in the calculation of particularized implicatures, those that are calculated uniquely for an utterance within a specific context:

> [A]ll implicatures that arise from observing the maxim of Relevance are particularized, since utterances are relevant only with respect to the particular topic or issue at hand. (1983: 127)

Levinson (1987b) points out that there is an important relationship between relevance and coherence, where coherence is defined as the ability of a discourse to mean more than the sum of its parts and where relevance is considered, in part, an interactional notion negotiated jointly by discourse participants. Drawing upon research in conversation analysis to provide examples of the type of coherence intimately connected with a notion of relevance, Levinson points to the interpretation of utterances within adjacency pairs (e.g., offer and acceptance) and other conversational sequences (e.g., giving directions) plus the interpretation of utterances with respect to a discourse topic:

> What seems to be going on here is that the ordinary notion of 'relevance' is constructed out of at least two notions of connectedness:
> (i)   rule-specified adjacency of two kinds of speech acts or activities, e.g., greetings or adjacency-pairs in general . . . thus what is 'relevant' is what should be done next;
> (ii)   teleological connectedness: a response is 'relevant' to the extent that it meets the other's need or interactional goals; thus what is 'relevant' is what is wanted or required.
> [(iii)] Yet a third notion that seems to be involved in the pretheoretical notion of relevance is topical connectedness. An important 'lay' notion, it has proved very resistant to theoretical understanding.
> (1987a: 78)

Levinson's remarks seem to indicate that there may be a variety of types of relevance that contribute to the interpretation of an utterance: a notion of relevance within adjacency pairs will sometimes be in effect; a notion of relevance with respect to topic will be in effect at other times, and so on. This notion of multiple relevancies is an idea that I use as the basis for the operation of particularized inference within the submodule of conversational context.

Within the pragmatic model, the submodule of conversational context is based on the notions of cooperation and relevance. Grice's Cooperative Principle describes the general assumption that an operation of inference can interpret an independent constituent utterance within a conversational context: interlocutors assume an utterance is a cooperative contribution to the conversation. Levinson's work on relevance suggests the general direction of the operation of particularized inference: assuming cooperation, interlocutors arrive at an interpretation by making inferences about the relevance of an utterance within a specific conversational context. Within the pragmatic model, the submodule of conversational context incorporates these notions of cooperation and relevance into its internal constructs of a structure-building principle, an operation of inference, and a condition governing acceptability.

The Cooperative Principle is central to the submodule of conversational context because pragmatic interpretation within specific contexts begins with an overt assumption of cooperation. Explicitly incorporating Grice's concept of an utterance as a cooperative contribution to a conversation, a Principle of Conversational Context describes the structure of conversational context for each utterance in a discourse sequence, building upon its input representation from the submodule of linguistic context:

(2)   *Principle of Conversational Context*
      In a discourse sequence, the representation of linguistic context for each utterance becomes the representation of an utterance with a potential structure of implicatures explaining its relevance as a cooperative contribution within the conversational context.

The Principle describes the modular interaction between the two submodules of the pragmatic model: a representation of linguistic context for an utterance becomes a representation within the submodule of conversational context. After applying the Principle, the structure of conversational context for an independent constituent utterance looks like (3) (the symbol $+\rangle$ means 'implicates'):

(3)   A: The White House staff doesn't visit Tip O'Neill in his Congressional office.
      B: Old grudge.
           $[_{NP}$ old grudge$]$
           $+\rangle$RELEVANCE

Applying the Principle creates a structure of conversational context that allows an utterance to have, in Levinson's words, "an unstable, context-specific pragmatic overlay — namely a set of implicatures" (1983: 99). These implicatures are based on the assumption of cooperation and an (as yet undifferentiated) notion of relevance.

Although the Principle creates a structure of conversational context, it requires an associated operation of inference for the elaboration of that structure. Within the submodule of conversational context, this operation of inference is called Cooperative Inference because it creates implicatures which explain how an utterance is a cooperative contribution to the conversation. In general, the operation of Cooperative Inference aims at an interpretation of the relevance of a constituent utterance within a specific conversational context. The notion of conversational context, however, is broad enough to encompass a great deal of information, and a determination of relevance can be based on any subset(s) of contextual information. I propose, therefore, that a number of specific domains of relevance are associated with the operation of Cooperative Inference. The domains correspond to subsets of information from the conversational context that interlocutors use as a set of boundaries for a particularized operation of inference; each subtype of Cooperative Inference incorporates a different domain of information and relevance:

(4)   *Cooperative Inference*
   (i)   If the utterance is relevant based on information from knowledge of the physical context of situation, then . . .
   (ii) If the utterance is relevant based on information from knowledge of the topic of conversation, then . . .
   (iii) If the utterance is relevant based on information from the background knowledge of the interlocutors, then . . .
   (iv) If the utterance is relevant based on information from knowledge about the world, then . . .

The subtypes of Cooperative Inference are open-ended *if-then* statements because they describe the general form of a particularized inference outside of the specific context that will instantiate both the *if* and the *then* portions of a particular inference. When a discourse participant makes an inference based on information drawn from knowledge of one of the domains of relevance, the resulting implicature(s) elaborate the structure of conversational context; the structure of implicatures then describes the representation of conversational context for an utterance.[3]

Proposing multiple domains of relevance within the submodule of conversational context has two theoretical advantages: first, it explicitly associates an implicature with the subset of contextual information that it is based upon; and second, it offers a way of accounting for the indeterminacy of particularized pragmatic interpretation. Indeterminacy is defined here as the possibility of different interpretations for an utterance.[4] The operation of Cooperative Inference accounts for indeterminacy in two ways: first, it predicts that multiple interpretations based on the physical context of situation, the topic, the background knowledge of the interlocutors and their general knowledge about the world are possible for an utterance; second, it explains that privileging one domain of relevance over others produces different interpretations. In the following subsection, I present examples of interpretation within each of the domains of relevance, arguing that the multiple domains of relevance incorporated into the operation of Cooperative Inference account for this notion of indeterminacy in a principled way.

5.1.2 *Interpretation within the submodule of conversational context*

This subsection presents examples of the interpretation of independent constituent utterances within the submodule of conversational context. After a short discussion of the nature of the data presented here, a set of examples illustrates interpretation within each domain of relevance incorporated into the operation of Cooperative Inference. The discussion of these examples suggests a way of representing each domain of contextual information in the description of the structure of conversational context for an utterance; it also shows how the pragmatic model accounts for indeterminacy within domains. A second set of examples illustrates the effect of privileging a domain of relevance in the interpretation of a constituent utterance; the discussion of these examples shows how the pragmatic model accounts for indeterminacy across domains. A final set of examples illustrates the interaction of the subtypes of Cooperative Inference as they make different contributions to the interpretation of an independent constituent utterance within the submodule of conversational context.

The pragmatic model, like a competence model, must account for the intuitions of a native speaker, and as is standard in linguistic investigations, the intuitions presented in this work are my own. Working with a notion of intuition in pragmatics, though, is more difficult than working with this concept in grammar. Within the idealization of a competence model, a grammar is determinate; in most cases, a native speaker's intuitions are limited to a binary judgment — a structure is either well-formed or not well-formed. These binary judgments then serve as the evidence in arguments motivating a particular structural representation or other grammatical construct.[5] Because a pragmatic model has to describe interpretation, however, intuitions of native speakers often vary. As a result, verifying intuitions about interpretation thus has to be a matter of reasonable agreement rather than strict judgment. Verifying an interpretation generated by the pragmatic model is a matter of native speakers agreeing that a particular interpretation is possible, reasonable, probable, or likely. These intuitions are considerably more indirect than intuitions concerning grammaticality.

Fortunately, rather than relying exclusively on the rather vague concept of intuitions of satisfaction, there is another method of verifying the interpretations generated by the operation of inference within the pragmatic model. In "Validating Pragmatic Explanations," Nunberg suggests:

> [T]he best we can say is that the explanations we offer are consistent with the capacities and beliefs of the speakers we are interested in, and that speakers behave as if they had worked them out. (1981: 207)

Speakers usually behave as though a particular pragmatic interpretation is in effect, and evidence of this can be gathered from an analysis of the continuing utterances within a discourse.

In order to illustrate interpretation within the submodule of conversational context, the data presented in this chapter are a mix of constructed and attested examples. Unless I am specifically discussing indeterminacy, I usually present only one interpretation of an utterance, which represents my best attempt at representing what speakers might have meant and what hearers might have interpreted as they conversed about Watergate. These interpretations are necessarily my own intuitions about interpretation, based on a close reading of the *Transcripts* as well as other sources about Watergate (Cooke 1979; Dash 1976; Dean 1976; Doyle 1977; Ervin 1980; Haldeman and DiMona 1978; Labovitz 1978; Lang and Lang 1983; Sirica 1979; WETA 1983, 1984; Woodward and Bernstein 1974; for a bibliography about Watergate, see Smith, M. 1983). Whenever possible, I use continuing utterances as evidence that some particular interpretation is in place. In the actual discourse sequences from the *Transcripts*, though, discourse participants do not always respond in a way that directly reflects the interpretation of a previous utterance, so in some cases I construct possible continuing utterances in order to analyze a discourse sequence. In any case, I try to present interpretations which other speakers might find satisfactory as possible interpretations, even though they might not agree with every detail.

Within the submodule of conversational context, the operation of Cooperative Inference incorporates four domains of relevance. The examples in (5) illustrate the operation of the subtypes of Cooperative Inference within each domain:

(5a)   A: What did John say about the drive around Washington?
       B: Red lights!

(5b) A: They always put cash campaign contributions in a passbook savings account.
      B: Cautious.
(5c) A: The White House staff doesn't visit Tip O'Neill in his Congressional office.
      B: Old grudge.
(5d) A: John doesn't know what the best defense against criminal charges would be.
      B: Ask any lawyer.

Example (5a) could be interpreted based on information from the physical context of situation; example (5b) could be interpreted based on information from the topic of conversation; example (5c) could be interpreted based on information from the shared background knowledge of the interlocutors; and example (5d) could be interpreted based on information from general knowledge about the world.

Of the four domains of relevance incorporated into the operation of Cooperative Inference, one with a fairly well-developed model is the physical context of situation. Brown and Yule, summarizing Hymes (1964), list the following features within a communicative event: addressor, addressee, audience, setting (place, time, physical relations of interlocutors, including posture, gesture, and facial expressions), channel (spoken or written language), and code (language or dialect) (1983: 38).[6] Since each utterance occurs within a unique configuration of these features, the domain of context of situation obviously encompasses a great deal of indeterminacy: within different contexts of situation, there is the potential for a different interpretation of an utterance.

Consider example (5a) above, which was discussed briefly in §4.2. If the context of situation consists of two interlocutors, with no audience, in the setting of a car in which A is the driver and B is the front seat passenger, and at the time B utters the NP he reaches over and touches A's arm with his left hand, then this information could be used as the basis for an inference interpreting the relevance of the constituent utterance NP within the domain of the physical context of situation:

(6) A: What did John say about the drive around Washington?
     B: Red lights!

Context of Situation[7]
Event: conversation

Addressor	Addressee	Setting
B	A	car
passenger	driver	B grabs A

$[_{NP}$ red lights]

$+\rangle$RELEVANCE If the utterance is relevant based on information from the physical context of situation, then B warns A that A should stop for upcoming red lights.

In this representation of conversational context, the opening part of the *if-then* inference states the domain of relevance in operation, and the representation of the physical context of situation shows the information in effect as the basis for the inference. The conclusion of the inference is the particularized implicature explaining the relevance of this constituent utterance. Within this sequence, several continuing utterances might provide evidence that an implicature warning about red lights is in effect:

(7a) A: What did John say about the drive around Washington?
      B: Red lights!
      A: Just in time.
(7b) A: Thanks for the warning.
(7c) A: Thanks.

These continuing utterances indicate that the implicature in (6) has been calculated and successfully acted upon. In this case, a continuing event in the physical context of situation, such as a screeching halt in front of a set of red lights, also would indicate that the interpretation in (6) is in effect as the interpretation for the NP *red lights*.

A second type of information triggering the operation of a subtype of Cooperative Inference is based on knowledge of the topic, a domain within which there is considerable indeterminacy of interpretation based on different topics of conversation. As noted by Levinson (cf. §5.1.1) and by many others (cf. Brown and Yule 1983: 68ff.; cf. also note 4 in Ch. 4 and references therein), the notion of topic is an intuitively powerful one, but one which is difficult to describe precisely within a theoretical framework. Consider, then, the example in (5b) with an intuitive statement of the topic drawn from a consideration of previous utterances within the discourse; this information about the topic of conversation provides the basis for an inference interpreting the ADJP constituent utterance:

(8) B: What does the Committee to Re-Elect the President do with cash contributions?
     A: They always put cash campaign contributions in a passbook savings account.
     B: Cautious.
     Topic: deposit of cash campaign contributions
     [$_{ADJP}$ cautious]
     +)RELEVANCE If the utterance is relevant based on information about the topic of the conversation, then putting cash campaign contributions in a passbook savings account is cautious.

Several continuing utterances could provide evidence that this implicature is in effect as the interpretation for the constituent utterance:

(9a) A: Yes, putting money in a savings account keeps it safe.
(9b) A: They won't be worried about security that way.
(9c) A: They don't want to keep cash in the office.

These utterances all continue the topic of the deposit of cash campaign contributions.

Suppose, however, based upon previous utterances within the discourse, that the topic of the conversation is different; the interpretation of the constituent utterance will differ, too:

(10) B: How do donors protect their anonymity when donating money to the Committee to Re-Elect the President?
     A: They always put cash campaign contributions in a passbook savings account.
     B: Cautious.
     Topic: anonymity of donors
     [$_{ADJP}$ cautious]
     +)RELEVANCE If the utterance is relevant based on information about the topic of the conversation, then a cautious way of protecting the anonymity of donors is by putting cash contributions in a passbook savings account.

Again, a number of continuing utterances would indicate that an implicature about protecting the anonymity of donors is in effect as the interpretation for the constituent utterance:

(11a) A: The money is under the name of the Committee this way.
(11b) A: The money is all mixed together when it is in one account.
(11c) A: No one knows who made the deposits that way.

These utterances all continue the topic of protecting the anonymity of donors. In (9) and (11), continuing utterances provide evidence that different implicatures are in effect as the interpretation of the ADJP constituent utterance. The indeterminacy in interpretation is the result of inferences based on different topics of conversation.

A third type of information triggering the operation of a subtype of Cooperative Inference is shared background knowledge that interlocutors have (or assume) about each other. Shared background knowledge is a powerful source of implicatures, so it has to be incorporated into the description of conversational context in some way, but it is difficult to describe because it is so variable. One possible way to represent background knowledge is to list the set of assumptions that are in effect as the basis for an inference. Different background assumptions would then generate different implicatures as in these contrasting interpretations for the constituent utterance NP in (5c):

(12a) A: The White House staff doesn't visit Tip O'Neill in his Congressional office.
      B: Old grudge.
          Background assumptions
          - B believes A knows that the White House staff has an old grudge against Tip O'Neill.
          [$_{NP}$ old grudge]
          +⟩RELEVANCE If the utterance is relevant based on information about the background knowledge of the interlocutors, then the White House staff doesn't visit Tip O'Neill because the staff has an old grudge against Tip O'Neill.

(12b) A: The White House staff doesn't visit Tip O'Neill in his Congressional office.

B: Old grudge.
Background assumptions
- B believes A knows that Tip O'Neill has an old grudge
against the White House staff.
[$_{NP}$ old grudge]
+⟩RELEVANCE If the utterance is relevant based on
information about the background knowledge of the
interlocutors, then the White House staff doesn't visit
Tip O'Neill because Tip O'Neill has an old grudge
against the White House staff.

Both operations of inference arrive at a causal conclusion; the specific
implicatures, however, are different because the assumptions forming the
basis for the operation of Cooperative Inference are different. A continuing
utterance in the conversation might indicate that one particular interpretation is in effect:

(13a) A: The White House staff doesn't visit Tip O'Neill in his Congressional office.
B: Old grudge.
A: They won't visit him because he refused to support their
economic program.
(13b) A: The White House staff doesn't visit Tip O'Neill in his Congressional office.
B: Old grudge.
A: He won't even let them make appointments.

The two different sequences show that different implicatures are in effect as
the interpretation of the constituent utterance: in (13a), the interpretation
of (12a) is in effect; in (13b), the interpretation of (12b) is in effect. The
operation of this particular subtype of Cooperative Inference depends upon
information drawn out of discourse participants' shared background knowledge; this information is represented as the assumptions providing the basis
for the inference.

A fourth type of information triggering the operation of a subtype of
Cooperative Inference is general knowledge about the world, including
knowledge of the similar (or different) cultures of the interlocutors. Like
background knowledge, knowledge about the world is difficult to represent, but it, too, could be represented as the assumptions that are in effect
as the basis for an inference. For example, consider the interpretation of

the VP constituent utterance in (5d):

(14) A: John doesn't know what the best defense against criminal charges would be.

B: Ask any lawyer.
Assumptions about the world
- Lawyers know how to construct defenses against criminal charges.
[$_{VP}$ ask any lawyer]
+⟩RELEVANCE If the utterance is relevant based on information from knowledge about the world, then John could find out what the best defense against criminal charges is by asking any lawyer.

A number of continuing utterances could indicate that this implicature is in effect as the interpretation for the constituent utterance:

(15a) A: That's a good idea.
(15b) A: Any lawyer could advise him.
(15c) A: Any lawyer could build a defense for him.

The operation of this particular subtype of Cooperative Inference depends upon information drawn from the discourse participants' general knowledge about the world; this information is represented as the assumptions providing the basis for the inference.

The statements describing the subtypes of Cooperative Inference within the four different domains of relevance make a distinction between knowledge and information. The term 'knowledge' refers to a cognitive construct, such as a representation of the physical context of situation or a model of background knowledge or knowledge about the world. The term 'information' refers to the activated portions of that knowledge in a specific conversational context, the pieces of information that are in effect as assumptions providing the basis for the operation of the subtypes of Cooperative Inference. The partially autonomous interaction of the sub-module of conversational context with a model of knowledge is a matter of using activated pieces of information to serve as assumptions, although I do not address the question of how the actual process of activation takes place (cf. the discussion of this issue in §4.1.3).

At first, the statements describing the subtypes of Cooperative Inference may seem vague because they do not explain what information is involved in making an inference within a domain of relevance and because they do not specify a conclusion within their *if-then* statements. This vagueness, though, is necessary in order to provide a theoretical account of pragmatic interpretation that accounts for indeterminacy within domains of relevance. The pragmatic model cannot provide an unchanging and determinate representation of the features of the physical context of situation, the statement of a topic of conversation, or the assumptions from background knowledge and knowledge about the world as a part of the description of conversational context, nor can it supply any specific conclusion from an operation of a subtype of Cooperative Inference. Information from different conversational contexts varies; when the information varies within the description of the information within a specific conversational context, the resulting implicatures vary as well, as shown in the discussion of examples (5b) as (8) or (10) and (5c) as (12a) or (12b). Nothing in the statements describing the general form of the inferences can predict specific implicatures because the inferences are particularized. This nonspecificity is theoretically necessary, and it is built into the formal statement of the operation of inference by leaving open the conclusion of the *if-then* statements which describe the subtypes of Cooperative Inference. The operation of Cooperative Inference must allow such indeterminacy because an indefinite number of implicatures are technically possible as an interpretation of an utterance.

Within the pragmatic model, indeterminacy arises from the fact that there are many possible interpretations for an utterance: theoretically, a constituent utterance could receive an interpretation based on (at least) the linguistic context, the physical context of situation, the topic of conversation, the shared background knowledge of the interlocutors, and their general knowledge about the world, and, as shown above, an utterance can even receive more than one interpretation within a domain. Within the submodule of conversational context, privileging one domain over another leads to different interpretations, which provides a way of accounting for indeterminacy across domains. The following discussion illustrates interpretations in which one particular domain of relevance is privileged over other domains.[8]

When information from the physical context is privileged, an interpretation can be quite different from interpretations based on any other domain of relevance and even from interpretations based on the linguistic context. Consider the following situation: the interlocutors are President Nixon and his Chief of Staff H. R. Haldeman; the setting is the Oval Office with Nixon sitting behind his desk and Haldeman sitting opposite. Haldeman has just asked a question when the phone rings, Nixon answers it and listens to the White House operator, who identifies the caller. While looking at Haldeman, Nixon then says, perhaps in a low tone, a whisper, or even by mouthing silently, the name of the Attorney General of the United States. This information from the physical context of situation can form the basis for an operation of the first subtype of Cooperative Inference:

(16) H: Who grants immunity?
      P: John Mitchell.

Context of Situation
Event: conversation

Addressor	Addressee	Setting
P	H	office
$[_{NP}$ John Mitchell]		P on phone

+⟩RELEVANCE If the utterance is relevant based on
     information from the context of situation, then P is
     speaking to John Mitchell on the phone.

The fact that the President is on the phone but addressing Haldeman, which is represented in the model of the context of situation (P as addressor; H, and not the person on the phone, as addressee), provides the basis for the operation of Cooperative Inference to create the implicature that P is telling H with whom he is speaking on the telephone.

The particular implicature in (16) is the result of an inference based on information about the context of situation, and when this domain is privileged, this interpretation is different from a number of other possible interpretations of the NP. First of all, the interpretation in (16) is different from an interpretation arising from the operation of Discourse Inference, which would interpret the NP as functioning in the discourse role of Agent in answer to the question. Second, the interpretation is different from interpretations arising from the operation of other subtypes of Cooperative Inference within different domains of relevance, which might interpret the NP in terms of some connection between John Mitchell and immunity: even though the topic of the discourse is a discussion of immunity, even though general knowledge about the world would provide the information that the Attorney General of the United States can grant immunity, and even though the shared background knowledge of the participants could include assumptions about John Mitchell as a crony who might act favorably toward the Administration with respect to granting immunity, when information from the physical context of situation is privileged, the interpretation of the NP constituent utterance *John Mitchell* does not connect him with the action of granting immunity. Instead, when the context of situation is privileged as a domain of relevance, it generates an interpretation connecting the NP with the identity of Nixon's caller.

Privileging the domain of topic also generates interpretations that are different from others in different domains. Consider the following situation: the interlocutors are President Nixon and his Chief of Staff Haldeman, and the topic of conversation is the possibility of seeking immunity for the members of the Executive staff. Nixon indicates his desire to get immunity, and Haldeman follows up Nixon's comment with an independent constituent utterance asking a question:

(17) P: We have to get immunity for the Executive staff somehow.
      H: John Mitchell?

Based on information about the topic, one interpretation of the NP is that Haldeman is suggesting a possible source of immunity:

(18) Topic: immunity for the Executive staff
      [$_{NP}$ John Mitchell]
      +⟩RELEVANCE If the utterance is relevant based on informa-
      tion about the topic of the conversation, then John Mitchell
      might be able to get immunity for members of the Executive
      staff.

This particular implicature, which is based on the topic of conversation, is different from a number of other interpretations for the NP based on other domains of relevance. First, the interpretation in (18) is different from an interpretation based on general knowledge that Mitchell is a member of the Executive staff, one who might need immunity; it also is different from an interpretation based on the interlocutors' shared background knowledge that the reason Mitchell might need immunity is because of certain illegal actions.

The shared background knowledge that interlocutors have about each other often functions to generate interpretations that are different from those that might be based solely on general knowledge about the world. Consider the following example:

(19) P: I wonder if there's a way to get immunity for members of
            the Executive staff.
      H: Speak to John Mitchell?

Here, an inference based on general knowledge about the world might
utilize information about John Mitchell in his position as Attorney General
of the United States:

(20) Assumptions about the world
      - John Mitchell is Attorney General of the United States.
      - The Attorney General of the United States has the power to
      grant immunity.
      [$_{VP}$ speak to John Mitchell]
      +⟩RELEVANCE If the utterance is relevant based on informa-
      tion from knowledge about the world, then H suggests that
      speaking to John Mitchell could reveal whether members of
      the Executive staff might be able to get immunity.

Although this is certainly a reasonable interpretation of the suggestion
made with the VP constituent utterance, if additional assumptions based on
shared background knowledge are privileged within the conversational context, then the interpretation of the VP could be quite different. One piece
of information that both the President and Haldeman could share is the fact
that John Mitchell, as a political appointee of the Nixon administration,
usually is favorably inclined toward requests from the White House. An
inference based on the information from this domain of relevance would
arrive at a different conclusion in the interpretation of the VP constituent
utterance:

(21) P: I wonder if there's a way to get immunity for members of
            the Executive staff.
      H: Speak to John Mitchell?
            Background assumptions
            - John Mitchell usually is favorably inclined toward requests
            from the White House because he is a political appointee
            of the Nixon administration.
            Assumptions about the world
            - John Mitchell is Attorney General of the United States.
            - The Attorney General of the United States has the power
            to grant immunity.

[$_{VP}$ speak to John Mitchell]
+) RELEVANCE If the utterance is relevant based on information from the background knowledge of the interlocutors, then speaking to John Mitchell might persuade him to use his position as Attorney General to obtain immunity for members of the Executive staff.

This particular implicature is more an interpretation concerning the influence of cronyism rather than an interpretation concerning the jurisdiction of the Attorney General; in other words, the interpretation in (20) is about the Attorney General while the interpretation in (21) is about John Mitchell. What makes the latter interpretation possible is the shared background knowledge that the President and Haldeman have about John Mitchell as a person in addition to their general knowledge about the position of U.S. Attorney General. To arrive at the interpretation in (21), the background assumptions are privileged with respect to the assumptions about the world.

The sequences above show that a constituent utterance may have different interpretations within different domains of relevance; they also show the effect of privileging a domain of relevance. Within all of these sequences, though, the operation of Cooperative Inference has calculated implicatures based on the assumption that each constituent utterance represents a cooperative contribution within a specific conversational context. These implicatures are what Levinson calls "standard implicatures," that is, implicatures that arise from observing the Cooperative Principle; standard implicatures contrast with conversational implicatures which arise from exploiting the maxims of the Cooperative Principle (1983: 104). In this work, I concentrate upon standard implicatures rather than conversational implicatures, because the use of independent constituent utterances is made possible by the assumption that discourse participants have the ability to calculate standard implicatures. The examples above were constructed in order to provide relatively straightforward illustrations of the operation of each subtype of Cooperative Inference as well as the effect of privileging one domain of relevance over others. The analysis of sequences from natural language, though, is more complicated, and the domain of topic seems to play an especially important role interacting with other domains. The following examples from *The Presidential Transcripts* illustrate the operation and interaction of subtypes of Cooperative Inference in the creation of standard implicatures.[9]

An interesting way in which discourse participants use independent constituent utterances is to give suggestions, which are sometimes interpreted through the subtype of Cooperative Inference based on topic. Consider the following sequence:

(22) D: One way to do it is for you to tell the Attorney General that you finally know. Really, this is the first time you are getting all the pieces together.

P: Ask for another Grand Jury?

D: Ask for another Grand Jury.

(*Transcripts* 1974: 116)

Knowledge of the topic of conversation provides some crucial information for the operation of Cooperative Inference to arrive at an interpretation of the constituent utterance VP as a suggestion. In the utterances previous to the sequence above, Dean is explaining that the White House staff, specifically Dean himself, Haldeman, and Ehrlichman, as well as Attorney General Mitchell, can no longer hide their attempts to cover up the Watergate affair; he warns Nixon that the publicity and investigations are going to involve the Presidency. Nixon then brings up the possibility of complete disclosure as a way to handle public knowledge of the cover-up:

(23) D: And the person who will be hurt by it most will be you and the Presidency. . . .I am not confident that we can ride through this. . . .[S]ince the publicity has increased on this thing again . . .

P: Let's suppose that you and Haldeman and Ehrlichman and Mitchell say we can't hold this? What then are you going to say? What are you going to put out after it[?] Complete disclosure, isn't that the best way to do it?

(*Transcripts* 1974: 115-116)

With information about the current topic of conversation as complete disclosure, an operation of Cooperative Inference can interpret the President's constituent utterance VP as a suggestion:

(24) Topic: complete disclosure
[$_{VP}$ ask for another Grand Jury]
+⟩RELEVANCE If the utterance is relevant based on information from the topic of the conversation, then asking for another Grand Jury is one way, possibly the best way, to achieve complete disclosure.

Dean's repetition of the VP in the next utterance indicates his agreement with the implicature that asking for another Grand Jury might be the best way to achieve complete disclosure.

An inference based on information from the domain of topic often interacts with inferences based on information from other domains of relevance in order to create a representation of the full interpretation for an independent constituent utterance in its conversational context. Consider the following sequence:

(25) D: You've got, then an awful lot of the principals involved who know. Some people's wives know. Mrs. Hunt was the savviest woman in the world. She had the whole picture together.

P: Did she?

D: Yes. Apparently, she [Mrs. Hunt] was the pillar of strength in that family before the [her] death.

P: Great sadness. As a matter of fact . . .
(*Transcripts* 1974: 109)

This particular sequence illustrates the fluidity of a topic of discourse: in the first sequence, Dean narrows the topic from *principals who know* to *wives who know* to *Mrs. Hunt*. The topic of Mrs. Hunt lasts for several utterances, including an utterance mentioning her death, and serves as the basis for an inference interpreting the NP constituent utterance:

(26) Topic: Mrs. Hunt's death
      [$_{NP}$ great sadness]
      +⟩RELEVANCE If the utterance is relevant based on information from the topic of the conversation, then Mrs. Hunt's death is a great sadness.

Knowledge of the topic, however, is not the only type of information contributing to the interpretation of this constituent utterance. A full interpretation of the NP is also based on some general knowledge of the (American) social convention that a mention of death is usually accompanied by a remark of condolence or regret (condolence if a mourner is present, regret if not). This information from knowledge about the world is the basis for an additional implicature interpreting the NP constituent utterance:

(27) Assumptions about the world
      - Mention of a death conventionally calls for a remark of condo-
      lence or regret.
      $[_{NP}$ great sadness]
      +⟩RELEVANCE If the utterance is relevant based on informa-
      tion from knowledge about the world, then this remark is a
      conventional expression of regret regarding Mrs. Hunt's
      death.

One particularly interesting feature of this sequence is that the speaker,
President Nixon, does not wait for any response from his interlocutor,
Dean. The President simply moves on to another topic, signalling his intention to do so with the introductory phrase *as a matter of fact*. The President
seems to assume that his NP constituent utterance will be fully interpreted
as a conventional response mentioning regret about a death. His assumption that Dean will interpret his implicated meaning is so strong that he
does not need to wait for any evidence, in the form of a continuing utterance, for confirmation of the implicatures. If the President had uttered the
NP *great sadness* and then paused, Dean could have made a comment to
indicate his recognition of and agreement with the President's implicature
that Mrs. Hunt's death was a great sadness; Dean, too, then, would be
uttering a conventional statement of regret:

(28a) D: Yes.
(28b) D: I agree.
(28c) D: An unfortunate tragedy.
(28d) D: A great pity.

But the President, in the actual performance of the discourse, did not wait
for any overt confirmation that Dean interpreted his constituent utterance
correctly, nor did he wait for Dean to respond with a matching expression
of regret; he simply moved on to another topic, secure in his assumption
that what he meant (and what is represented in the submodule of conversational context as a structure of implicatures) became part of the shared conversational context between Dean and himself.

   In the *Transcripts*, some of the most interesting examples of independent constituent utterances are ones whose interpretation is the result of
inferences based on the interaction of the domain of shared background
knowledge with other domains of relevance, particularly the domain of
topic. Consider the following sequences:

(29a) P: The *Post* didn't have it until after you continued to the back section. It is the (adjective [expletive]) thing I ever saw.

D: Typical.

(29b) D: Maybe we could invite the Committee down to the Roosevelt Room or the Blair House.

H: Maintain informality.

(*Transcripts* 1974: 46, 164)

In example (29a), the ADJP constituent utterance *typical* occurs within a conversation in which Dean and the President are discussing newspaper coverage of the revelation of an illegal campaign contribution from Robert Vesco, a controversial financier, to Maurice Stans, chairman of the Finance Committee within the Committee to Re-Elect the President. Specifically, Dean and the President are referring to the fact that the contribution was returned to Vesco, which the *New York Times* reported in the second paragraph of its story; the *Washington Post's* placement of this fact in the back section is the referent of *it* in the first utterance of the discourse sequence. This knowledge of the topic contributes to an interpretation of the ADJP:

(30)   Topic: return of Vesco contribution

[$_\text{ADJP}$ typical]

+ ⟩ RELEVANCE If the utterance is relevant based on information from the topic of the conversation, then it is typical of the *Post* not to emphasize the fact of the return of the contribution.

This implicature connects the constituent utterance to the specific topic, but it does not fully explain why it is typical of the *Post* not to emphasize the return of the contribution. Additional implicatures, however, could result from an operation of Cooperative Inference based on the background knowledge that Dean and the President share about the *Washington Post*, the newspaper most dedicated to publishing unfavorable reports about the conduct of Nixon and the Executive staff during the Watergate scandal:

(31)   Background assumptions

- In general, the *Post* does not regard the Nixon Administration favorably.

[$_\text{ADJP}$ typical]

+ ⟩ RELEVANCE If the utterance is relevant based on information from the background knowledge of the interlocutors, then it is typical of the *Post* not to emphasize the return of the contribution because this fact is favorable to the Nixon Administration.

The full interpretation of the ADJP is composed of two implicatures based on the topic and the shared background knowledge of the discourse participants: information from the topic generates an implicature that is specific to the fact under discussion; information from background knowledge generates an implicature that is a generalization about how this fact fits into a larger pattern.

In the conversation of (29b), the President, Haldeman, and Ehrlichman are discussing the topic of meeting with the Senate Watergate Committee, and the first utterance in the sequence suggests inviting the Committee down to the Roosevelt Room, which is a room in the White House, or to the Blair House, which is the residence for guests of the President of the United States and a location for many meetings and functions. An implicature based on knowledge of the topic provides an interpretation for the VP constituent utterance:

(32)   Topic: meeting the Watergate Committee
       [$_{VP}$ maintain informality]
       +)RELEVANCE If the utterance is relevant based on information from the topic of the conversation, then meeting the Committee in the Roosevelt Room or the Blair House would maintain informality.

The background knowledge of the participants, however, might include a shared assumption that an informal meeting with the Senate Watergate Committee would be advantageous to the members of the Executive staff; this background assumption provides the basis for a variety of implicatures:

(33)   [$_{VP}$ maintain informality]
       Background assumptions
       - An informal meeting with the Watergate Committee would be advantageous to the members of the Executive staff.
       +)RELEVANCE If the utterance is relevant based on information from the background knowledge of the interlocutors, then the advantages of maintaining informality might include avoiding sworn testimony, allowing the staff to lie without risking criminal charges of perjury or contempt of Congress.

+)RELEVANCE If the utterance is relevant based on information from the background knowledge of the interlocutors,
then the advantages of maintaining informality might include
avoiding public hearings and the attendant media coverage.

The combination of an inference based on topic and a series of inferences
based on background knowledge provide the full interpretation for the constituent utterance VP.

One final example of a discourse sequence from the Watergate conversations illustrates the contribution of the submodule of linguistic context to
an interpretation within the submodule of conversational context:

(34)   P: Who is going to be the first witness up there?
       D: Sloan.
       P: Unfortunate.
       D: No doubt about it.
       (*Transcripts* 1974: 80)

After the operation of Discourse Inference, the NP constituent utterance
Sloan functions in the discourse of Theme as an answer to the question. The
interpretation of the next utterance, the ADJP constituent utterance *unfortunate* takes place within the submodule of conversational context:

(35)   Topic: witnesses at the hearing
       [$_{ADJP}$ unfortunate]
       +)RELEVANCE If the utterance is relevant based on informa-
       tion from knowledge of the topic of conversation, then it is
       unfortunate that Sloan is going to be the first witness.

The interpretation of the ADJP incorporates knowledge of the discourse-
based interpretation of the previous NP plus knowledge of the topic of conversation. Further interpretation based on the interlocutors' shared
background knowledge about Sloan could generate additional implicatures
explaining why it is unfortunate that Sloan will be the first witness at the
hearing:

(36)   Background assumptions
       - Sloan knows about illegal financial transactions.
       +)RELEVANCE If the utterance is relevant based on informa-
       tion from the background knowledge of the interlocutors,
       then it is unfortunate that Sloan is going to be the first witness
       because he knows about illegal financial transactions.

The same interdependence of interpretation characterizes the NP in next utterance:

(37) [$_{NP}$ no doubt about it]
+ 〉 RELEVANCE If the utterance is relevant based on information from knowledge of the topic of conversation, then there is no doubt that it is unfortunate that Sloan is going to be the first witness up there.

Here, too, the interpretation of the idiomatic NP incorporates knowledge of previous implicatures, including the discourse function of the NP *Sloan* as well as the interpretation of the ADJP *unfortunate*. In sequences like (34), the submodule of linguistic context makes a significant contribution to interpretation within the submodule of conversational context; knowledge of the representation of linguistic context is incorporated into interpretation within the submodule of conversational context. The operation of Cooperative Inference has access to information from the linguistic context because the representation of linguistic context is the input to the submodule of conversational context.

This subsection has presented examples of the pragmatic interpretation of independent constituent utterances within the submodule of conversational context. Interpretation within this submodule is particularized within domains of relevance; the multiple domains of relevance reflect the indeterminacy of pragmatic interpretation, which takes place within specific conversational contexts. Within this submodule, the particularized operation of Cooperative Inference generates standard implicatures which explain the relevance of a constituent utterance as a cooperative contribution to the conversation and thus function, in Grice's words, to "yield results according to the Cooperative Principle" (1975: 45).

5.1.3 *The condition of acceptability within the submodule of conversational context*

Within the submodule of conversational context, the operation of Cooperative Inference is triggered by the assumption of cooperation incorporated into the Principle of Conversational Context; this assumption is so strong that discourse participants strive to make enough inferences to arrive at an explanation of the relevance of an utterance in order to come to an understanding of what has been meant by an independent constituent utterance.

It is possible, though, to construct some discourse sequences in which intuitions of pragmatic acceptability are violated:

(38a) A: Nixon was President from 1968 to 1974.
      B: #Stickball
(38b) A: John Mitchell was Attorney General during the Nixon administration.
      B: #Stained glass windows

In another discourse sequence, however, the same constituent utterances would be acceptable:

(39a) A: Philadelphia has a famous street sport.
      B: Stickball.
(39b) A: Some medievalists study theological art in cathedrals.
      B: Stained glass windows?

Utterances are judged as acceptable or unacceptable within the boundaries of the specific conversational contexts associated with their discourse sequence.

The notion of acceptability and unacceptability within the submodule of conversational context seems to be associated with the ability of the discourse participants to arrive at a set of implicatures which explains the relevance of an utterance. If the discourse sequences in (38) actually occurred, the continuing utterances probably would indicate a breakdown in communication by asking, in a more or less overt fashion, for clarification:

(40a) A: Nixon was President from 1968 to 1974.
      B: #Stickball
      A: What?/Huh?/What are you talking about?/
           I don't know what you mean./(silence)
(40b) A: John Mitchell was Attorney General during the Nixon administration.
      B: #Stained glass windows
      A: What?/Huh?/We're talking about politics here./
           What do windows have to do with politics?/(silence)

The different reactions function as a request for clarification, which indicates that the problem with an unacceptable constituent utterance seems to be an inability to infer a set of implicatures that determines the relevance of an utterance; in other words, the operation of Cooperative Inference does not arrive at any result. The breakdown in communication can be seen as a request for a specification of the implicatures that make the utterance relevant.

Formulating a specific condition of acceptability to govern the representation of conversational context incorporates this notion of a breakdown in communication as a reflection of a judgment of unacceptability. The Condition of Acceptability is an attempt to describe the conditions that prevail when a constituent utterance is acceptable and interpretable through the operation of Cooperative Inference; if these conditions do not prevail, a constituent utterance is unacceptable:

(41) *Condition of Acceptability within the Submodule of Conversational Context*
A constituent utterance is pragmatically acceptable if a set of implicatures establishes its relevance as a cooperative contribution in the representation of conversational context; otherwise, it is deemed unacceptable (and marked #) because a set of implicatures cannot be inferred to establish relevance. An unacceptable constituent utterance often causes a breakdown in communication.

An unacceptable constituent utterance, followed by silence or a breakdown in communication, requires an overt clarification of the implicatures that make it a relevant contribution to the conversation.[10]

Claiming that the Condition marks a constituent utterance as unacceptable if a set of implicatures cannot be inferred for it describes several types of breakdowns in communication. One kind of breakdown in communication governed by the Condition of Acceptability is an unsuccessful attempt to introduce or shift a topic of conversation. Yanofsky points out that discourse participants often use initial NPs to draw attention to a new topic in the context of situation or to introduce a new topic within a conversation; she cites the following examples:

(42a) Fire!
(42b) The phone.

In (42a) and (42b), the NPs introduce new topics based on information from the physical context of situation. Sometimes, however, the use of a constituent utterance in an attempt to introduce or shift a topic fails. Consider example (42b); if the addressee has not heard the ringing of the phone and therefore is unaware of this feature of the context of situation, the constituent utterance would be unacceptable:

(43) A: #The phone
      B: What?/ What are you talking about?/Is the phone ringing?/I
            don't hear anything.

Each of the continuing utterances indicates that the constituent utterance
has failed to introduce a new topic. The unacceptability of the constituent
utterance, though, could be quickly corrected by the original speaker's
specifying the relevance of the utterance; if the addressee is not aware of
the information from the context of situation that makes the NP relevant,
then the speaker can supply that information:

(44) A: #The phone
      B: What are you talking about?
      A: The phone is ringing; answer it.

A's response to the indication of unacceptability specifies the implicatures
that he or she originally expected B to calculate.

Another type of breakdown in communication occurs when a discourse
participant mistakenly assumes that some piece of information is shared
background knowledge or knowledge about the world. Consider the following sequence, in which speaker A uses an independent constituent utterance under the assumption that A and B share the information that provides the assumption for the operation of Cooperative Inference:

(45) A: John's late for the committee meeting.
      B: Late night at Alvin's.
            Background assumptions
            - Alvin's is a bar.
            $[_{NP}$ late night at Alvin's]
            +〉RELEVANCE If the utterance is relevant based on
                information from the background knowledge of the
                interlocutors, then John is late because he stayed too
                late at Alvin's bar last night.

If B, however, used this constituent utterance in a conversation with
another person, C, who is not aware or who has forgotten that Alvin's is a
bar, C would be unable to arrive at the implicature above, and the Condition of Acceptability would mark the utterance as unacceptable. Continuing utterances might indicate the breakdown in communication:

(46) C: John's late for the committee meeting.
      B: #Late night at Alvin's

C: Who's Alvin?/What do you mean?/What are you talking about?/Pardon?

It is important to note here that the constituent utterance is unacceptable within a specific conversational context, which can change across different participants with different background knowledge. In (45), the utterance, *late night at Alvin's* is acceptable for A and B because they share the background knowledge that Alvin's is a bar; in (46) the same utterance is unacceptable for B and C because they do not share that piece of information. In the latter case, B can respond to the breakdown in communication by specifying the information that he or she had expected C to be aware of:

(47) C: John's late for the committee meeting.
B: #Late night at Alvin's
C: Who's Alvin?
B: Alvin's is a bar./I thought you knew — Alvin's is a bar./You know Alvin's — it's that bar across the street.
C: Oh.
+⟩RELEVANCE If the utterance is relevant based on information from the shared background knowledge of the interlocutors, then C now realizes that John is late because he stayed too late at Alvin's bar last night.

In this case, C's confirming utterance, *oh*, indicates that he or she is now able to calculate the implicature associated with B's utterance *late night at Alvin's* because the identification of Alvin's as a bar is now shared knowledge. By specifying this piece of information, C allows B to interpret the originally unacceptable constituent utterance.

In conclusion, this section of Chapter Five has described interpretation within the submodule of conversational context in the pragmatic model of the interpretation of independent constituent utterances. The essence of the conversational context for an utterance is the assumption that each utterance is a cooperative contribution to the conversation; this version of Grice's Cooperative Principle is built into the statement of the Principle of Conversational Context. Once cooperation is assumed, then an operation of Cooperative Inference fills in the structure of context by generating a set of implicatures that explains the relevance of a constituent utterance. Inferences aimed at explaining the relevance of an utterance can draw upon information from different domains within the conversational context; these domains include the physical context of situation, the topic of conversation, the shared background knowledge of the interlocutors, and their general knowledge about the world. These different domains account for a dimension of indeterminacy in pragmatic interpretation: utterances may receive an interpretation within different domains, and inferences within domains generate different interpretations. An acceptable constituent utterance is one which has been interpreted according to the operation of Cooperative Inference. An unacceptable constituent utterance is one which has not been interpreted successfully because the operation of Cooperative Inference does not arrive at any implicatures that explain relevance. An unacceptable constituent utterance usually causes a breakdown in communication and requires a specification of the implicatures that describe its relevance within the conversational context.

5.2 Arguments supporting the submodule of conversational context

In this section, I present arguments supporting the claim that the submodule of conversational context offers a theoretically principled way of describing the information-based interpretation of independent constituent utterances. In §5.2.1, I discuss similarities and differences between the submodule of linguistic context and the submodule of conversational context. In §5.2.2, I consider the ways in which the submodule of conversational context complements work in neo-Gricean pragmatics and contrasts with work in post-Gricean pragmatics.

5.2.1 Distinguishing submodules

In the course of the previous chapters, I have argued that a pragmatic model of the interpretation of independent constituent utterances requires two submodules for the representation of implicated meaning. In §4.2.1, I motivated the submodule of linguistic context as one which is theoretically distinct from its input component of Logical Form representation by arguing that the submodule of linguistic context represents the discourse-based interpretation of constituent utterances as generalized implicatures. In this subsection, I motivate the submodule of conversational context as one which is theoretically distinct from its input submodule of linguistic context by arguing that the submodule of conversational context represents the information-based interpretation of constituent utterances as particularized implicatures.

The main contrast between the two submodules within the pragmatic model is reflected by their different operations of inference. Within the submodule of linguistic context, the operation of Discourse Inference generates implicatures based solely on information from the linguistic context of an utterance. Implicatures within the submodule of linguistic context are generalized since they are calculated for a constituent utterance unless canceled either by the Condition of Acceptability or by an operation of Cooperative Inference as in, for example, the ability of information from the physical context of situation to generate an interpretation that is different from an interpretation based on the operation of Discourse Inference (cf.the discussion of examples (51) and (52) in §4.2.1 and examples (6) and (16) in §5.1.2). The operation of Cooperative Inference, in contrast, generates particularized implicatures that are based on a variety of types of information defined as domains of relevance; these particularized implicatures are calculated for an individual constituent utterance within its specific conversational context.

These familiar examples illustrate the contrast between the submodules of linguistic context and conversational context in the pragmatic model:

(48a) A: What stops the White House staff from visiting Tip O'Neill in his Congressional office?

     B: Old grudge.

(48b) A: The White House staff doesn't visit Tip O'Neill in his Congressional office.

     B: Old grudge.

The constituent utterance in (48a) is interpreted within the submodule of linguistic context; the NP functions in the discourse role of Agent for the predicate *stop*, and the interpretation of the constituent utterance does not require any information from beyond the discourse itself. In the discourse sequence of (48b), however, the independent constituent utterance does not receive an interpretation within the submodule of linguistic context because it does not match any expansion possibilities to trigger the operation of Discourse Inference. Under the assumption that the constituent utterance is a cooperative contribution to the conversation, its interpretation takes place within the submodule of conversational context, and different interpretations of the constituent utterance are possible across and within the domains of relevance.

Although the submodule of linguistic context and the submodule of conversational context contrast in the type of information that triggers their operation of inference, within both submodules the operation of inference generates implicatures that elaborate the structure of context for an independent constituent utterance. In §4.2.1, I showed that the implicatures generated by the operation of Discourse Inference fulfilled all of the tests for an implicature: they are indeterminate, (somewhat) defeasible, reinforceable, non-detachable, non-conventional, and calculable. Within the submodule of conversational context, implicatures generated by the operation of Cooperative Inference also satisfy all of these diagnostics for implicatures, as I show below.

Consider the discourse sequence in (48b) once more. The interpretation of the constituent utterance *old grudge* is indeterminate because the constituent utterances could occur in different conversational contexts, generating different interpretations based on different assumptions from the background knowledge of the interlocutors: in one case, the White House staff doesn't visit Tip O'Neill because they hold an old grudge against him; in another case, the White House staff doesn't visit Tip O'Neill because he holds an old grudge against them (cf. the different interpretations of this example as (12a) and (12b) in §5.1.2).

The implicatures forming an interpretation for this constituent utterance also are defeasible and reinforceable. Any particular implicature associated with the constituent utterance can be canceled with the addition of explanatory material:

(49a) B: Old grudge, but not a real one between the White House staff and Tip O'Neill; it's just that White House staff members historically have a grudge against the Speaker of the House which prohibits them from visiting the Speaker's office.

(49b) B: Old grudge, but not a real one between Tip O'Neill and the White House staff; it's just that the Speaker of the House historically holds a grudge against the members of the White House staff and never lets them visit his office.

The statement in (49a) cancels the implicature that the members of the Executive staff have an old grudge against Tip O'Neill; the statement in (49b) cancels the implicature that Tip O'Neill has an old grudge against the White House staff. Both cancellations indicate that there is no real grudge, there is only a political game being played out. The implicatures associated with the constituent utterance *old grudge* also are reinforceable; they can be explicitly stated without anomaly:

(50a) B: Old grudge; the White House staff doesn't visit Tip O'Neill in his Congressional office because of they hold an old grudge against him.

(50b) B: Old grudge; Tip O'Neill won't let the White House staff visit him in his Congressional office because he holds an old grudge against them.

In (49) and (50), the addition of material cancels or reinforces the implicatures associated with the interpretation of the NP *old grudge*.

In addition to being indeterminate, defeasible, and reinforceable, the implicatures associated with the constituent utterance in (48b) also are non-detachable; they are not associated with a particular form of the utterance. Substituting synonyms or paraphrases for the constituent utterances does not affect the calculation of the implicatures:

(51) A: The White House staff doesn't visit Tip O'Neill in his Congressional office.

       B: Long-standing feud.

In addition, the implicatures associated with the constituent utterance are non-conventional, that is, they are not solely associated with the meanings of the words; they are associated with the employment of the constituent utterance in (48b) within a particular conversational context consisting of background knowledge that licenses the implicatures.

Finally, the submodule of conversational context describes the calculation of the implicatures associated with the constituent utterance in (48b). This description of interpretation follows Grice's specification of the working-out process. Consider the inferential argument that could be constructed for the example; below the steps in Grice's description of the calculation process are numbered (1975: 49-50); the corresponding steps for the calculation of the implicature within the submodule of conversational context are indented and lettered:

(52) A man who, by (in, when) saying (or making as if to say) that p
has implicated that q, may be said to have [implicated] that q,
    B, who has said *old grudge* has implicated that *the White
    House staff doesn't visit Tip O'Neill because the White
    House staff has an old grudge against Tip O'Neill*
PROVIDED THAT
(i)   he is to be presumed to be observing the conversational maxims,
or at least the Cooperative Principle:
        (a) the Principle of Conversational Context creates a
        potential structure of implicatures explaining the rele-
        vance of the constituent utterance under the assump-
        tion of cooperation
(ii) the supposition that he is aware that, or thinks that, q is required
in order to make his saying or making as if to say p (or doing so
in THOSE terms) consistent with this presumption:
        (b) B thinks that the implicature *the White House staff
        doesn't visit Tip O'Neill because the White House staff
        has an old grudge against him* will make the NP *old
        grudge* consistent with the assumption of cooperation
        by explaining the relevance of the constituent utterance
(iii) the speaker thinks (and would expect the hearer to think that the
speaker thinks) that it is within the competence of the hearer to
work out, or grasp intuitively, that the supposition mentioned in
(ii) is required:
        (c) B thinks that A can arrive at the implicature in (b)
        based upon the assumption from their shared
        background knowledge that an old grudge exists
        between the White House staff and Tip O'Neill.

Within the submodule of conversational context, knowledge of the
Cooperative Principle is built into the Principle of Conversational Context;
knowledge of the maxim of Relation, the maxim most important to a determination of particularized conversational implicatures, is built into the
statement of the operation of Cooperative Inference. Different types of
background knowledge and of other types of knowledge necessary for making inferences are built into the domains of relevance, which describe
specific conversational contexts. All together, the constructs within the submodule of conversational context generate a particularized interpretation

for an independent constituent utterance.

The representation of conversational context in the pragmatic model describes the structure of implicatures that inferences create for an utterance; these implicatures constitute participants' shared knowledge of the conversational context. The notion of shared knowledge is somewhat controversial, although Prince offers a working definition: "The speaker assumes that the hearer 'knows,' assumes, or can infer a particular thing" (1981: 230).[11] This definition works well within the pragmatic model presented here because it describes two types of shared knowledge: what discourse participants know and assume plus what they can infer. Within the submodule of conversational context, what discourse participants know is the Principle of Cooperative Context and the description of subtypes of Cooperative Inference based on domains of relevance; what they assume is that these are in effect in the interpretation of utterances. What discourse participants can then infer is an interpretation of an utterance, an interpretation consisting of implicatures about the relevance of a constituent utterance within its conversational context. Prince's definition of shared knowledge captures a generalization about the active relationship between inference and shared knowledge within the pragmatic model: inferences can create shared knowledge.

The description of interpretation within the submodule of conversational context offered in this chapter has both strengths and weaknesses. I have argued that this account of information-based pragmatic interpretation has several strengths: it suggests that the operation of pragmatic inference takes place within domains, which narrows the scope of inference from a general operation of thinking to a more specialized act of interpretation within boundaries; it also explicitly connects an inference to the boundaries of the domain of relevance within which it takes place. In addition, this account of interpretation also offers a theoretical account of the indeterminacy that characterizes information-based interpretation through the constructs of the domains of relevance and the mechanism of privileging a domain: the pragmatic model predicts indeterminacy because there are multiple domains of relevance, each of which could give rise to interpretations; it also explains that different interpretations arise from privileging different domains of relevance.

The account of interpretation presented here, however, has two significant weaknesses. First, it does not explain why one particular domain of relevance might be privileged at any particular time; in other words, I have not offered any mechanism for weighting the domains, and I leave this issue open for future research. More seriously, though, as presented here, the statements describing the operation of Cooperative Inference do not explain how an inference arrives at a specific conclusion; in other words, I have not completely described how an inference works. Even though some vagueness in the statement of the operation of inference is necessary (cf. the discussion of this issue in §5.1.2), the operation of Cooperative Inference falls short of offering a specific description of arriving at conclusions within pragmatic interpretation. I stand with many other researchers in not providing a general account of inference (cf. the comments of Fodor and Levinson about this issue in §1.2), but I hope that my more specific claims, the connection between particularized inference and its multiple domains of relevance, and the place of domains of relevance in an account of indeterminacy, have contributed to a better understanding of the operation of pragmatic inference.[12]

5.2.2 *The wider framework*

The pragmatic model of the interpretation of independent constituent utterances is partially modular because its two submodules share crucial properties. The similarity between the two submodules is in their internal structure: each has a principle describing the structure of context, an operation of inference elaborating the structure of context, and a condition governing the results of the operation of inference. The differences between the two submodules arise out of their respective definitions of context: within the submodule of linguistic context, the context is limited to the discourse structure of an utterance; within the submodule of conversational context, the context is expanded to a much broader notion. In this subsection, I consider the Principle of Conversational Context and the operation of Cooperative Inference, showing how each one characterizes the nature of the autonomy and modularity that define the submodule of conversational context and the pragmatic model. I then discuss the ways in which the work presented here complements and contrasts with other recent work in pragmatics.

Like the Principle of Linguistic Context, which describes a modular interaction between the grammar of nonsentential constituent structures and the pragmatic model, the Principle of Conversational Context also

describes a modular interaction: within the pragmatic model, the representation of the linguistic context of an utterance becomes a representation
within the submodule of conversational context. The Principle of Conversational Context also contributes to the distinctness of the submodule of conversational context in comparison to the submodule of linguistic context.
Whereas the statement of the Principle of Linguistic Context (cf. (7) in
§4.1.1) quite specifically defines the structure of linguistic context as a
series of utterances, the statement of the Principle of Conversational Context (cf. (2) in §5.1.1) more loosely defines the structure of conversational
context as one in which an utterance has a potential structure of implicatures. The contrast in the specificity of the principles reflects the different
natures of the linguistic context and the conversational context: the linguistic context is a specific construct within which discourse-based interpretation takes place; in contrast, the conversational context is a more open construct within which cooperation and relevance could be based on a variety
of information.

The operation of Cooperative Inference is the specific mechanism for
interpretation within the submodule of conversational context; its statement (cf. (4) in §5.1.1) incorporates four domains of relevance. Together,
these domains of relevance constitute the conversational context for an
utterance; individually, each domain functions as a limited area for the calculation of a particularized inference. Having multiple domains of relevance incorporates a constraint limiting the submodule of conversational
context to describing information-based interpretation within individual
domains, which explicitly ties the operation of a subtype of Cooperative
Inference to one specific type of context. The domains of relevance also
serve as the interface points between the partially autonomous pragmatic
model and other systems. This partial autonomy of the submodule of conversational context is fairly restricted since it takes place only through the
domains within the operation of Cooperative Inference.

The pragmatic model of the interpretation of independent constituent
utterances is not autonomous like a grammar because it does not conform
to the condition of informational encapsulation, which Fodor defines as a
necessary characteristic of a fully autonomous system (1983: 64). The partially autonomous pragmatic model draws upon knowledge about the world
at two points, the Condition of Acceptability within the submodule of linguistic context and the domains of relevance within the submodule of conversational context. An interesting contrast between the submodules of the

pragmatic model is that the partially autonomous relationship between each submodule with a cognitive model is different. Within the submodule of linguistic context, the interpretation is discourse-based and the governing Condition of Acceptability represents the contact point between the pragmatic model and a cognitive model; knowledge from a model of the world functions to confirm or overrule the likelihood of a constituent utterance performing its implicated function. Within the submodule of conversational context, the interpretation is information-based, and it is the subtypes of Cooperative Inference that represent contact points with a model of the world; activated knowledge from such a model serves as the information in effect as the basis for an operation of inference. Within the submodule of conversational context, the governing Condition of Acceptability relies on a discourse-based criterion, some indication, such as a pause, an expression of confusion, or an overt statement of lack of understanding, that the hearer has failed to arrive at a set of implicatures that explains the relevance of a constituent utterance.

Much recent work in pragmatics, especially within the neo-Gricean framework generally adopted here, concentrates upon the calculation of generalized implicatures only, and the description of the submodule of linguistic context fits in with this work (cf. §4.2.2). Horn and Levinson (1987), however, have called for an extension of a theory of pragmatic interpretation in order to account for particularized pragmatic inference, and Levinson suggests that relevance is one of the key notions involved in the calculation of particularized implicatures (cf. quote in §5.1.1). What I have attempted to do in the development of the submodule of conversational context in the pragmatic model is to explore exactly what kind of relevance is needed within a theoretical apparatus that generates particularized implicatures. My conclusion is that the notion of relevance needs to be specified into domains, four of which I have considered in this chapter. Arguments motivating four separate domains of relevance have shown that having multiple domains of relevance predicts indeterminacy in interpretation; they also have shown that privileging different domains generates different interpretations for an utterance because each domain provides a different type of information as the basis for an operation of Cooperative Inference. The domains of relevance thus account for this dimension of indeterminacy in pragmatic interpretation.

The final question I wish to address here is why multiple domains of relevance have theoretical advantages over a single concept of relevance.

Sperber and Wilson (1986; Wilson and Sperber 1986) offer a pragmatic theory based on a single principle of relevance, one, they claim, which is powerful enough to generate a single, determinate, interpretation of an utterance, especially when that interpretation consists of particularized implicatures. I believe that the concept of multiple domains of relevance as presented here has two advantages over the work of Sperber and Wilson: first, it attempts to explain rather than dismiss indeterminacy; and second, it offers a richer and more explanatory concept of context.

Sperber and Wilson claim that their Principle of Relevance eliminates indeterminacy because of its dual subdefinitions that combine information and processing effort. Their definition of relevance is repeated here:

[(i)] Other things being equal, the greater the contextual effects, the greater the relevance.

[(ii)] Other things being equal, the smaller the processing effort, the greater the relevance.

(Wilson and Sperber 1986: 74)

Sperber and Wilson identify three types of contextual effects: the most important of these is the set of contextual implications, which are defined as the deductions that give rise to new knowledge based on an utterance plus a context (defined as a set of propositions); the other two types of contextual effects are the strengthening or the contradiction of existing contextual assumptions. The following sequences illustrate contextual effects:

(53a) You wake up with the following thought:
If it's raining, I'll stay at home.
You look out the window and discover:
It's raining.
In this case from your existing assumption and the new information, you can deduce some further information not deducible from either the existing assumption or the new information:
I'll stay at home.

(53b) You wake up, hearing a pattering on the roof, and form the hypothesis that:
It's raining.
You open your eyes, look out of the window, and discover that:
It IS raining.

(53c) You wake up, as in case (b), hearing a pattering on the roof, and
form the hypothesis that:
It's raining.
This time, when you open your eyes and look out of the window,
you discover that the sound was made by leaves falling on the
roof, and that actually:
It's not raining.
(Wilson and Sperber 1986: 72-73)

Example (53a) illustrates reasoning, which, incidentally, Sperber and Wilson claim is deductive in nature, arriving at a contextual implication; examples (53b) and (53c) illustrate the strengthening and contradiction, respectively, of contextual assumptions.[13] Sperber and Wilson identify processing cost as the effort involved in producing contextual effects. They consider the following example:

(54) You wake up, thinking:
If it rains, I'll stay at home.
Then EITHER
You look out of the window and see:
(i) It's raining.
OR you look out of the window and see:
(ii) It's raining and there's grass on the lawn.
(Wilson and Sperber 1986: 74)

Both (54i) and (54ii), given the context of *If it rains, I'll stay at home*, have the same contextual effect, which is the implication *I'll stay at home*. The example in (54i), however, achieves the same contextual effect with less processing effort that the example in (54ii), which, basically, has an extra clause that requires processing but does not add any effects to the context. The Principle of Relevance defines the most relevant interpretation as the one which has the greatest increase in information along with the least effort in processing.

Wilson and Sperber claim that this specification of relevance solves the problem of indeterminacy, which they see as a major flaw in previous work: "The problem of providing an explicit account of the indeterminacy of implicatures has defeated many pragmatists" (1986: 79). They rely upon the notion of cognitive processing to eliminate indeterminacy, which is a dubious argument given the current lack of knowledge about processing steps, time, effort, or other components of the process. Consider their explanation of the extra processing cost of example (54i) over example (54ii):

> This difference, we suggest, can be explained in terms of the intuition underlying Grice's Manner maxims, which itself derives from some basic facts about cognition. The intuition is that speakers should make their utterances easy to understand. . . .Now is it clear that though [(54i)] and [(54ii)] above have exactly the same contextual effects in this context [(54)], you would have to work harder to recover them from [(54ii)] than [(54i)]. . . .This extra processing effort detracts from the relevance of the information in [(54ii)], and of any utterance used to communicate it. (Wilson and Sperber 1986: 74)

Sperber and Wilson have claimed to shift what is essentially a matter of intuition to an empirical matter of the evaluation of processing costs. But they have failed in this attempt because they have not proposed any reduplicatable method for evaluating processing costs, so their evaluation still remains a matter of intuition.[14] The ability of the second part of their definition of relevance to constrain interpretation is questionable, which brings into doubt their claim that the principle of relevance can function to determine one determinate interpretation for an utterance. Furthermore, in this work I have argued that it is theoretically necessary for a pragmatic model to account for indeterminacy. Different interpretations for an utterance are possible, especially if a model takes into account the differences in context that are brought to bear upon the operation of inference. Sperber and Wilson's claim is far too strong; they are attempting to force pragmatics into a determinate, logical mold, which contradicts some of the reasons for the development of the field of pragmatics in the first place. Pragmatics, by its nature, deals with the indeterminate, context-specific aspects of interpretation. Denying that nature leads to a fundamental flaw in Sperber and Wilson's theory.

A second problem with Sperber and Wilson's theory of relevance is that they have an extremely narrow view of the concept of context. For them, a context is a set of propositions, one that is augmented by inference. The context is further defined as encyclopedic entries for constants, terms in the propositions that make up a context (Sperber and Wilson 1986: 87ff.). In other words, for the following proposition, which could be a contextual assumption in a cognitive model, there would be encyclopedia entries for the italicized terms:

(55) *Elephants* are *mammals*.

Participants in a discourse can access the encyclopedia entry in order to determine the contextual effects of utterances. For instance, in the pair of utterances below, both could have access to the previous utterance as well as its encyclopedia entries:

(56a) Elephants live underwater.
(56b) Elephants live in the forest.

Presumably, the encyclopedia entry under *mammal* will help determine that the proposition in (56a) contradicts a contextual assumption while the proposition in (56b) strengthens it, which would make (56b) more relevant in a context consisting of the following question:

(57)   Where could elephants live?

Sperber and Wilson's view of context is limited to encyclopedic knowledge, or what I have discussed using the term general knowledge about the world.

The problem with such a narrow view of context is that it does not allow other types of information to figure in the calculation of an inference. As I have shown in this chapter, however, information from the physical context of situation or the topic of conversation often plays a crucial role in interpretation. The shared background knowledge of the interlocutors as well as their general knowledge about the world also generate different interpretations. In contrast to a theory of a single domain of relevance, the division of relevance into domains seems to explain the range and variety of interpretations in a more principled way because it explicitly connects the operation of inference to the specific context that licenses it.

5.3 Conclusion

This chapter described the interpretation of constituent utterances within the submodule of conversational context in the pragmatic model. Each of the theoretical constructs within the submodule is based on Grice's Cooperative Principle: the Principle of Conversational Context creates a structure for the explanation of an utterance as a cooperative contribution to the conversation; the operation of Cooperative Inference elaborates that structure by generating implicatures that explain the relevance of an utterance within different domains; and the Condition of Acceptability checks to make sure that the operation of Cooperative Inference has arrived at a satisfactory result. The submodule of conversational context describes information-based interpretation within domains of relevance, which are defined as knowledge of the physical context of situation, knowledge of the topic of conversation, shared background knowledge of the interlocutors, and their general knowledge about the world. Each of these domains of relevance represents a subset of the conversational context for an utterance, a subset which provides a limited area for the calculation of particularized inference.

This chapter also presented arguments supporting the claim that the submodule of conversational context provides a theoretically satisfying description of the information-based interpretation of independent constituent utterances. Arguments in §5.1.2 showed that having multiple domains of relevance predicts a dimension of indeterminacy in pragmatic interpretation and that privileging a domain of interpretation accounts for the different information-based interpretations of an independent constituent utterance. Arguments in §5.2.1 showed that the submodule of conversational context is both different from and similar to the submodule of linguistic context: the submodules contrast in their definition of context, which is reflected in their different structure-building principles and operations of inference, but they are similar in the generation of implicatures that satisfy all of the diagnostics of indeterminacy, defeasibility, reinforceability, non-detachability, non-conventionality, and calculability. Finally, arguments in §5.2.2 showed that the submodule of conversational context in the pragmatic model is an extension of work in neo-Gricean pragmatics, extending this framework to account for the generation of particularized inference based on relevance; arguments also suggested that the concept of domains of relevance has significant theoretical advantages over a single concept of relevance as postulated in competing work in post-Gricean pragmatics.

Conclusion

This work has explored the similarities and differences in the following paradigm of utterances:

(1a) A: The White House staff doesn't visit Tip O'Neill in his Congressional office because of an old grudge.

(1b) A: What stops the White House staff from visiting Tip O'Neill in his Congressional office?

      B: Old grudge.

(1c) A: The White House staff doesn't visit Tip O'Neill in his Congressional office.

      B: Old grudge.

Native speakers use both sentential and nonsentential utterances in discourse, which suggests that theories of language have to account for the structure and interpretation of sentences as well as nonsentential constituents. Previous research, perhaps because of its historical emphasis on the sentence as its object of study and its exclusive use of question and answer sequences as data, collapsed the explanation of (1a) - (1c) above, identifying independent major lexical categories like those in (1b) and (1c) as sentence fragments and offering analyses based on ellipsis from full sentence sources. Upon close inspection of a wider variety of data, however, such ellipsis analyses have been proved to be empirically and theoretically inadequate as an explanation for the structure and interpretation of independent constituents, especially with respect to examples like (1c), which is clearly not derived and interpreted by ellipsis. This work has offered a new perspective on independent major lexical categories by developing a theory of nonsentential constituents with two interacting models: an autonomous competence model of the grammar of nonsentential constituent structures and a modular pragmatic model of the interpretation of independent constituent utterances in context.

The research presented here has general implications for the development of linguistic theory. The proposed generalization of X-bar theory, by suggesting that X^{max} is the initial node of a generative grammar, accounts for all of the structures generated by a grammar: an initial node of INFL" generates a sentence structure like example (1a), and an initial node of X" generates a nonsentential constituent structure like examples (1b) and (1c). This generalization to X^{max} equalizes the status of sentences and constituents as two classes of structures generated by the grammar.

This research also has general implications for the development of pragmatic theories, especially in terms of their interaction with theories of grammar. First, it suggests that imposing a strict condition of autonomy on a grammar makes interesting claims about the structure and interpretation of nonsentential constituents. Specifically, autonomy allows the competence model of grammar to account for the well-formedness of nonsentential constituents solely as syntactic structures generated by the grammar; the grammar takes no account of discourse, contextual, or other factors affecting interpretation and acceptability. The major consequence of the constraint of autonomy is the shift of interpretive labor from a context-free domain of semantics to a context-based domain of pragmatics, which takes over the majority of the interpretation of independent constituent utterances in context. Thus, the interaction between a competence model of grammar and a pragmatic model of interpretation is a modular one: the competence model accounts for the limited amount of the determinate semantic meaning of a nonsentential constituent structure; the pragmatic model accounts for the large amount of the indeterminate implicated meaning of an independent constituent utterance. A second implication of this work suggests that pragmatic models may be partially autonomous and partially modular. The partial autonomy of a pragmatic model establishes its differences from and connections to knowledge about the world: a pragmatic model specifically describes the interpretation of utterances, which is distinct from other operations of thinking and reasoning, yet these interpretations are crucially based on knowledge about the world; the pragmatic model developed here has interface points of contact between its operations and representations and external systems of knowledge. The partial modularity of a pragmatic model arises from differences in context, which correspond to the different types of inference resulting in different representation of meaning. Within the two submodules of the pragmatic model developed here, speakers use different kinds of information as the basis for inferences. The first submodule is defined as the submodule of linguistic context, which is constrained to discourse-based interpretation like that required for interpreting examples like (1b). The second submodule is defined as the submodule of conversational context, which incorporates the information-based interpretation required for interpreting examples like (1c). Functioning together, the two submodules contribute an account of the context-based interpretation of independent constituent utterances to the theory of nonsentential constituents.

Notes

Introduction

1. The use of the term 'constituent structure' to refer to syntactic structures dominated by major lexical categories as initial nodes may cause some initial confusion, since linguists are used to thinking of constituent structure as the representation of the internal structure of categories within a tree diagram or labeled bracketing of a sentence. My extension of the term, though, is theoretically justifiable because constituents within sentences and nonsentential constituents are the same grammatical constructs: major lexical categories such as NP, VP, ADJP, and so on, are constituents within sentences as well as independent nonsentential constituents. To help maintain this distinction at the risk of some wordiness, I preface my use of the term 'constituent structure' with the word 'nonsentential' when I am referring to those syntactic structures dominated by a major lexical category as their initial node.

2. I use the terms 'constituent structures' and 'constituent utterances' in an attempt to maintain a principled distinction between the domain of grammar and the domain of pragmatics. The term 'nonsentential constituent structure' is a grammar-internal one, referring to syntactic structures dominated by a major lexical category initial node. The term 'independent constituent utterance' (or just 'constituent utterance') is within the domain of pragmatics; it refers to the use of an independent major lexical category within a specific context. In general, the terms 'meaning' and 'interpretation' encode a similar distinction between grammar and pragmatics. As used here, 'meaning' refers to the semantic representation of a constituent structure in an autonomous grammar; within a Chomskyan framework, this is limited to the representation of Logical Form. 'Interpretation' refers to a larger concept, broadly defined as the understanding of an utterance; this notion of understanding is within the domain of pragmatics because it is the result of inferences based on information from a variety of contextual sources.

3. Chomsky, of course, was not the only person to suggest that the concept of competence extends to domains other than grammar and that one of these domains is the use of language in context. Dell Hymes (1964, 1972, 1974), for example, proposes the concept of communicative competence, defining it as the ability to use language appropriately in sociocultural situations, an idea which seems to have informed Chomsky's later definitions of pragmatic competence.

4. Most researchers working in the area of pragmatics agree that the notion of inference is somehow central to an account of pragmatic interpretation. For similar comments on the centrality of inference from a variety of theoretical approaches to pragmatics, cf. Thomason 1977; Morgan 1981; Gumperz 1982; Fodor 1983; Joshi, Webber and Sag 1981; and Sperber and Wilson 1986.

5. In this representation, I provide only the relevant details of an interpretation within the submodule of linguistic context; in Chapter Four, I discuss the representation of linguistic context in more detail.

6. In this representation, I provide only the relevant details of an interpretation within the submodule of conversational context; in Chapter Five, I discuss the representation of conversational context in more detail.

7. Discourse sequences drawn from the Watergate conversations are taken from the 1974 Dell paperback edition of *The Presidential Transcripts*, which was prepared by the staff of the *Washington Post*; this reference is abbreviated as *Transcripts* 1974, in the text. Discourse participants in these conversations are identified by their initials:

    P: President Richard Nixon
    D: John W. Dean, Counsel to the President
    H: H. R. Haldeman, White House Chief of Staff
    E: John D. Ehrlichman, Assistant to the President for Domestic Affairs
    M: John M. Mitchell, U. S. Attorney General
    K: Richard G. Kleindienst, U. S. Attorney General (succeeding Mitchell)
    HP: Henry E. Petersen, Assistant U. S. Attorney General
    LH: Lawrence M. Higby, Deputy Assistant to the President

    Other figures associated with Watergate and mentioned in examples include the following:

    Thomas P. (Tip) O'Neill (D. MA), Speaker of the U.S. House of Representatives
    Senator Sam J. Ervin (D. NC), Chairman of the Senate Watergate Committee
    Senator Howard H. Baker (R. TN), Vice Chairman of the Senate Watergate Committee
    John J. Sirica, Federal Justice
    Charles W. Colson, Special Counsel to the President
    E. Howard Hunt, Jr., Assistant to Charles Colson
    Frederick C. LaRue, Committee to Re-Elect the President
    G. Gordon Liddy, Committee to Re-Elect the President
    Jeb S. Magruder, Committee to Re-Elect the President
    Robert C. Mardian, Committee to Re-Elect the President
    James W. McCord, Committee to Re-Elect the President
    Maurice Stans, Committee to Re-Elect the President

Chapter 1

1. In the literature, the use of the terms 'autonomy' and 'modularity' to describe models (of grammar, of pragmatics, etc.) has not been consistent. An autonomous model is one that is informationally independent and internally motivated as described in §1.1. Some researchers (e.g., Fodor 1983) call an autonomous grammar a module because of its self-contained nature; Harnish and Farmer call this "externally modular" (1984: 257). The concept of modularity is discussed in §1.2; briefly, modularity refers to the internal organization of a model into independent (modular) subsystems; modularity also refers to the interaction a set of independent systems or subsystems. Some researchers (e.g., Sadock 1983, whose work is discussed in §1.2) call this view of organization and interac-

tion strong autonomy. In this work, I use the term 'autonomy' to refer to an independent, internally motivated model; I use the term 'modularity' to refer to the internal organization of a model or to the interaction within and between models.

2. Since this goal necessarily limits the scope of the pragmatic model to be developed here, I will not draw upon a great deal of interesting work in pragmatics under a broader definition, including work in conversation analysis (cf. the overview remarks in Schegloff 1981, 1988; and Schiffrin 1988, a review article with an extensive bibliography); sociolinguistics (cf. Wardhaugh 1985; Gumperz 1982; Stubbs 1983; Goffman 1981); or speech act theory (cf. Bach and Harnish 1979; Searle 1969, 1975, 1979; Labov and Fanshell 1977), even though an analysis of independent constituent utterances within these frameworks surely would be interesting and revealing.

3. A fuller discussion of the internal modularity of a Government-Binding grammar is in Chapter Three.

4. As a counterexample to the subhypothesis of Formal Distinctness, Sadock points out that the two hemispheres of the brain are formally similar, yet their functions are quite different. As a counterexample to the subhypothesis of Sharpness of Boundaries, Sadock mentions the atmosphere of the earth and outer space, two separate systems with no distinct boundary. Sadock does not provide a specific counterexample to the subhypothesis of Interactional Simplicity, merely noting that "complex mechanisms of feedback and control are operative among the systems of living things." Finally, as a counterexample to the hypothesis of Submodularity, Sadock notes that the human body consists of submodules like the eye; the eye itself, though, has some non-modular subparts like the aqueous humor (1983: 199-200). Since Sadock's examples here are non-linguistic, it is not clear what relevance they have in terms of the assumption of modularity within linguistic theory.

5. Not all linguists would agree that the semantic and phonological components are strongly autonomous. Ratliff (1986), for example, cites sound symbolism in Hmong as an example of phonological properties that are meaning-bearing; Rhodes and Lawler (1981) and Rhodes (1986) make a similar argument for English and other languages.

Chapter 2

1. These examples and their explanations are presented within the Standard Theory framework; few details of such Standard Theory analyses are still accepted in current research in generative grammar. In particular, the Interrogative Transformation illustrated in (2b) is one which underwent significant changes almost immediately after its introduction and initial discussion in Chomsky (1964).

2. The exact definition of syntactic identity became a significant controversy in research during the late 1960s (cf. Ross 1967, 1969; Grinder and Postal 1971; Dahl 1973). Later developments in Extended Standard Theory, however, particularly Sag's (1976) proposal that identity for the purpose of deletion is defined at the level of Logical Form rather than at any syntactic level, make much of the literature on syntactic identity obsolete, so the definition of identity will not be discussed here. Sag's work is discussed later in §2.1 and in note 4 below.

3.   The formal arguments supporting a Condition of Recoverability began with the work of Lees, who suggested that segregating deletion rules to the end of the grammar would partially solve the problem of decidability: "Moreover, if all elliptical rules could be placed last, the grammar preceding them would then be decidable" (1960: 34). (Newmeyer (1986) notes that Lees' proposal reappears without acknowledgment in later work in generative grammar; cf. note 4 below.) G. Matthews (1961) also considered the issue of decidability in an article on machine translation. He examined sentences such as *John was frightened* with the deletion of the agent phrase *by something*, noting that restricting deletion to certain specified environments such as the deletion of an unspecified agent phrase restricts the grammar to generating a decidable set of sentences: the sentence *John was frightened* necessarily derives from *John was frightened by something* rather than deriving from an undecidable and infinite set through free deletion of agent phrases such as *John was frightened by the burglar, by the noise, by the man, . . .*

The empirical arguments supporting a Condition of Recoverability considered the operation of specific transformations. In one such argument concerning the Standard Theory transformation of Relativization, Chomsky demonstrates that a Condition of Recoverability allows grammatical relativization and blocks ungrammatical relativization in the sentences below:

(a)   Δ fired the man (the man persuaded John to be examined by a specialist)
[→ by Relativization]
Δ fired the man who persuaded John to be examined by a specialist
[→ by Passive]
the man who persuaded John to be examined by a specialist was fired

(b)   Δ fired the man (the boy persuaded John to be examined by a specialist)
(1965: 137-138)

In (a), Relativization can operate because the NPs are identical and the deletion (and substitution of *who*) is recoverable; in (b), however, Relativization is blocked because the NPs are not identical and the deletion of *the boy* would be unrecoverable. This particular analysis of Relativization is no longer accepted in current research; it does, however, illustrate Standard Theory argumentation in support of a Condition of Recoverability on Deletion.

Even though the details of these analyses are no longer generally accepted, this combination of formal and empirical arguments has proved strong enough to motivate the Condition of Recoverability on Deletion as a constraint on grammars through twenty-five years of subsequent research.

4.   Sag presents a variety of arguments supporting his theory of deletion based on identity at Logical Form; I summarize only one of the most convincing ones here. By analyzing the following set of sentences with quantifiers, Sag demonstrates the inadequacy of a syntactic version of VP Deletion:

(a)   Someone hit everyone.
(b) $(\exists x) (\forall y) [x \text{ hit } y]$
(c) $(\forall y) (\exists x) [x \text{ hit } y]$
(d)   Someone hit everyone, and then Bill hit everyone.
(e)   Someone hit everyone, but Bill didn't hit everyone.
(f)   Someone hit everyone, and then Bill did.
(g)   Someone hit everyone, but Bill didn't.
(1976: 57-61)

Sag points out that sentence (a) is ambiguous:

> First if there was some individual [A] who hit every individual in the relevant
> domain of discourse (with the possible exception of himself) [reading (b)], and
> secondly, if everyone (in the relevant domain of discourse) was hit by some-
> one, but not necessarily by the same person [reading (c)]. (1976: 58)

The (b) reading includes the universal quantifier within the scope of the existential quantifier; the (c) reading includes the existential quantifier within the scope of the universal
quantifier. Sentences (d) and (e) also admit both readings of the left conjunct. A transformation of VP Deletion based on a syntactic definition of identity would generate sentences (f) and (g) from sentences (d) and (e). But the ambiguity of the left conjunct disap-
pears in (f) and (g); the only reading possible is that one individual hit everyone in the relevant domain of discourse [reading (b)]. A syntactic definition of identity does not restrict
VP Deletion to operate only in sentences with reading (b) in the left conjunct because
syntactic representation within the transformational component does not indicate scope
of quantifiers. Sag's logical theory of deletion, however, predicts that sentences (f) and
(g) derive from sentences with reading (b) in the left conjunct because a logical definition
of identity constrains VP Deletion from operating unless the Logical Form representations of the VPs in the left and right conjuncts are identical, a situation that occurs with
reading (b) but not with reading (c), so the lack of ambiguity in sentences (f) and (g) is
explained. Sag's statement of the rule of VP Deletion utilizes Logical Form as the relevant level for a definition of identity:

> With respect to a sentence S, VP Deletion can delete any VP in S whose rep-
> resentation at the level of Logical Form is [identical with] another [VP] present
> in Logical Form of S. (1976: 105-106)

Commenting on his proposed shift to a definition of identity using Logical Form representation, Sag says: "Now surely in some sense, 'sameness of meaning' is what all the previous discussions of deletion identity conditions have been trying to get at" (1976: 92).

5. In spite of fairly widespread agreement that deletion rules probably are general state-
    ments, researchers continue to talk about specific deletion rules, especially VP Deletion.
    Most often, this is a convenient way to focus on a particular construction rather than a
    theoretical statement that such a specific rule exists. This also reflects the fact that a com-
    prehensive theory of deletion has not been worked out within the current framework of
    Government-Binding, as pointed out by van Riemsdijk and Williams (1986: 141, 160).

6. The details of these transformational analyses are no longer generally accepted in current
    research on generative grammar. At the time Morgan was writing, though, presenting
    analyses based upon the necessary application of transformations was an accepted form of
    argumentation.

7. Napoli uses the term 'base-generated' to describe nonsentential major lexical category
    structures dominated by major category initial nodes; I, too, have used this term in the
    past (cf. Barton 1986a,b; 1987). Steven Lapointe (personal communication) has pointed
    out, however, that the technical term 'base-generated' refers to a structure generated by
    the base and then not changed by any operations within the transformational component.
    This description, though, does not apply to all nonsentential constituent structures since
    movement can occur within nonsentential constituents; for example, in the nonsentential
    structure *the rumor that Nixon is likely t to fire his entire staff*, NP-movement has taken

place (cf. §3.2 for a brief discussion of movement within nonsentential constituent structures). Consequently, I no longer use the term 'base-generated' to refer to nonsentential constituent structures dominated by a major lexical category initial node.

8.   In Chapter Two, I use the nonformal abbreviations NP, VP, ADJP, ADVP, and PP for major lexical categories, ignoring for now the question of whether ADVP is a major category. I also use the general term 'major category' to refer to the set of these categories, ignoring for now the question of whether any other non-lexical categories such as S or S' are defined as major categories. In Chapter Three, I discuss nonsentential constituent structures using the more precise notation and definitions of X-bar theory. I also discuss the status of ADVP and the relationship between major lexical categories and major non-lexical categories within the total set of major syntactic categories generated by a grammar.

9.   In the literature, there is one additional analysis that could account for fragments. At the same time that Sag (1976) proposed a rule of VP Deletion based on identity at Logical Form (cf. §2.1 and note 4 above), Williams (1977) proposed a rule of VP Copying, which operates on incomplete S-structures to create full Logical Form representations. Sag and Williams offer different, yet similar, analyses of B's sentence with a missing VP:

(a)   A: Who can do it?
        B: John can.

In Sag's theory, the structure *John can* would derive from the complete sentence *John can do it*. At S-structure, the VP *do it* would be deleted under Logical Form identity with the VP *do it* in the question. In Williams' theory, the structure *John can* would derive from the complete sentence *John can [VP Δ]*. At Logical Form, the empty VP would be filled in with a copy of the VP *do it* from the VP in the question. These analyses differ in their specific mechanisms: Sag proposes a deletion rule while Williams proposes a copying rule. These analyses are similar, though, in one crucial way: both rules require identity at Logical Form to trigger their operation. By incorporating identity into their theories, both Sag and Williams preserve the Condition of Recoverability.

Although the rule of VP Copying is, strictly speaking, an instance of anaphora rather than ellipsis, Williams' work is relevant to an overview of deletion and to a consideration of fragments because he attempts to replace a deletion analysis for missing VPs and because his work could be extended in an attempt to account for independent major lexical category structures as fragments. Consider one of the examples from the text above:

(b)   A: What happened in 1974?
        B: A scandal in the White House.

Although Williams himself does not make any specific claims regarding copying rules as an explanation for fragments, in an extension of his general framework the NP *a scandal in the White House* would be the only lexically filled constituent in a sentential S-structure; deltas would fill the lexical nodes of the empty portions of the sentence. A copying rule would then build the full sentence Logical Form representation in (c) by filling in the deltas with a copy of the VP from the Logical Form representation of the question:

(c)   A scandal in the White House (happened in 1974).

For the purposes of this work, Williams' copying analysis is merely a notational variant of Sag's ellipsis analysis since both analyses are alike in two fundamental ways: first, they assume that fragments are derived from full sentence sources, and second, they require identity at Logical Form to trigger the operation of ellipsis or copying rules. In the remainder of this book, I argue explicitly against the ellipsis analyses of Morgan and Sag; the arguments should, however, hold against the extension of Williams' copying analysis.

10. In this chapter, I present only a nonformal representation of the relevant details of syntactic structure.

11. In Chapter Three, I present a more formal description of the conditions governing the grammatical well-formedness of nonsentential constituent structures.

12. These examples, especially (17a), (17b), and (17c), will be used throughout the book in order to illustrate grammatical derivation and pragmatic interpretation within the theory of nonsentential constituents.

13. The absence of a determiner within the nonsentential constituent structure NP *old grudge* is discussed in §3.1.3.

Chapter 3

1. The version of GB I use to develop the competence model of nonsentential constituent structures is that presented in Chomsky's *Lectures on Government and Binding* (1981) and *Some Concepts and Consequences of the Theory of Government and Binding* (1982). Where relevant, chiefly in the discussion of X-bar theory, I have incorporated recent revisions from *Knowledge of Language* (1986a) and *Barriers* (1986b). I also have drawn upon lecture notes from a course on GB given by Rizzi (1987) at the 1987 Linguistic Institute, Stanford University. For updated discussion, cf. Barton (forthcoming).

2. In GB, the combination of the Projection Principle and the Predication Principle as the conditions that describe a well-formed sentence developed out of an earlier concept called the Extended Projection Principle, which included the Projection Principle plus a statement of the base rule expanding S (S → NP INFL VP), thereby stipulating that sentences must occur with subjects (Chomsky 1982: 10). Rizzi (1987) points out that the Predication Principle is a more significant theoretical statement because it explains why sentences have subjects: the Predication Principle ensures that the subject and predicate elements within a sentence are licensed so that the sentence structure satisfies the Principle of Full Interpretation at Logical Form.

3. There are several definitions of c-command in the generative grammar literature with major proposals in the work of Reinhart (1976, 1983) and Aoun and Sportiche (1983). In addition to the strong version of c-command presented in the text above, Sells also defines the weak version of c-command: "α c-commands β iff every maximal projection dominating α dominates β" (1985: 39).

He points out that the two definitions differ in their analysis of the VP structure of (2) in the text:

$$[_{V''} [_{V'} [_{V}] [_{N''}]] [_{P''}]]$$

In the weaker version of c-command defined here, V c-commands both N" and P" because the maximal projection dominating V, V", also dominates N" and P". In the stronger version of c-command in the text, V c-commands N" but not P". Rizzi (1987) points out that both definitions of c-command seem to be operative at different points in

GB theory (the strong version of c-command, for example, is operative in the explanation of the backward anaphora constraint in example (4) of §2.1). The differences between the two definitions, though, do not seem to play any crucial role in the grammar of nonsentential constituent structures, so I use the strong definition in the rest of this chapter.

4.   This background material has emphasized the interaction between the theory of GB and the grammars of individual languages because this relationship is of crucial importance in the development of the grammar of nonsentential constituent structures. For a comprehensive introduction that more fully explains the principles within each module of the theory of GB, see Sells (1985) or van Riemsdijk and Williams (1986). Chomsky has an article-length overview of GB theory in Hornstein and Lightfoot (1981).

5.   Although this argument holds for the order of complements within phrases, it is not clear whether the interaction of X-bar theory, the Projection Principle, and Case theory automatically accounts for the proper constraints on the order of modifiers within phrases.

6.   As it stands, Chomsky's schema for X-bar theory in (6) does not allow direct recursion of the head term (X" → X" or X'; X' → X' or X), although Hornstein and Lightfoot (1981) have argued that at least the category of NP requires such direct recursion.

Also, the schema could be misleading in one respect: while rules like those in (6) incorporate the constraint that a phrasal head X" must match its intermediate (X') and lexical (X) projections, it may indicate that specifiers and complements (X"*) also have to match the phrasal head, which is not correct. A modification of Chomsky's schema might be as follows:

$$X" \rightarrow Y"* \; X'$$
$$X' \rightarrow X \; Y"*$$

where X and Y = any major category

This schema explicitly allows specifiers and complements to be different from the head.

7.   Chomsky's extension of the X-bar principles as in (9) expands some earlier uses of the term 'major category', which usually referred only to the phrasal level of categories with a lexical head (XP). In the extended schema, Chomsky includes sentences and sentential complements, calling them major non-lexical categories. The generalization captured here is that the major syntactic structures of languages are sentences (INFL"), clauses (C"), and phrases (X"), all of which are unified under the term 'major categories' with a distinction between major lexical categories (X"), which have a lexical head, and major non-lexical categories (INFL" and C"), which do not have a lexical head. I use this extended terminology consistently throughout this work.

8.   The technically correct analysis of C" is that it is the initial node for both sentence structures and for sentential complements, following Bresnan's (1970) analysis of all sentence structures as COMP-S. Although C" is the initial node for all sentential structures, usually it is acknowledged as the initial node only when the matrix sentence has a topicalized constituent or a moved wh-phrase. I will conform to this usage, calling INFL" the initial node for a matrix sentence structure and calling C" the initial node for an embedded complement sentence structure.

It is possible, though, that C" could be the initial node for a nonsentential clausal structure. Such an hypothesis would explain many independent subordinate clauses, assuming that some subordinate clauses are of the structure COMP-S:

(a)   A: John doesn't know where the Library of Congress is.
       B: Whether he'll admit it or not.
       $[_{C''} [_{C'} [_C \text{ whether}] [_{INFL''} \text{ he'll admit it or not}]]]$
(b)   A: If only he would ask a police officer.
       $[_{C''} [_{C'} [_C \text{ if}] [_{INFL''} \text{ only he would ask a police officer}]]]$

Some speakers, though, find independent clausal structures with the complementizers *for* and *that* somewhat awkward (example (c) was suggested to me by James McCawley):

(c)   A: It was stated that someone is naming names.
       B: That John Dean is?
(d)   A: He said that he took drastic action in the cover-up of Watergate.
       B: For the FBI to stop the spread of scandal.

Many speakers, though, find both of these sequences perfectly acceptable. In looking for examples of independent clausal structures in *The Presidential Transcripts*, I did not find any independent *for*-clauses, but I did find numerous independent *that*-clauses as in the following examples:

(e)   E: I have a commitment to Ervin and Baker.
       P: That you won't discuss that?
(f)   D: He said, "Well, I was pushed without mercy by Magruder to get in there
          and to get more information. That the information was not satisfactory.
          That Magruder said, 'The White House is not happy with what we are
          getting'."
       (*Transcripts* 1974: 262, 103)

Even though it would be interesting to pursue this analysis of independent clausal structures further, I will not do so here since the focus of this work is on the contrast between sentence structures and nonsentential major lexical category constituent structures.

9.   I often use the expressions 'X'' as an initial node' and 'X^{max} as an initial node', though these expressions technically are incorrect as X is a variable in X-bar theory, not an actual node in any individual grammar. By using these expressions, though, I am taking advantage of the ability of the term X'' to refer to the set of major lexical categories in a language; I also am taking advantage of the ability of the term X^{max} to refer to the set of major syntactic categories in a language, a set that includes the major non-lexical categories INFL'' and C'' as well as the major lexical categories represented by X''.

10.   A more detailed discussion of the set of θ-roles in a GB grammar is in §4.1.1.

11.   In recent work, Chomsky and others debate the precise formulation of the Projection Principle; the most substantive change is that the Principle is now formulated in terms of chains of arguments and their positions (Chomsky, 1986a,b). These developments, though, do not substantially affect the proposals here, so I continue to use the version of the Projection Principle described above.

12.   In recent work, Chomsky and others have investigated the precise nature of the Predication Principle; one possible change is that the Principle is now formulated in terms of saturation conditions: INFL is ill-formed when it is "unsaturated" without a subject (Chomsky 1986a: 116). This formulation, however, does not substantially affect the proposals here, so I will continue to refer to the combination of the Projection Principle and the Predication Principle as the licensing conditions for sentence structures.

13. It is not clear exactly what kind of contrast there is between an imperative VP and a non-sentential constituent structure VP. If imperatives are generated with either full or empty nodes in the subject and INFL positions and deletion to an imperative still exists as an operation of the grammar, then an imperative is one more example of a structure that has undergone recoverable intrasentential deletion. Emonds, for one, suggests that such a deletion analysis still holds for imperatives (1985: 318). It also is possible, though, that imperatives are a special instance of nonsentential constituent structure VPs. The origin and derivation of an imperative VP, however, is an open question which I leave for future research; in the text above, I assume a deletion analysis of imperatives.

14. There is an interesting contrast between the imperative in (18c) and the nonsentential constituent structure VP in (18f), even though the surface form of both structures is the same. One possible test for distinguishing nonsentential constituent structure VPs from imperatives is an intonational one: nonsentential constituent structure VPs can occur with question intonation; imperative VPs, in contrast, cannot. Consider the contrast between the following two VPs:

   (a)   A: Do your homework!
   (b)   B: Do your homework?

The VP in (a) is an imperative command, the VP in (b), in contrast, could be described as an offer, a reminder, or a check upon whether the addressee has finished his or her homework. Whatever (b) is, though, with its question intonation, I do not believe that it is an imperative.

   The intonation of nonsentential constituents raises interesting questions. Yanofsky points out that initial NP utterances seem to occur with statement, question, and exclamatory intonation (1978: 500). In general, it seems that nonsentential constituents generally occur with intonational patterns of independent units rather than with patterns of phrasal units within larger sentence structures. The contrast between imperative VPs and nonsentential question VPs is one example; another example is the difference between the intonation and stress contours of a NP within a sentence as in (c) and its possible intonations as a nonsentential NP in (d):

   (c)   A: The White House staff has an old grudge against Tip O'Neill.
   (d)   A: The White House staff doesn't visit Tip O'Neill in his Congressional
             office.
          B: Old grudge.   (statement intonation)
          B: Old grudge?   (question intonation)
          B: Old grudge!   (exclamatory intonation)

I cannot, unfortunately, pursue these interesting questions here, but I believe that a study of the phonological properties of nonsentential constituents would be an interesting one.

15. Gregory Ward (personal communication) suggested this example.

16. At first, it might seem that Napoli's rule of phonological deletion (cf. §2.1) might be relevant here, generating a nonsentential NP like *Thief!* from *A thief!* or *The thief!* with deletion of the unstressed determiner. But Napoli's deletion rule has to be constrained by the Condition of Recoverability since it takes place within the grammar, and many nonsentential NPs do not have a recoverable determiner. Consider one of the sequences under discussion:

(a)   A: The White House staff doesn't visit Tip O'Neill in his Congressional office.
     B: Old grudge.

Here, the NP *old grudge* could be either indefinite (*an old grudge*) or definite (*the old grudge*), and deletion of the determiner cannot take place since it would not be recoverable (cf. note 17 below).

17.   This analysis is somewhat unsatisfactory because it does not explain why NPs within sentences do require a determiner with singular count nouns. The argument simply explains why nonsentential NPs are under no such restriction at D-structure by virtue of the licensing interaction between X-bar theory and the Projection Principle. Further explanation of the obligatory vs. optional status of determiners might arise from some combination of grammatical rules plus semantic and/or pragmatic factors having to do with reference. Although the presence of a determiner for a singular count noun in a sentence is obligatory by grammatical or semantic rule, the presence of a determiner within a nonsentential constituent structure NP seems to depend upon the reference of the NP in a discourse or pragmatic sense:

(a)   A: The White House staff doesn't visit Tip O'Neill.
     B: An old grudge.
(b)   B: The old grudge.
(c)   B: Old grudge.

In (a), the NP and its reference are indefinite, and in (b), the NP and its reference are definite. In (c), however, the NP is neither indefinite nor definite, so its reference is left open for a discourse interpretation.

    James McCawley (personal communication) offers a different discourse/pragmatic explanation of the discourse acceptability of nonsentential constituent structure NPs without determiners. He suggests that nonsentential constituent structure NPs without determiners seem best when the determiner is semantically empty; he sees a contrast in the acceptability of the following examples:

(d)   A: Mary is an alto.
     B: No, soprano.
(e)   A: John is dating a soprano.
     B: ?No, alto.

To McCawley, the NP without a determiner seems less acceptable in a discourse when the NP is specific; in other words, there is one specific alto in (e). Not all native speakers, however, agree with McCawley's judgments; many find both of the sequences in (d) and (e) acceptable. Gregory Ward (personal communication) suggests the following counterexample to (e):

(f)   A: John is dating a formal syntactician.
     B: No - formal semanticist.

18.   In some versions of GB, aspectual *have* and *be* are assumed to be part of INFL (cf. van Riemsdijk and Williams 1986: 274). Lapointe (1980), however, following Akmajian, Steele, and Wasow (1979), argues that these elements occur within the VP, an analysis which I will assume here. When the first aspectual verb is tensed, it appears in INFL; if it is untensed, it appears within VP.

19. For the purposes of this argument, the structures in (34) - (35) are analyzed as INFL', not S-structures that have undergone phonological deletion as in Napoli (1982). Phonological deletion might generate examples that are similar to these with the subject or subject plus INFL deleted:

(a) A: What does John do for a living?
   B: Plays baseball.
   (John) plays baseball.

(b) A: What does John do for a living?
   B: Playing baseball.
   (John is) playing baseball.

(c) A: Will he go to spring training this year?
   B: Leaving any day now.
   (He is) leaving any day now.

(d) A: I wonder whether he'll make the big leagues this year.
   B: Been wondering about that lately.
   (I have) been wondering about that lately.

These examples are not counterexamples to the argument in the text because the inflected forms of the verbs indicate that they derive from full sentence sources.

20. In this argument, I do not consider *do* as a marker of emphasis or as an element in an imperative.

21. Jackendoff's (1977a,b) proposal integrating S into the X-bar system by making it equivalent to the maximal projection of V is the most commonly cited analysis, although Jackendoff was not the only person to suggest this. Bresnan (1976b); Koster (1978); and van Riemsdijk (1978) all offered similar analyses of S as a bar projection of V. Hornstein (1977) argues against Jackendoff's proposal by showing that a separate set of rules for S is necessary to account for the distribution of negative elements, which differs across phrases and sentences. Marantz (1980) supports Jackendoff's claim, arguing that making S equivalent to V^{max} explains the parallel distribution of subjectless VPs like gerunds and embedded sentences as well as the distribution of negative elements (*contra* Hornstein).

There has been much research on the status of the category sentence in X-bar theory within other syntactic theories. Modifying a proposal suggested by Gazdar (1982), in which S and S' are instances of V" with the contrasting feature of [±Complementizer], Borsley (1983) presents a GPSG analysis in which VP and S are the same category with different features: VP is [-Subject] while S/S' is [+Subject] and S' is [+Complementizer]. This is the GPSG analysis reviewed in Sells (1985: 81-82). In her work on Lexical Functional Grammar, Bresnan (1982) suggests that S is not integrated into X-bar theory because it is an exocentric category, not the projected from any lexical category; this analysis, too, is reviewed in Sells (1985: 139-140). McCloskey (1983) provides arguments in support of Bresnan's position with an analysis of Irish as a VSO language.

In the text above, I, too, argue against Jackendoff's proposal, although my arguments will be based upon a consideration of nonsentential constituent structures in comparison to sentence structures within the framework of GB.

22. Jackendoff uses the term 'complement' to refer to obligatory complements at the single-bar level as well as modifiers of different types at double or triple-bar levels. In my discussion of Jackendoff, I use the more neutral term 'expansion' to refer to the total set of complements and modifiers, restricting the term 'complement' to obligatory selections at

the single-bar level. In this discussion of Jackendoff, I use the abbreviations NP and VP instead of the more precise N" and V" as the initial node of nonsentential constituent structures. This is to avoid confusion with Jackendoff's system in which a triple-bar V''' or N''' is a maximal projection.

23. The examples in this discussion are slightly modified forms of Jackendoff's original examples (1977b: 57ff.).

24. These examples were suggested by Steven Lapointe (personal communication).

25. In what follows in the text, I offer some preliminary arguments for including the category ADVP into the set of major categories. This analysis is tentative, though, because I do not go on to consider the category of ADVP in terms of any feature matrix. A full analysis of the status of ADVP with respect to a feature matrix I leave as an open issue for future research.

26. This constraint restricting the participating categories in X-bar theory to major categories already exists in the theoretical framework of Generalized Phrase Structure Grammar (GPSG). Sells points out that GPSG incorporates the following stipulation:

A category C is a minor category iff C (BAR) is undefined.
(1985: 83)

For major categories, namely, nouns, verbs, adjectives, and prepositions, the feature BAR = 2 (for maximal projections), which has the effect of eliminating minor categories from participating in X-bar theory.

27. In the brief analysis that follows, I discuss determiners as the sole example of a minor category because it is a relatively uncontroversial example of a minor category in English.

28. In these examples, *this* and *these* are assumed to be instances of determiners and not pronouns. Both forms would be grammatical as instances of independent pronouns dominated by the initial node of NP as in sequences like the following:

    (a)   A: What smells?
            B: This. (holding up a skunk)
    (b)   A: What smells?
            B: These. (holding up a cage with several skunks)

Also, Gregory Ward (personal communication) points out that in some instances, determiners do occur as independent utterances. One instance is the mention of a determiner as a name as in examples like the following sequence:

    (c)   A: Name a three letter determiner in English.
            B: *The.*

In this instance, the determiner is actually a NP (Lyons 1977: 5-10). Another instance is the repetition of a determiner in an echo:

    (d)   A: John is the expert around here.
            B: The?

Echoes can copy any part of a previous utterance (McCawley 1987; Tannen 1987).

29. Pullum (1985) excoriates much work on X-bar theory within the GB framework, especially the claim that X-bar theory restricts the set of possible base systems to a finite number (as, e.g., proposed in Chomsky 1981, 1986a). He then presents a series of possi-

ble conditions on X-bar theory and discusses their mathematical implications. He also discusses some aspects of X-bar theory within the GPSG framework. In the text above, I discuss only the set of conditions explicated by Pullum.

30. In §3.2 and 3.3, I provide only the relevant details of syntactic structure; in addition, for ease of representation and exposition, I sometimes use the conventional abbreviations S and S' for INFL" and C" and NP, VP, etc. for N", V", and so on.

31. Case interacts in intricate ways with movement and Binding within the theory of GB, but most of these interactions are more relevant for sentence structures than for nonsentential constituent structures. The brief outline of the rules and principles of Case theory presented above should serve as sufficient background for a consideration of Case in terms of the S-structure representation of nonsentential constituent structures. For a fuller discussion of Case, see Stowell (1981); Koopman (1984); and Travis (1984).

Some recent research has attempted to subsume the Case Filter under θ-theory, particularly if the θ-Criterion is reformulated in terms of chains (Chomsky 1986a,b). Other recent research has attempted to reformulate the Case Filter in terms of visibility and the Principle of Full Interpretation: a NP is visible in the phonological component of the grammar only if it has Case; a NP without Case violates the Principle of Full Interpretation because it is not licensed in the phonological component (Rizzi 1987). These proposals, however, do not significantly affect the following discussion of Case in relation to nonsentential constituent structures.

32. Even though it is not a general pattern, some speakers also use the first person singular nominative case as an independent form even when the discourse interpretation of the pronoun is not that of an agent:

    (a)   A: John gave a book to someone.
              B: ?I
    (b)   A: Who did John give a book to?
              B: ?I

Native speaker judgments vary considerably, however, with regard to first person plural and third person independent pronouns in the nominative case when the discourse interpretation is not that of an agent. Very few speakers agree that the pronouns within the sequences in (c) - (e) are well-formed:

    (c)   A: Who did John give a book to?
              B: ??He/She
    (d)   B: ??We
    (e)   B: ??They

Native speakers differ considerably in their reactions to the nominative case examples in (a) - (e). Many, if not most, speakers judge all of these pronouns to be completely ungrammatical.

For some reason, though, an independent first person singular form as in (a) or (b) is most acceptable to those native speakers who accept any of the pronouns in (a) — (e). One use of an independent first person form without regard to the discourse interpretation of the pronoun can be a stylistic variant for the purposes of emphasis. I have heard the independent first person nominative form used by young black and white speakers in Detroit in sequences like the following:

(f)   A: She gave that to *someone*. (heavy stress on *someone*)
       B: I. (heavy stress)

Some hypercorrection may be involved in the varying judgments concerning the acceptability of the independent use of the first person singular nominative, especially if speakers
are being influenced by fuzzy recall of prescriptive rules about the use of *I* vs. *me*:

(g)   A: Who is it?
       B: It is I.
(h)   A: Who is it?
       B: It's me.

Prescriptive grammars claim that only the form in (g) is grammatically correct because
predicate nominals are in the nominative case (cf., for example, Follett 1966; Quirk et al.
1972). Almost all native speakers of English, however, use the form in (h), and many
speakers use the objective form in (h) more often than the form in (g), especially if the
pronoun is an independent one:

(i)   A: Who is it?
       B: Me.

There is a fair amount of confusion, however, about the prescriptive rules for the correct
use of first person pronouns, as many linguists point out when they are attempting to
demonstrate the distinction between prescriptive and descriptive grammars (cf. Akmajian, Demers, and Harnish 1984). The descriptive grammar of nonsentential constituent
structures, though, must be able to generate both nominative and objective pronouns as
independent structures because speakers actually produce both forms (cf. the discussion
of examples (65) - (68) above).

33.   This argument could be strengthened by considering languages with more elaborate mor-
       phological case systems than the case system of English. In a language like Russian, for
       instance, with multiple cases for both nouns and pronouns, it would be impossible to
       specify a workable set of rules for an autonomous grammar to generate just those pro-
       nouns that are acceptable in a variety of discourse sequences; again, the best solution
       seems to be to allow the grammar to generate pronouns in any morphological case and
       allow the pragmatic component of a theory to mark particular examples as acceptable or
       unacceptable within specific discourse sequences.

34.   For a speaker whose dialect or idiolect does not allow any independent pronouns except
       in the objective form, there could be a marked version of the Case Rule for NP Con-
       stituent Structures:

       If N" is the initial node, then assign objective Case.

       I propose the more general rule assigning any Case above because it accounts for the
       attested examples of independent pronouns in the nominative, genitive, and objective
       cases. It is possible, however, that the marked Case Rule formulated here is more wide-
       spread than the general one in the text because there does seem to be a fairly strong pre-
       ference for the consistent use of objective forms as independent pronouns.

35.   Of the two aspects of Logical Form representation, the distribution of θ-marked argu-
       ments has received less attention in the literature, even though Chomsky has noted that
       at LF, "The fundamental notion is that of θ-role" (1981: 101). The fact that Logical Form
       representation describes the distribution of θ-marked arguments is crucial for the

interpretation of nonsentential constituent structures, although the precise reasons for this will not become clear until Chapter Four. Not all of the aspects of Logical Form with respect to anaphors, quantifiers, and empty categories, though, are relevant for a discussion of the semantic representation of nonsentential constituent structures. In this section, I discuss only anaphor/antecedent relations within Binding theory since the movement and relations of quantified expressions and their traces as well as the specification of the reference of empty categories basically describe sentence-based rather than constituent-based aspects of meaning.

36.   The situation with regard to independent reflexive pronouns appears to be undergoing some kind of stylistic change in English: in certain instances, reflexives are used as R-expressions. As in the case of independent first person nominative pronouns (cf. note 32 above), some hypercorrection may be involved in the use of a reflexive as an R-expression as in the following attested examples:

(a)   When you come in, just ask for myself.
(b)   She invited John and myself.

There are other instances, though, in which R-expression reflexives seem to occur as an emphatic form. Such independent reflexives occur without antecedents in sayings as in the following attested example:

(c)   A: That shouldn't happen to anybody.
       B: Especially to a nice person like myself.

The use of a reflexive pronoun without an antecedent also appears to be a viable stylistic alternative for speakers who use the independent reflexive to convey the fact that the referent of the pronoun is somehow larger than life. Consider the following exchange in which I (EB) bring a copy of *Barriers* into my office which I share with another linguist (SL):

(d)   EB: I just bought a new book on GB.
       SL: By whom?
       EB: Himself.

Because my colleague knows that Chomsky is the central figure in GB, and, in general, is (arguably) a larger than life figure in the field of linguistics, he should be able to identify the referent of the pronoun and the author of the book as Noam Chomsky. A similar example is in a quote from an interview with the TV talk show hostess Oprah Winfrey:

(e)   When they told me *60 Minutes* was coming and it was going to be himself — Mike Wallace — I said, "Lordy be . . . is there something the matter with my taxes? (quoted in "Lessons We Can Learn from TV's Female Superstars," *New Woman* July, 1987)

Although Winfrey immediately identifies the referent of *himself* as Mike Wallace, identification does not always seem to be necessary. The following attested example is from an exchange between two members of an English department; Professor A is holding a copy of Michel Foucault's *The Order of Things*, and Professor B says, during a discussion of a point of literary criticism:

(f)   And what does himself have to say about it?

The independent reflexive refers to Foucault, the author of the book Professor A was carrying and the critic most championed by Professor A in his work and teaching. Another attested example is from a conversation between two professors discussing the Pope:

(g)   I don't know how many people will actually lay eyes upon himself.

In these latter two examples, explicit identification of the reflexive does not seem neces-sary, although the two speakers, being literary scholars, might be using the independent reflexive as a form of language play upon the archaic usage of the third person masculine singular reflexive as a pronoun referring to the master or head of a household, to some other socially important person, or to God. *Webster's New International Dictionary* (2nd ed.) cites the following archaic usage of *himself* as an antecedent of the head of a house-hold: *Himself ordered it*; the *Oxford English Dictionary* cites the following 19th century usage of *himself* with an elevated antecedent: *Neither did he mix with the crowd of populace: indeed he had much the appearance of being a himself, at least to the aggregation about him.* I am grateful to Dorothy Huson (personal communication) for pointing out this historical explanation of the use of a R-expression reflexive. I also am grateful to John Sherry (personal communication) for pointing out that the use of a R-expression reflexive is a common feature of Irish English as in the following example from the play *Riders to the Sea* by John Synge; two women are discussing a third woman who may have lost her husband in a drowning accident: "We're to find out if it's Michael's they are [some articles of clothing]; some time herself will be down looking by the sea" (1904: l. 10-11).

Chapter 4

1.   In the representations in Chapters Four and Five, I provide only the relevant details of structure. For convenience of reading, I use S and S' rather than INFL" and C"; I also use NP, VP, and so on for phrasal projections rather than N", V", or N^{max}, V^{max}. I place labels of θ-roles underneath the NP, PP, or *wh*-phrase that carries the role. If a θ-bearing element moves, I continue to place the label underneath that element; this is for the con-venience of reading representations only and does not indicate a position within the con-troversy of the assignment of a θ-role to one or another end in a chain.

2.   The term 'θ-role' is a grammar-internal one, referring to the role of a NP argument selected by a lexical element, usually a predicate. The term 'discourse role' is within the domain of the pragmatic model. It refers to the discourse function of an independent con-stituent utterance within the linguistic context.

3.   Within a Government-Binding framework, the principles of X-bar theory, for example, are structure-building; the θ-Criterion and Projection Principle, in contrast, are licensing principles.

4.   Brown and Yule point out that speakers have intuitions about where discourse sequences begin and end, decisions which often are based on their understanding of topic; they also point out such a pretheoretical notion of topic is powerful but difficult to define in any formal sense (1983: 69-70). With respect to the issues surrounding the demarcation of topics within discourse sequences (cf. Chapter 3 of Brown and Yule 1983; Keenan and Schieffelin 1976; Tyler 1978; Grimes 1981; Coulthard 1977; Shuy 1981; Venneman 1975; van Dijk 1977; de Beaugrande 1980; Reinhart 1982), an analysis of constituent utterances can contribute only positive evidence rather than any defining evidence. The fact that a constituent utterance interacts with another utterance within a structure of linguistic con-text might serve as evidence that one topic is under discussion because no instances of

interaction across intuitive topic boundaries have occurred in the discourse sequences that I have examined for this research, but this is certainly not a necessary feature of a topic unit within a discourse, nor does it contribute to describing the features that begin or end topic units within discourse.

5. I use ADVP as a default category label for discourse particles such as *yes, no, well*, and so on.

6. My notion of linguistic context is similar to other descriptions, such as Lewis' (1969) notion of previous discourse (discussed in Brown and Yule 1983: 41), or Hirschberg's definition of context (C_h) as temporally ordered sequences of utterances in the current discourse (1985: 9). One important difference between previous discussions and my discussion above is that I make explicit the relationship and interaction between a grammar and a linguistic context through the Principle of Linguistic Context. Another important difference is my conception of a structure of linguistic context as a dynamic construct, one that can be elaborated by means of the operation of Discourse Inference. My notion of linguistic context also differs significantly from definitions which claim that a context consists of a set of propositions, as, for example, in the work of Gazdar (1979) or Sperber and Wilson (1986). The notion of linguistic context in this work is utterance-based rather than proposition-based; cf. §4.2 for additional discussion of the differences between a proposition-based vs. an utterance-based accounts of pragmatic interpretation.

7. For a discussion of discourse anaphora, cf. Chapter 6 of Brown and Yule 1983; Halliday and Hasan 1976; Tyler 1978; Clark and Clark 1977; Bolinger 1979; Linde 1979; Reinhart 1983; Levinson 1987c; *inter alia*. For a discussion of pragmatic anaphora, cf. Hankamer and Sag 1976; Sag and Hankamer 1977. Later in §4.1.2 I discuss some aspects of discourse-based anaphora in which the pronoun conventionally follows its antecedent.

8. In the brief discussion in the text, I introduce the phenomenon of the specification of pronouns with constituent utterance NPs; I do not, however, fully explore the motivation for this phenomenon. Upon first reflection, it seems that speakers specify pronouns when they realize that they have used a pronoun without an antecedent or when they suspect that their interlocutors have not understood the reference of a pronoun. I believe, though, that the situation may be much more complicated because specification of pronouns occurs even when a pronoun should, theoretically, be interpretable within a linguistic context. Consider the larger discourse context for example (29b) in the text:

> H: . . . one thing you might consider is that O'Brien and Parkinson who are getting a little shaken now themselves are retained by the Committee . . .
> P: They aren't involved in the damn thing are they? O'Brien and Parkinson?
> (*Transcripts* 1974: 186)

Even though the NP *O'Brien and Parkinson* already exists in the discourse context and could potentially serve as the discourse antecedent for the pronoun *they*, the speaker still chooses to specify the pronoun. Some of my current research involves a closer examination of the motivation for the specification of pronouns with independent NPs.

9. Steven Lapointe (personal communication) suggests that I am covertly referring to properties of X-bar theory and D-structure rather than Logical Form in this discussion of independent constituent utterances that modify previous elements in the structure of linguistic context. A lexical entry in Logical Form, though, in addition to allowing access to selec-

tion possibilities for argument roles, allows access to expansion possibilities for modifiers. In support of this claim, I offer a brief discussion of the following examples:

(a)   A: What is John cutting down?
      B: The tree inside his property line.
      B: The tree between his cottage and the lake.

(b)   A: When will John cut down the tree?
      B: One day inside the next month.
      B: One day between Tuesday and Friday.

(c)   A: What is John cutting down?
      B: The tree above his property line.
      B: The tree across the street.
      B: The tree beside the lake.
      B: *The tree next week
      B: *The tree before the weekend
      B: *The tree during the coming month

(d)   A: When will John cut down the tree?
      B: One day next week.
      B: One day before the weekend.
      B: One day during the coming month.
      B: *One day above his property line
      B: *One day across the street
      B: *One day beside the lake

Although both head nouns seem to allow expansion with PP modifiers as a general property as in the examples of (a) and (b), this expansion is not completely general. The head noun *tree* allows expansion with PP modifiers of place, but not time, as shown in the examples of (c); the head noun *day* allows expansion with PP modifiers of time, but not place, as shown in the examples of (d). The type (and perhaps even form) of modifiers is part of the lexical entry for an item; this property, therefore, has to be a part of the Logical Form representation for a lexical item since the Projection Principle preserves such selection or expansion properties of lexical structure throughout a syntactic derivation (cf. §3.1). The operation of Discourse Inference in the pragmatic model, then, can draw upon this aspect of Logical Form representation as a potential match possibility in determining the discourse function of an independent constituent utterance functioning as a modifier.

10.   The examples in the following discussion include all of the sequences mentioned in §3.2 and §3.3 as examples of independent pronouns that require a specification of their discourse-based interpretation.

11.   Many others have noticed a general constraint that grammatically uninterpreted pronouns must receive an interpretation through discourse or pragmatic anaphora; cf. the references in note 7.

12.   Many of the examples in this subsection were suggested by Judy Levi (personal communication).

13.   Further discussion of the Relevance theory of Sperber and Wilson (1986) is in Chapter 5.

14.   The operation of Discourse Inference is not a type of conversational inference as described in Grice's later work (1975) because its operation is based on a limited amount of information, specifically, the information in the structure of linguistic context for an

utterance. Conversational inferences, in contrast, are based on information from a variety of sources beyond knowledge of discourse. Cf. Chapter 5 for discussion of an operation of inference that is not constrained by the linguistic context.

15.   I am indebted to Deirdre Wilson (personal communication) for suggesting examples like (51b).

16.   Gregory Ward (personal communication) suggested this example.

17.   Horn points out that the principles of least effort and sufficient effort have been suggested by a number of different researchers, citing the work of Zipf (1949) and its reappearance in Martinet (1962) *inter alia*; he also mentions the Minimax Principle of Tanenhaus and Carroll (1975) as a similar principle in psycholinguistics.

18.   The following quotations of the maxims are from Grice (1975: 45-46); the quotations describing the Q and R-Principles are from Horn's handout for the Pragmatics Seminar of the 1987 Linguistic Institute, Stanford University (Horn and Levinson 1987).

19.   Gazdar (1979) and Hirschberg (1985) also have extensive discussion of scalar and clausal implicatures.

20.   Levinson (1987a) provides full references to previous discussions of each of these categories of inference.

Chapter 5

1.   I do not mean to imply here that the Cooperative Principle is not applicable within the submodule of linguistic context in the pragmatic model; the operation of Discourse Inference does depend upon the assumption that speakers and hearers are acting cooperatively as they use and interpret constituent utterances that fit into the linguistic context. The operation of Discourse Inference, however, is generalized, so that it calculates discourse functions in any context. The Cooperative Principle has a more active role within the submodule of conversational context because the inferences that operate to interpret utterances at this submodule of the pragmatic model are particularized, which means that they require overt reference to the Cooperative Principle.

2.   I believe that Sperber and Wilson's most significant contribution to current research is their identification of relevance as central to pragmatic interpretation, which is an idea that I follow here. As is clear from my discussion of their work in §4.2, however, I do not agree with the nature of the theory that Sperber and Wilson have built from this idea, and I offer additional arguments against Sperber and Wilson in §5.2. In this work, I offer my own view of how relevance is operationalized in a theory of pragmatic interpretation. I acknowledge my indebtedness, though, to Sperber and Wilson's fundamental insight about the centrality of relevance in pragmatic interpretation.

3.   It is entirely possible that these four areas do not exhaust the domains of relevance; following Levinson's remarks about relevance (cf. quote in text), another obvious candidate for a domain would be relevance based on adjacency or some other notion of conversational interaction. The number and nature of additional domains of relevance is an open issue for future research; in this chapter, I limit myself to exploring the ability of the four domains listed in the text to serve as the basis for inferences interpreting independent constituent utterances within their conversational contexts.

4. This notion of indeterminacy as the possibility of different interpretations for an utterance is one specific type of indeterminacy, one that is theoretically interesting from the perspective of developing a pragmatic model of the interpretation of independent constituents. It is not, however, the only notion of indeterminacy; another kind of indeterminacy might include the variations and/or mismatches in speakers' intentions and hearers' interpretations; yet another kind of indeterminacy might arise from expressions that are ambiguous or misleading, whether deliberately or unintentionally. I do not specifically address other types of indeterminacy in this work, restricting my account of indeterminacy to the notion defined above.

5. Even in the supposedly determinate domain of grammar, working with native speaker intuitions often raises issues of indeterminacy. Chomsky (1981, 1986a) and Sells (1985), among others, have commented on the delicacy and fuzziness of native speaker intuitions, and van Riemsdijk and Williams note that there is no such thing as a generally accepted "methodology of sentence judgments" (1986: 2). The system of a grammar, however, is set up as a binary one in which a structure is either well-formed or ill-formed, even though this represents a considerable idealization. Newmeyer discusses the controversies surrounding the use of such introspective and idealized data, pointing out that it is historically and methodologically the standard form of data used in linguistic investigation (1983: 48-67).

6. Hymes also includes topic and message-form (genre) in his model of the context of situation (Brown and Yule 1983: 38); since these are text-related features rather than features connected with some aspect of the physical context, I eliminate them from the list of features within the domain of the physical context of situation. I discuss topic as a separate domain of relevance. I do not consider message-form at all since all of the examples in this work are from the single genre of casual conversational discourse.

7. This representation of Hymes' model of the context of situation is for the convenience of reading only. It is not meant as any indication of how knowledge of a context of situation might be represented in the minds of native speakers, but indicates only that the manifestation of these features of the physical context contains information that could be used in making cooperative inferences. For convenience in reading representations, I do not list the channel (spoken language) and code (English) common to all of the examples; also, I do not list audience unless it is relevant to a particular interpretation.

8. I am grateful to Dawn Bates for a discussion of the examples that illustrate the privileging of different domains of relevance.

9. In this section, I do not discuss any examples in which a speaker uses an independent constituent utterance in order to create a conversational implicature. As I mentioned above, I concentrate upon interpretation involving standing implicatures because this is the way in which the vast majority of constituent utterances are interpreted. Unfortunately, a full treatment of the ways in which speakers use constituent utterances to exploit the Cooperative Principle is beyond the scope of this book, and I leave this study to future research.

   In the discussion that follows, I concentrate upon interpretations based on information from the topic, from background knowledge, and from knowledge about the world because an analysis of the written *Transcripts* cannot provide examples for which I can accurately reconstruct the physical context of situation.

10. The criterion of a breakdown in communication as an indicator of an unacceptable utterance is similar to ideas proposed by Levinson (1985, 1987a,b) in his work in conversation analysis.

11. This definition of shared knowledge from Prince is not the only definition of this concept; she herself points out that the term has "given rise to great confusion" (1981: 232). Researchers in many different fields, including linguistics, philosophy, psychology, sociolinguistics, and artificial intelligence, have proposed definitions of the concept (cf. the Introduction to Smith, N. 1982; Clark and Marshall 1981). Some researchers even argue that the entire concept of shared knowledge is misleading and unnecessary in pragmatic theories (cf. Sperber and Wilson, 1986).

12. For further discussion of the pragmatic model with respect to other work on inference and context, cf. Barton 1989.

13. Although I have not developed a full critique of Sperber and Wilson's notion that pragmatic inference takes place through deductive logic, it is troubling for several reasons. First, a number of researchers, including Brown and Yule (1983) and Geis (1984), point out that discourse participants often do not seem to use deductive inferences as they work towards understanding an utterance or a discourse. Second, Levinson (1987) points out that one non-deductive characteristic of pragmatic inference is that it often functions to arrive at premises as well as conclusions. Finally, pragmatic inference, at least in the case of the interpretation of independent constituent utterances, seems to operate more closely in connection with a notion of discourse or conversational context rather than a set of deductive rules. Consider an example of interpretation from the submodule of linguistic context:

    (a)   P: Mitchell has given a sworn statement, hasn't he?
            D: Yes, Sir.
            P: To the Jury?
            D: To the Grand Jury.
            (*Transcripts* 1974: 105)

The PP constituent utterances are interpreted as functioning in the discourse role of Goal for the predicate *give* (cf. the discussion of this example as (10) in §4.1.1). But the connection between the constituent utterance and the previous utterance is language-based, not logic-based; there is no deductive connection between the utterances and their function. The inference takes place within a linguistic context rather than a logical context. The connections between independent constituent utterances and the conversational context also do not seem to be logic-based; in Chapter Five, connections include suggestions, reasons, generalizations, and so on; again, because they take place within a specific context, these connections seems information-based rather than logic-based.

14. Jerry Delahunty (personal communication) points out that a processing constraint within a theory is possible in principle. Pointing to the development of parallel processing in computer science, he notes that if a number of interpretations are processed in parallel, then the interpretation that "pops out" first is the one with the least processing cost. Sperber and Wilson, however, develop their concept of processing within a cognitive model rather than a computational model, so I believe that my criticisms in the text still stand.

References

Akmajian, A. and F. Heny.
   1975. *An Introduction to the Principles of Transformational Syntax*. Cambridge, MA: MIT Press.

Akmajian, A., S. Steele, and T. Wasow.
   1979. "The Category AUX in Universal Grammar". *Linguistic Inquiry* 10.1-64.

Akmajian, A., R. Demers, and R. Harnish.
   1984. *Linguistics: An Introduction to Language and Communication*. (2nd ed.) Cambridge, MA: MIT Press.

Aoun, J. and D. Sportiche.
   1983. "On the Formal Theory of Government". *The Linguistic Review* 2.211-236.

Atlas, J. and S. Levinson.
   1981. "It-Clefts, Informativeness, and Logical Form: Radical Pragmatics (Revised Standard Version)". Cole 1981.1-61.

Bach, K. and R. Harnish.
   1979. *Linguistic Communication and Speech Acts*. Cambridge, MA: MIT Press.

Baker, C.
   1979. "Syntactic Theory and the Projection Problem". *Linguistic Inquiry* 10.533-581.

Barton, E.
   1986a. "Interacting Models: Constituent Structures and Constituent Utterances". *Papers from the Parasession on Pragmatics and Grammatical Theory*, 140-151. Chicago: Chicago Linguistic Society.

Barton, E.
   1986b. "Levels of Representation in a Pragmatic Model". Paper presented to the 61st Annual Meeting of the Linguistic Society of America.

Barton, E.
   1987. "Domains of Relevance". Paper presented to the 62nd Annual Meeting of the Linguistic Society of America.

Barton, E.
   1989. "Autonomy and Modularity in a Pragmatic Model". *Papers from the Parasession on Language in Context*, 1-14. Chicago: Chicago Linguistic Society.

Barton, E.
    Forthcoming. "Nonsentential Constituents and Theories of Phrase Structure". To
        appear in *Views on Phrase Structure* ed. by D. Bouchard and K. Leffel. Dor-
        drecht: Kluwer.

Beaugrande, R. de.
    1980. *Text, Discourse, and Process*. London: Longman.

Bloomfield, L.
    1933. *Language*. New York: Holt, Rinehart and Winston.

Bolinger, D.
    1972. *Degree Words*. The Hague: Mouton.

Bolinger, D.
    1977. *Meaning and Form*. London: Longman.

Bolinger, D.
    1979. "Pronouns in Discourse". Givón 1979b.289-309.

Borsley, R.
    1983. "A Welsh Agreement Process and the Status of VP and S". Gazdar, Klein,
        and Pullum, 57-74.

Brame, M.
    1979. "A Note on COMP S Grammar vs. Sentence Grammar". *Linguistic Analysis*
        5.383-386.

Bresnan, J.
    1970. "On Complementizers: Toward a Syntactic Theory of Complement Types".
        Fundamentals of Linguistics 6.297-321.

Bresnan, J.
    1976a. "Evidence for a Theory of Unbounded Transformations". *Linguistic
        Analysis* 2.353-394.

Bresnan, J.
    1976b. "On the Form and Functioning of Transformations". *Linguistic Inquiry* 7.3-
        40.

Bresnan, J., ed.
    1982. *The Mental Representation of Grammatical Relations*. Cambridge, MA: MIT
        Press.

Brown, G. and G. Yule.
    1983. *Discourse Analysis*. Cambridge: Cambridge University Press.

Carnap, R.
    1939. "Foundations of Logic and Mathematics". *Foundations of the Unity of Sci-
        ence: Toward an International Encyclopedia of Unified Science* (1969) ed. by
        O. Neurath, R. Carnap, and C. Morris, 139-214. Chicago: University of
        Chicago Press.

Carston, R.
    1985a. "Saying and Implicating". Unpublished ms., University College of London.

Carston, R.
    1985b. "A Reanalysis of Some 'Quantity Implicatures'". Unpublished ms., University College of London.
Chafe, W.
    1970. *Meaning and the Structure of Language*. Chicago: University of Chicago Press.
Chomsky, N.
    1957. *Syntactic Structures*. The Hague: Mouton.
Chomsky, N.
    1964. "Current Issues in Linguistic Theory". *The Structure of Language: Readings in the Philosophy of Language* ed. by J. Fodor and J. Katz, 50-118. Englewood Cliffs, NJ: Prentice-Hall.
Chomsky, N.
    1965. *Aspects of the Theory of Syntax*. Cambridge, MA: MIT Press.
Chomsky, N.
    1970. "Remarks on Nominalization". *Readings in English Transformational Grammar* ed. by R. Jacobs and P. Rosenbaum, 184-221. Waltham, MA: Ginn.
Chomsky, N.
    1977a. *Essays on Form and Interpretation*. New York: Elsevier North-Holland.
Chomsky, N.
    1977b. "On Wh-Movement". Culicover, Wasow, and Akmajian 1977.71-132.
Chomsky, N.
    1980. *Rules and Representations*. New York: Columbia University Press.
Chomsky, N.
    1981. *Lectures on Government and Binding*. Dordrecht: Foris.
Chomsky, N.
    1982. *Some Concepts and Consequences of the Theory of Government and Binding*. Cambridge, MA: MIT Press.
Chomsky, N.
    1986a. *Knowledge of Language*. New York: Praeger.
Chomsky, N.
    1986b. *Barriers*. Cambridge, MA: MIT Press.
Chomsky, N. and G. Miller.
    1963. "Introduction to the Formal Analysis of Natural Languages". *Handbook of Mathematical Psychology* ed. by R. Luce, R. Bush, and E. Galanter, 269-321. New York: Wiley.
Clark, H. and E. Clark.
    1977. *Psychology and Language*. New York: Harcourt Brace Jovanovich.
Clark, H. and C. Marshall.
    1981. "Definite Reference and Mutual Knowledge". Joshi, Webber, and Sag 1981.10-63.

Cole, P., ed.
1978. *Syntax and Semantics*. Vol. 9: *Pragmatics*. New York: Academic Press.

Cole, P., ed.
1981. *Radical Pragmatics*. New York: Academic Press.

Cole, P. and J. Morgan, eds.
1975. *Syntax and Semantics*. Vol. 3: *Speech Acts*. New York: Academic Press.

Cooke, A.
1979. *The Americans: Fifty Talks on Our Lives and Times*. New York: Knopf.

Coulthard, M.
1977. *An Introduction to Discourse Analysis*. London: Longman.

Culicover, R., T. Wasow, and A. Akmajian, eds.
1977. *Formal Syntax*. New York: Academic Press.

Curme, G.
1931. *Syntax*. Boston: D. C. Heath.

Dahl, O.
1973. "On So-Called 'Sloppy Identity'". *Synthese* 26.81-112.

Dash, S.
1976. *Chief Counsel: Inside the Ervin Committee — The Untold Story of Watergate*. New York: Random House.

Dean, J.
1976. *Blind Ambition: The White House Years*. New York: Simon and Schuster.

Dijk, T. van.
1972. *Some Aspects of Text Grammars*. The Hague: Mouton.

Dijk, T. van.
1977. *Text and Context*. London: Longman.

Doyle, J.
1977. *Not Above the Law: The Battles of Watergate Prosecutors Cox and Jaworski*. New York: Morrow.

Emonds, J.
1985. *A Unified Theory of Syntactic Categories*. Dordrecht: Foris.

Ervin, S.
1981. *The Whole Truth: The Watergate Conspiracy*. New York: Random House.

Fauconnier, G.
1985. *Mental Spaces*. Cambridge, MA: MIT Press.

Fillmore, C.
1968. "The Case for Case". *Universals in Linguistic Theory* ed. by E. Bach and R. Harms, 1-90. New York: Holt, Rinehart and Winston.

Fillmore, C.
1975. *Santa Cruz Lectures on Deixis 1971*. Bloomington: Indiana University Linguistics Club.

Fillmore, C.
  1977. "The Case for Case Reopened". *Syntax and Semantics*. Vol. 8: *Grammatical Relations*. ed. by P. Cole and J. Sadock, 59-82. New York: Academic Press.

Firth, J. R.
  1957. *Papers in Linguistics*. London: Oxford University Press.

Fodor, J.
  1983. *The Modularity of Mind*. Cambridge, MA: MIT Press.

Foley, W. and R. Van Valin.
  1984. *Functional Syntax and Universal Grammar*. Cambridge: Cambridge University Press.

Follet, W.
  1966. *Modern American Usage*. New York: Hill and Wang.

Fowler, H.
  1926. *A Dictionary of Modern English Usage*. (2nd ed., 1965 rev. by E. Gowers). Oxford: Oxford University Press.

Gazdar, G.
  1979. *Pragmatics: Implicature, Presupposition and Logical Form*. New York: Academic Press.

Gazdar, G.
  1982. "Phrase Structure Grammar". *The Nature of Syntactic Representation* ed. by P. Jacobson and G. Pullum, 131-186. Dordrecht: Reidel.

Gazdar, G., E. Klein, and G. Pullum, eds.
  1983. *Order, Concord and Constituency*. Dordrecht: Foris.

Gazdar, G., E. Klein, G. Pullum, and I. Sag.
  1985. *Generalized Phrase Structure Grammar*. Cambridge, MA: Harvard University Press.

Geis, M.
  1984. "On Semantic and Pragmatic Competence". Schiffrin 1984.71-84.

Givón, T.
  1979a. *On Understanding Grammar*. New York: Academic Press.

Givón, T., ed.
  1979b. *Syntax and Semantics*. Vol. 12: *Discourse and Syntax*. New York: Academic Press.

Goffman, E.
  1981. *Forms of Talk*. Philadelphia: University of Pennsylvania Press.

Green, G. and J. Morgan.
  1979. "A Guide to the Study of Syntax". Unpublished ms., Department of Linguistics, University of Illinois at Champaign-Urbana.

Greenberg, J., ed.
  1963. *Universals of Language*. (2nd ed., 1966) Cambridge, MA: MIT Press.

Grice, H. P.
    1957. "Meaning". *Semantics* (1971) ed. by D. Steinberg and L. Jakobovits, 53-59.
           Cambridge: Cambridge University Press.
Grice, H. P.
    1968. "Utterer's Meaning, Sentence-Meaning, and Word-Meaning". Searle
           1971.54-70.
Grice, H. P.
    1975. "Logic and Conversation". Cole and Morgan 1975.41-58.
Grimes, J.
    1981. "Topics within Topics". Tannen 1981.164-176.
Grinder, J. and P. Postal.
    1971. "Missing Antecedents". *Linguistic Inquiry* 2.269-312.
Grossman, R., L. San, and T. Vance, eds.
    1975. *Papers from the Parasession on Functionalism*. Chicago: Chicago Linguistic
           Society.
Gumperz, J.
    1982. *Discourse Strategies*. Cambridge: Cambridge University Press.
Haldeman, H. R. and J. DiMona.
    1978. *The Ends of Power*. New York: Times Books.
Hale, K., L. Masayesva, and P. Platero.
    1977. "Three Cases of Overgeneration". Culicover, Wasow, and Akmajian
           1977.379-416.
Halliday, M. A. K.
    1973. *Explorations in the Functions of Language*. London: Edward Arnold.
Halliday, M. A. K.
    1978. *Language as a Social Semiotic*. London: Edward Arnold.
Halliday, M. A. K.
    1985. *An Introduction to Functional Grammar*. London: Edward Arnold.
Halliday, M. A. K. and R. Hasan.
    1976. *Cohesion in English*. London: Longman.
Hankamer, J.
    1973. "Unacceptable Ambiguity". *Linguistic Inquiry* 4.17-68.
Hankamer, J. and I. Sag.
    1976. "Deep and Surface Anaphora". *Linguistic Inquiry* 7.391-428.
Harnish, R. and A. Farmer.
    1984. "Pragmatics and the Modularity of the Linguistic System". *Lingua* 63.255-
           277.
Heim, I.
    1982. *The Semantics of Definite and Indefinite Noun Phrases*. Unpublished doc-
           toral dissertation, University of Massachusetts.

Hirschberg, J.
1985. *A Theory of Scalar Implicature.* Unpublished doctoral dissertation, University of Pennsylvania.

Horn, L.
1984. "Toward a New Taxonomy for Pragmatic Inference: Q-Based and R-Based Implicature". Schiffrin 1984.11-42.

Horn, L. and S. Levinson.
1987. Lectures for the Pragmatics Seminar, 1987 Linguistic Institute, Stanford University.

Hornstein, N.
1977. "S and X' Convention". *Linguistic Analysis* 3.137-176.

Hornstein, N.
1984. *Logic as Grammar.* Cambridge, MA: MIT Press.

Hornstein, N.
1986. "Pragmatics and Grammatical Theory". *Papers from the Parasession on Pragmatics and Grammatical Theory*, 234-247. Chicago: Chicago Linguistic Society.

Hornstein, N. and D. Lightfoot, eds.
1981. *Explanation in Linguistics: The Logical Problem of Language Acquisition.* London: Longman.

Hymes, D.
1964. "Toward Ethnographies of Communication: The Analysis of Communicative Events". *Language and Social Context* (1972) ed. by P. Giglioli, 21-44. Harmondsworth, Middlesex: Penguin.

Hymes, D.
1972. "Models of the Interaction of Language and Social Life". *Directions in Sociolinguistics: The Ethnography of Communication* ed. by J. Gumperz and D. Hymes, 35-71. New York: Holt, Rinehart and Winston.

Hymes, D.
1974. *Foundations in Sociolinguistics: An Ethnographic Approach.* Philadelphia: University of Pennsylvania Press.

Jackendoff, R.
1972. *Semantic Interpretation in Generative Grammar.* Cambridge, MA: MIT Press.

Jackendoff, R.
1977a. "Constraints on Phrase Structure Rules". Culicover, Wasow, and Akmajian 1977.249-283.

Jackendoff, R.
1977b. *X' Syntax: A Study of Phrase Structure.* Cambridge, MA: MIT Press.

Jesperson, O.
1924. *The Philosophy of Grammar.* London: George Allen and Unwin.

Jesperson, O.
  1933. *Essentials of English Grammar.* New York: Holt.
Jesperson, O.
  1949. *A Modern English Grammar on Historical Principles.* Vols. I - VII. London: George Allen and Unwin.
Johnson, M.
  1987. *The Body in the Mind: The Bodily Basis of Meaning, Reason and Imagination.* Chicago: University of Chicago Press.
Johnson-Laird, P.
  1983. *Mental Models: Towards a Cognitive Science of Language, Inference, and Consciousness.* Cambridge, MA: Harvard University Press.
Joshi, A., B. Webber, and I. Sag, eds.
  1981. *Elements of Discourse Understanding.* Cambridge: Cambridge University Press.
Kamp, H.
  1981. "A Theory of Truth and Semantic Representation". *Formal Methods in the Study of Language* ed. by J. Groenendijk et al., 277-322. Amsterdam: Mathematical Centre.
Katz, J. and J. Fodor.
  1963. "The Structure of a Semantic Theory". *Language* 39.170-210.
Kayne, R.
  1984. *Connectedness and Binary Branching.* Dordrecht: Foris.
Keenan, E. O. and B. Schieffelin.
  1976. "Topic as a Discourse Notion". *Subject and Topic* ed. by C. Li, 337-384. New York: Academic Press.
Kempson, R.
  1986. "Ambiguity and the Semantics-Pragmatics Distinction". *Meaning and Interpretation* ed. by C. Travis, 77-103. Oxford: Basil Blackwell.
Kempson, R.
  1988. "Grammar and Conversational Principles". Newmeyer 1988b.139-163.
Koopman, H.
  1984. *The Syntax of Verbs.* Dordrecht: Foris.
Koster, J.
  1978. *Locality Principles in Syntax.* Dordrecht: Foris.
Labov, W.
  1972. *Sociolinguistic Patterns.* Philadelphia: University of Pennsylvania Press.
Labov, W. and D. Fanshell.
  1977. *Therapeutic Discourse: Psychotherapy as Conversation.* New York: Academic Press.
Labovitz, J.
  1978. *Presidential Impeachment.* New Haven: Yale University Press.

Lakoff, G.
   1987. *Women, Fire and Dangerous Things: What Categories Reveal about the Mind*. Chicago: University of Chicago Press.

Lang, G. and K. Lang.
   1983. *The Battle for Public Opinion: The President, the Press, and the Polls During Watergate*. New York: Columbia University Press.

Lapointe, S.
   1980. "A Lexical Analysis of the English Auxiliary Verb System". *Lexical Grammar* ed. by T. Hoekstra, H. v. d. Hulst, and M. Moortgat, 215-254. Dordrecht: Foris.

Lees, R.
   1960. *The Grammar of English Nominalizations*. The Hague: Mouton.

Levinson, S.
   1983. *Pragmatics*. Cambridge: Cambridge University Press.

Levinson, S.
   1985. "What's Special about Conversational Inference?" Paper presented to the Annual Conference of the British Psychological Society.

Levinson, S.
   1987a. "Minimization and Conversational Inference". *The Pragmatic Perspective* ed. by J. Verschueren and M. Bertuccelli-Papi, 61-129. Amsterdam: John Benjamins.

Levinson, S.
   1987b. Lectures on Approaches to Interactive Discourse, 1987 Linguistic Institute, Stanford University.

Levinson, S.
   1987c. "Pragmatics and the Grammar of Anaphora". *Journal of Linguistics* 23.379-434.

Lewis, D.
   1969. *Convention: A Philosophical Study*. Cambridge, MA: Harvard University Press.

Linde, C.
   1979. "Focus of Attention and the Choice of Pronouns in Discourse". Givón 1979b.337-354.

Lyons, J.
   1968. *Introduction to Theoretical Linguistics*. Cambridge: Cambridge University Press.

Lyons, J.
   1977. *Semantics*. Vols. 1-2. Cambridge: Cambridge University Press.

Marantz, A.
   1980. "English S is the Maximal Projection of V". *Cahiers Linguistiques d'Ottawa* 9.303-314.

Marantz, A.
   1984. *On the Nature of Grammatical Relations*. Cambridge, MA: MIT Press.

242 NONSENTENTIAL CONSTITUENTS

Martinet, A.
1962. *A Functional View of Language*. Oxford: Clarendon Press.

Matthews, G.
1961. "Analysis by Synthesis of Sentences of Natural Languages". *First International Conference on Machine Translation*, 532-540. Teddington, England.

Matthews, P.
1981. *Syntax*. Cambridge: Cambridge University Press.

May, R.
1985. *Logical Form: Its Structure and Derivation*. Cambridge, MA: MIT Press.

McCawley, J.
1987. "The Syntax of English Echoes". *Papers from the Twenty-third Regional Meeting of the Chicago Linguistic Society*, 246-258. Chicago: Chicago Linguistic Society.

McCloskey, I.
1983. "A VP in a VSO Language?" Gazdar, Klein, and Pullum 1983.9-55.

Miller, G.
1977. "Practical and Lexical Knowledge". *Thinking: Readings in Cognitive Science* ed. by P. Johnson-Laird and P. Wason, 400-410. Cambridge: Cambridge University Press.

Morgan, J.
1973. "Sentence Fragments and the Notion 'Sentence'". *Issues in Linguistics* ed. by B. Kachru et al., 719-751. Urbana, IL: University of Illinois Press.

Morgan, J.
1981. "Discourse Theory and the Independence of Sentence Grammar". *Analyzing Discourse: Text and Talk* ed. by D. Tannen, 196-204. Washington, DC: Georgetown University Press.

Morris, C.
1938. "Foundations of the Theory of Signs". *Foundations of the Unity of Science: Toward an International Encyclopedia of Unified Science* (1969) ed. by O. Neurath, R. Carnap, and C. Morris, 77-138. Chicago: University of Chicago Press.

Napoli, D.
1982. "Initial Material Deletion in English". *Glossa* 16.85-111.

Newmeyer, F.
1983. *Grammatical Theory: Its Limits and Its Possibilities*. Chicago: University of Chicago Press.

Newmeyer, F.
1986. *Linguistic Theory in America*. (2nd ed.) New York: Academic Press.

Newmeyer, F., ed.
1988a. *Linguistics: The Cambridge Survey*. Vol. I: *Linguistic Theory: Foundations*. Cambridge: Cambridge University Press.

Newmeyer, F., ed.
   1988b. *Linguistics: The Cambridge Survey*. Vol. II: *Linguistic Theory: Extensions and Implications*. Cambridge: Cambridge University Press.

Newmeyer, F., ed.
   1988c. *Linguistics: The Cambridge Survey*. Vol. III: *Language: Psychological and Biological Aspects*. Cambridge: Cambridge University Press.

Newmeyer, F., ed.
   1988d. *Linguistics: The Cambridge Survey*. Vol. IV: *Language: The Socio-cultural Context*. Cambridge: Cambridge University Press.

Nunberg, G.
   1981. "Validating Pragmatic Explanations". Cole 1981.199-222.

Ochs, E.
   1979. "Transcription as Theory". *Developmental Pragmatics* ed. by E. Ochs and B. Schieffelin, 43-72. New York: Academic Press.

Peters, P. S. and R. Ritchie.
   1971. "On Restricting the Base Component of Transformational Grammars". *Information and Control* 18.483-501.

Peters, P. S. and R. Ritchie.
   1973. "On the Generative Power of Transformational Grammars". *Information Sciences* 6.49-83.

The Presidential Transcripts.
   1974. New York: Dell.

Prince, E.
   1981. "Towards a Taxonomy of Given-New Information". Cole 1981.223-255.

Pullum, G.
   1985. *Assuming Some Version of the X-Bar Theory*. Santa Cruz, CA: Syntax Research Center, Cowell College, University of California.

Pylshyn, Z.
   1984. *Computation and Cognition: Toward a Foundation for Cognitive Science*. Cambridge, MA: MIT Press.

Quirk, R., S. Greenbaum, G. Leech, and J. Svartvik.
   1972. *A Grammar of Contemporary English*. London: Longman.

Radford, A.
   1981. *Transformational Syntax: A Student's Guide to Chomsky's Extended Standard Theory*. Cambridge: Cambridge University Press.

Ratliff, M.
   1986. "Two Word Expressives in White Hmong". *The Hmong in Transition* ed. by G. Hendricks, B. Downing, and A. Deinard, 219-236. New York: Center for Migration Studies.

244 NONSENTENTIAL CONSTITUENTS

Reinhart, T.
1976. *The Syntactic Domain of Anapnora.* Unpublished doctoral dissertation, MIT.

Reinhart, T.
1981. "Definite NP Anaphora and C-command Domains". *Linguistic Inquiry* 12.605-635.

Reinhart, T.
1982. *Pragmatics and Linguistics: An Analysis of Sentence Topics.* Bloomington: Indiana University Linguistics Club.

Reinhart, T.
1983. *Anaphora and Semantic Interpretation.* Chicago: University of Chicago Press.

Rhodes, R.
1986. "Aural Images". Paper presented at the Conference on Sound Symbolism, University of California Berkeley.

Rhodes, R. and J. Lawler.
1981. "Athematic Metaphors". *Papers from the Seventeenth Regional Meeting of the Chicago Linguistic Society*, 318-342. Chicago: Chicago Linguistic Society.

Riemsdijk, H. van.
1978. *A Case Study in Syntactic Markedness.* Lisse: Peter de Ridder Press.

Riemsdijk, H. van and E. Williams.
1986. *Introduction to the Theory of Grammar.* Cambridge, MA: MIT Press.

Rizzi, L.
1987. Lectures on Government-Binding Theory, 1987 Linguistic Institute, Stanford University.

Rogoff, B. and J. Lave, eds.
1984. *Everyday Cognition: Its Development in Social Context.* Cambridge, MA: Harvard University Press.

Ross, J. R.
1967. *Constraints on Variables in Syntax.* Unpublished doctoral dissertation, MIT.

Ross, J. R.
1969. "Guess Who?" *Papers from the Fifth Regional Meeting of the Chicago Linguistic Society*, 252-286. Chicago: Chicago Linguistic Society.

Sadock, J.
1978. "On Testing for Conversational Implicature". Cole 1978.281-297.

Sadock, J.
1981. "Almost". Cole 1981.257-271.

Sadock, J.
1983. "The Necessary Overlapping of Grammatical Components". *Papers from the Parasession on the Interplay of Phonology, Morphology, and Syntax*, 198-221. Chicago: Chicago Linguistic Society.

Sadock, J.
    1984. "Whither Radical Pragmatics?" Schiffrin 1984.139-149.

Sag, I.
    1976. *Deletion and Logical Form*. New York: Garland.

Sag, I. and J. Hankamer.
    1977. "Syntactically vs. Pragmatically Controlled Anaphora". *Studies in Language Variation* ed. by R. Fasold and R. Shuy, 120-135. Washington, DC: Georgetown University Press.

Schegloff, E.
    1981. "Discourse as Interactional Achievement". Tannen 1981.71-93.

Schegloff, E.
    1988. "Discourse as Interactional Achievement II: An Exercise in Conversation Analysis". *Linguistics in Context: Connecting Observation and Understanding* ed. by D. Tannen, 135-158. Norwood, NJ: Ablex.

Schegloff, E., G. Jefferson, and H. Sacks.
    1977. "The Preference for Self-Correction in the Organization of Repair in Conversation". *Language* 53.361-382.

Schiffrin, D., ed.
    1984. *Meaning, Form, and Use in Context: Linguistic Applications*. Washington, DC: Georgetown University Press.

Schiffrin, D.
    1988. "Conversation Analysis". Newmeyer 1988d.251-276.

Searle, J.
    1969. *Speech Acts*. Cambridge: Cambridge University Press.

Searle, J., ed.
    1971. *The Philosophy of Language*. Oxford: Oxford University Press.

Searle, J.
    1975. "Indirect Speech Acts". Cole and Morgan 1975.59-82.

Searle, J.
    1979. *Expression and Meaning*. Cambridge: Cambridge University Press.

Searle, J.
    1986. "Introductory Essay: Notes on Conversation". *Contemporary Issues in Language and Discourse Processes* ed. by D. Ellis and W. Donohue, 7-19. London: Hillsdale, Erlbaum.

Sells, P.
    1985. *Lectures on Contemporary Syntactic Theories*. Stanford: Center for the Study of Language and Information.

Shuy, R.
    1981. "Topic as the Unit of Analysis in a Criminal Law Case". Tannen 1981.113-126.

Sirica, J.
1979. *To Set the Record Straight: The Break-in, the Tapes, the Conspirators, the Pardon.* New York: Norton.

Smith, M.
1983. *Watergate: An Annotated Bibliography of Sources in English 1972 - 1982.* Metuchen, NJ: Scarecrow Press.

Smith, N., ed.
1982. *Mutual Knowledge.* New York: Academic Press.

Sperber, D. and D. Wilson.
1986. *Relevance: Communication and Cognition.* Cambridge, MA: Harvard University Press.

Stalnaker, R.
1972. "Pragmatics". *Semantics of Natural Language* (2nd ed.) ed. by D. Davidson and G. Harman, 380-397. Dordrecht: Reidel.

Stillings, N., M. Feinstein, J. Garfield, E. Rissland, D. Rosenbaum, S. Weisler, L. Baker-Ward.
1987. *Cognitive Science: An Introduction.* Cambridge, MA: MIT Press.

Stowell, T.
1981. *Origins of Phrase Structure.* Unpublished doctoral dissertation, MIT.

Stowell, T.
1983. "Subjects across Categories". *The Linguistic Review* 2.285-312.

Stubbs, M.
1983. *Discourse Analysis.* Chicago: University of Chicago Press.

Sweet, H.
1900. *New English Grammar.* Oxford: Clarendon Press.

Synge, J.
1904. "Riders to the Sea". *Masterpieces of the Drama* (2nd ed., 1966) ed. by A. Allison, A. Carr, and A. Eastman, 507-518. New York: Macmillan Company.

Tanenhaus, M. and J. Carroll.
1975. "The Clausal Processing Hierarchy . . . and Nouniness". Grossman, San, and Vance 1975.499-511.

Tannen, D., ed.
1981. *Analyzing Discourse: Text and Talk.* Washington, DC: Georgetown University Press.

Tannen, D.
1987. "Repetition in Conversation: Toward a Poetics of Talk". *Language* 63.574-605.

Thomason, R.
1977. "Where Pragmatics Fits In". *Proceedings of the Texas Conference on Performatives, Presuppositions, and Implicatures*, 161-165. Arlington, VA: Center for Applied Linguistics.

Travis, L.
   1984. *Parameters and Effects of Word Order Variation*. Unpublished doctoral dissertation, MIT.

Tyler, S.
   1978. *The Said and the Unsaid*. New York: Academic Press.

Venneman, T.
   1975. "Topics, Sentence Accent, Ellipsis: A Proposal for their Formal Treatment". *Formal Semantics of Natural Language* ed. by E. Keenan, 313-328. Cambridge: Cambridge University Press.

Wardhaugh, R.
   1985. *How Conversation Works*. Oxford: Basil Blackwell.

WETA Public Broadcasting.
   1983. "Summer of Judgment: The Watergate Hearings". Washington, DC.

WETA Public Broadcasting.
   1984. "Summer of Judgment: The Impeachment Hearings". Washington, DC.

Williams, E.
   1977. "Discourse and Logical Form". *Linguistic Inquiry* 8.101-139.

Williams, E.
   1980. "Predication". *Linguistic Inquiry* 11.203-238.

Wilson, D. and D. Sperber.
   1981. "On Grice's Theory of Conversation". *Conversation and Discourse* ed. by P. Werth, 155-178. London: Croom Helm.

Wilson, D. and D. Sperber.
   1986. "Pragmatics and Modularity". *Papers from the Parasession on Pragmatics and Grammatical Theory*, 67-84. Chicago: Chicago Linguistic Society.

Woodward, B. and C. Bernstein.
   1974. *All the President's Men*. New York: Simon and Schuster.

Yanofsky, N.
   1978. "NP Utterances". *Papers from the Fourteenth Regional Meeting of the Chicago Linguistic Society*, 491-502. Chicago: Chicago Linguistic Society.

Zipf, G.
   1949. *Human Behavior and the Principle of Least Effort*. Cambridge: Addison-Wesley.

Zwicky, A.
   1984. "Autonomous Components and Limited Interfacing: Phonology-Free Syntax, the Hallean Syllogism, and their Kin". *Papers from the Twentieth Regional Meeting of the Chicago Linguistic Society*, 365-386. Chicago: Chicago Linguistic Society.

Index of Topics

Index of Names

In the PRAGMATICS AND BEYOND NEW SERIES the following titles have been published and will be published during 1990:

1. WALTER, Bettyruth: *The Jury Summation as Speech Genre: An Ethnographic Study of What it Means to Those who Use it.* Amsterdam/Philadelphia, 1988.
2. BARTON, Ellen: *Nonsentential Constituents: A Theory of Grammatical Structure and Pragmatic Interpretation.* Amsterdam/Philadelphia, 1990.
3. OLEKSY, Wieslaw (ed.): *Contrastive Pragmatics.* Amsterdam/Philadelphia, 1989.
4. RAFFLER-ENGEL, Walburga von (ed.): *Doctor-Patient Interaction.* Amsterdam/Philadelphia, 1989.
5. THELIN, Nils B. (ed.): *Verbal Aspect in Discourse: Contributions to the Semantics of Time and Temporal Perspectives in Slavic and Non-Slavic Languages.* Amsterdam/Philadelphia, 1990. n.y.p.
6. VERSCHUEREN, Jef (ed.): *Selected Papers from the 1987 International Pragmatics Conference. Vol. I: Pragmatics at Issue. Vol. II: Levels of Linguistic Adaptation. Vol. III: Intercultural and International Communication (ed. with Jan Blommaert).* Amsterdam/Philadelphia, 1990. n.y.p.
7. LINDENFELD, Jacqueline: *Speech and Sociability at French Urban Market Places.* Amsterdam/Philadelphia, 1990. n.y.p.
8. YOUNG, Lynne: *Language as Behaviour, Language as Code: A Study of Academic English.* Amsterdam/Philadelphia, n.y.p.
9. LUKE, Kang-Kwong: *Utterance Particles in Cantonese Conversation.* Amsterdam/Philadelphia, n.y.p.
10. MURRAY, Denise E.: *Conversation for Action. The computer terminal as medium of communication.* Amsterdam/Philadelphia, n.y.p.
11. LUONG, Hy V.: *Discursive Practices and Linguistic Meanings. The Vietnamese system of person reference.* Amsterdam/Philadelphia, n.y.p.
12. ABRAHAM, Werner (ed.): *Discourse Particles. Descriptive and theoretical investigations on the logical, syntactic and pragmatic properties of discourse particles in German.* Amsterdam/Philadelphia, n.y.p.
13. NUYTS, Jan, A. Machtelt BOLKESTEIN and Co VET (eds): *Layers and Levels of Representation in Language Theory: a functional view.* Amsterdam/Philadelphia, n.y.p.

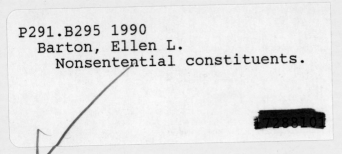